AMERICA
AT THE MALL

D0807262

AMERICA AT THE MALL

The Cultural Role of a Retail Utopia

LISA SCHAROUN

McFarland & Company, Inc., Publishers

Jefferson, North Carolina, and London

Library of Congress Cataloguing-in-Publication Data

Scharoun, Lisa, 1979–
    America at the mall : the cultural role of a retail utopia /
Lisa Scharoun.
        p.   cm.
    Includes bibliographical references and index.

    ISBN 978-0-7864-6272-8
    softcover : acid free paper ∞

    1. Shopping malls — United States — History.   2. Shopping
centers — United States — History.   I. Title.
HF5430.3.S28 2012
381'.110973 — dc23   2012010667

British Library cataloguing data are available

Front cover images © 2012 Jupiterimages and Shutterstock

Manufactured in the United States of America

McFarland & Company, Inc., Publishers
    Box 611, Jefferson, North Carolina 28640
        www.mcfarlandpub.com

Dedicated to my mother, Ann Scharoun.
Thanks for taking me shopping.

Table of Contents

Introduction

The design for the enclosed shopping mall has been attributed to the Austrian designer and shop fitter Victor Gruen. In 1952 Gruen was influential in creating the first fully enclosed shopping mall, Southdale Mall in Edina, Minnesota, with a vision to provide a space where "shoppers will be so bedazzled by a store's surroundings that they will be drawn — unconsciously, continually — to shop in a master-planned, mixed-use community."[1] The enclosed shopping mall, asserted Gruen, was "the nucleus of a utopian experiment."[2] With the movement of family life from urban to suburban environments at the end of the Second World War, the shopping mall became the natural "town center" and formed an essential place in the minds of the post-war consumer. It has evolved to become the heart of many suburban areas across the country. A veritable "temple of consumerism," the mall represents more than simply a place to shop. For some demographic groups, it is the primary place for community and social interaction and an essential element in their day-to-day life.

I grew up in the capital region of New York State, and I have lived the majority of my life in the United States. The shopping mall is for me, and for many of my generation, the only American town center that we have ever known. Whereas my mother and father can fondly recall shopping with their parents and friends in downtown Rochester, Buffalo and Syracuse, New York, for my siblings and me growing up in the '80s and '90s, the experience of downtown department stores and open air shopping was something altogether foreign.

For the children of the '70s, '80s and '90s, the shopping mall was the place to be, it was a space that we defined as our own and was more familiar and welcoming than the downtown shopping districts that it replaced. I have a wealth of happy childhood memories of the mall. It was where I felt my first real taste of adult independence; the mall was where I met my friends and played "dress-up" with the clothing in the stores in an attempt to define "grown up" identities. The mall taught me how to fit in, how to be a consumer,

1

ultimately, it taught me how to be American. And in this sense, the mall was an extremely important part of my upbringing.

For the past ten years I have been living overseas in a variety of countries including France, China, the United Kingdom and currently Australia. In my travels I have visited shopping malls in such geographically diverse places as Singapore, China, India and the Philippines. Every time I encounter one of these structures I feel a sense of the familiar, a sense of home. Viewing anything from a distance gives one a new perspective, and when I take yearly trips back to the U.S., things that would normally remain unnoticed in the daily cacophony have become more apparent. In 2009, I was intrigued when I came across an article in *Newsweek* ("Birth, Death and Shopping") proclaiming the death of the American mall.[3] After reading the article, I began to notice many "dead malls" near my hometown and across New York State. I felt an unexpected pang of sadness for the loss of this American institution and wished to learn more. Searching through user-driven web-blogs, *Deadmalls.com* and *Labelscar*, I was presented with hundreds of stories of individuals lamenting the loss of their local mall. As a teen "mall rat" myself, the stories resonated with me and heightened my awareness of the influence and importance of shopping malls in contemporary American society. Viewing this institution from a position outside of America, I recognized that across the globe, the shopping mall has come to represent the American Dream in a microcosm.

This book is a formal attempt to understand the spiritual, emotional and physical effects of the enclosed shopping mall on the American public. A current portrait of the shopping mall is presented with historical documentation and case studies. Through the medium of the shopping mall, this book explores the American condition with a focus on capitalism, optimism, control, patriotism, religion, globalization, adolescence, and death. It looks at the mall as not just a commercial site, but as a rich institution of American culture to shape an understanding of what it means to lose it. Observing Gruen's "experimental utopia" sixty years later, this book reflects on the current retail climate and the state of things to come.

The first section of this book sets the historical stage for the growth of the shopping mall and its role in shaping suburban and urban life in the United States. Chapter 1 explores the foundations of the American shopping mall through a discussion of retail models from urban department stores to "tax-payer strips" and enclosed shopping malls. Chapter 2 reflects on the rise of suburbia and the auto-dependent American dream of post-war America. Both chapters reveal the importance of the enclosed shopping mall in facilitating and supporting this new American dream and the implications of this dream on the growth of downtown areas across the country. Chapter 3 reflects on the factors that added to the decline of downtown areas and discusses attempts by designers and developers in the 1960s, '70s and '80s to re-vitalize the urban areas across the United States.

The positive and negative aspects of the shopping mall are explored in context with its rise as a popular retail development model. Chapter 4 and 5 provide the reader with an understanding of how the shopping mall is more than simply a consumer space. Chapter 4 explores the concept of the shopping mall as a "temple of consumerism" and discusses its role as a replacement for religion in American society. In chapter 5, an understanding of the symbolism of historic Main Street U.S.A is given as a means of comparison to the fabrication of Main Street in the enclosed shopping mall. An understanding of the importance of Main Street and the spiritual relevance of the shopping mall provides grounds for exploring the primary demographic groups that utilize the shopping mall as a community space. Chapters 6 and 7 explore demographic groups, elderly and teenage Americans, that utilize the shopping mall as their primary social space.

Problems with the shopping mall environment are discussed in Chapters 8 and 9. Since its inception, the shopping mall has had issues with being used as a public space. First Amendment rights and the issue of control in the privatized space of a shopping mall are explored in Chapter 8. This chapter also looks at the perception of safety and the problems with this assumption. As a development model, the shopping mall is culpable in the destruction of fragile ecosystems through the covering of arable land with large concrete structures. The shopping mall has also been cited as a secondary source of air pollution through its reliance on auto transport. Chapter 9 reviews the effects that the shopping mall has on the environment around it as well as how the synthetic environment inside has affected human behavior.

The enclosed shopping mall and its current role in the retail environment is discussed in Chapter 10. Through an understanding of the current retail climate, the shopping mall's future viability is questioned. An exploration of the big-box retail development model is covered in Chapter 11. Big Box power centers have been cited as a widespread replacement for the regional mall. Case studies of regional malls are presented in Chapter 12 as a means to provide evidence of the decline of this model. Chapter 13 presents current case studies of viable retail models as a means for comparison with the regional shopping mall. In the final chapters, I return to urban areas of the country to explore the "new urbanism" movement. A new "American Dream" of walkable urbanism in is discussed with the possibilities of new visions of retail and public space. Chapter 14 presents case studies of urban shopping malls as a means to uncover current and future possibilities. Chapter 15 looks toward the future with a focus on the assimilation of retail and public space in a more authentic and informed way.

According to Farrell, "Shopping is such a common part of America's pursuit of happiness that we usually take shopping centers for granted."[4] Embedded within the environment of the shopping mall are environmental, social, political, and community dialogues that at times conflict with each other. "Retailers routinely use our cultural values to stimulate sales," writes Farrell. "Shopping centers reinforce these values even as they distract us from other American values."[5] The idea of private and public space, for example, is frequently contested at the shopping mall and people find it difficult to realize that public space in the United States can be very limited. Therefore, the shopping mall has proven to be more than simply a place to buy consumer goods, but is also a site rich with symbolic influence, which in many ways serves as a mirror of the American condition. The purpose of this book, therefore, is not to simply represent the implied effectiveness of the mall in economic terms, but to explore the mall as an important cultural and social site. Statistics and examples are shown to help demonstrate the social, behavioral and visual effects of the mall on the consumer and as means to show how this institution has shaped generations of Americans.

This book employs case studies, interviews and photo documentation as means of representing the social importance of these structures. Case studies are an effective means of showing a current phenomenon and have been employed in publications by the Urban Land Institute, a non-profit body founded in 1936, as a way to illustrate change and innovation in the retail environment in the United States. Case studies in this book are balanced with comments, taken from both primary and secondary sources, which help to inform the reader of the social consequences of the decline of a shopping mall on the community surrounding it. While social media sites have not been traditionally recognized as academic research tools, the shopping mall represents a form of social interaction that both informs and feeds on popular culture and media; therefore, I felt it highly relevant to include comments from these forums. Through the case studies, the reader is presented with a current snapshot of the regional shopping mall and its importance to the community.

Case studies of other forms of retail space are compared to the regional shopping mall. The shopping malls in the case studies are all located in suburban areas of New York State and offer a cross-section of demographic areas, spanning from southern New York to Western New York. New York State cannot be said to represent the whole of the United States; however, with one of the largest state populations and GDP in the country, as well as being the home of the first suburb in Levittown and Gruen's first urban shopping mall in Rochester, it offers relevant insight to the current state of the regional shopping mall.

"Today's malls are an end product of a certain kind of American utopianism," says Farrell.[6] While the enclosed shopping mall was invented in the United States, it has now become a global phenomenon. Shopping malls can be found in countries as culturally varied as the United Arab Emirates and the People's Republic of China. This structure, mimicking a pedestrian street in an enclosed area, remains the same throughout the world; however, the meaning and symbolism of this retail environment varies dramatically. I focus on the United States in this book and explore the mall as an extension of the American capitalist vision. David Loy asserts: "Market capitalism has already become the most successful religion of all time."[7] Carrying onward from this statement, Pahl argues, "Malls are more than ordinary places, they function as sacred places in a religion of the market."[8] In this sense, the American shopping mall has functioned like other transportable forms of American culture: to inform a global norm based on the capitalist ethic.

This book, therefore, is an exploration of the importance of the shopping mall in American culture and forms a foundation for understanding its historical and current social relevance. I do not directly compare the American shopping mall to its manifestations in other countries, as a study of the global importance of its symbolic and social meaning in other countries is another research project although. However, from this American perspective, there is a foundation for future research on the importance of the shopping mall in other countries.

The International Council of Shopping Centers quantifies that only a third of a total 1,100 enclosed regional shopping malls in the United States are currently viable.[9] Post global financial crisis, as Americans have become more pocket conscious, big-box stores (such as Walmart), Internet shopping and several alternative development models have risen in popularity. Redell explains: "A driving force in the decline of the American shopping mall as we know it is a realization that the model is not sustainable, either economically or environmentally."[10] This book explores the effects of the decline of the regional mall on the community. "Malls are America's public spaces," asserts Farrell, "the town halls of the 20th and 21st centuries."[11]

Through a comparison with the big-box model, the shopping mall is shown as an important social environment for the young and old in many suburban communities across the country that is not easily replaced with the big-box center. Several books have been published on the subject of the social importance of the shopping mall in American culture. Books such as *The Malling of America* by William Kowinski, *The Call of the Mall* by Paco Underhill, and *One Nation Under Goods* by James Farrell are key texts in this area. The mentioned texts review the importance of the mall to certain demographic groups and the symbolisms inherent in the mall environment. While this book is also grounded in a foundation of knowledge of the importance of the shopping mall environment to certain demographic groups and provides an understanding of its symbolism, this work offers a point of difference in reviewing the viability of the shopping mall post global financial crisis. The above-mentioned books provide a perspective that reflects the dominance of this retail model, whereas this book provides an insight on its decline. This book provides solid evidence of the decline of the regional shopping mall and reflects on the implications of this decline on the demographic groups that utilize the mall as their primary social space.

"American life-styles, for all the material acquisition and the seeking after comforts and pleasures, are plagued by boredom, loneliness, alienation, and a high-price-tag," writes Oldenburg. "America can point to many areas where she has made progress, but in the area of informal public life she has lost ground and continues to lose it."[12] While the shopping mall has provided generations of Americans with a climate controlled "temple of consumerism," a fantasy world of retail goods on display, wrapped in the serene "faux-natural" environment of an enclosed concrete box, it has struggled to achieve the authenticity and community environment of a true Main Street.

After living abroad for over ten years, I have come to understand that an authentic feeling of community, which is very present in some nations, is lacking in the United States. In this respect, the global spread of the shopping mall is worrying. Through the documentation of the shopping mall I hope to relay its importance as a site of American culture; however, I also aim to reiterate the concept that the mall as a model for public space is flawed. The feeling of community that existed in post Second World War America has been damaged through the compartmentalization that came about by suburban living, which led to the decline of the urban areas and Main Street environments, leaving a community that was stratified and re-defined by individual desires. The shopping mall is a product of this compartmentalization and its enclosed nature has, in many cases, made it a very bland and homogenous environment that fosters conformity and control rather than creative expression and community.

Visiting vibrant community markets in India or China, one can at once sense the difference from a sterile, controlled shopping mall environment. The marriage of retail and public space has existed for centuries, and this is not likely to cease. The final chapter of this book forms an understanding of how the shopping mall can be improved with future development models that come closer to the utopian vision of Victor Gruen. With this book, I hope to assert that, despite current economic woes, the optimism of the post-war generation may yet re-surface and the public spaces of the United States may be re-generated with a new outlook. In the words of Bel Geddes, the designer of the 1939-40 World Fair exhibition "Futurama," "All eyes to the future!"[13]

1. The Birth of the Mall

The term "shopping center" originated in 1947 to describe "a group of architecturally unified commercial establishments built on a site that is planned, developed, owned and managed as an operating unit related by its location, size and type of shops to the trade area that it serves."[1] Defined by the Urban Land Institute (ULI), this commercial establishment must provide "on-site parking in definite relationship to the types and total size of the stores."[2] As this phrase asserts, the enclosed shopping center was constructed as a means to address the rise of automobile dependency in the United States. Suburban development and the mass-production of the automobile inspired a new type of shopping center, one that blended the ideals of an ancient European town square and turn of the century arcades with Modernist architectural ethics. Victor Gruen, credited as the "father" of the enclosed shopping mall, created the blueprint for the enclosed shopping center, a model that has endured fifty years of retail flux. Due to many factors, which will be discussed in-depth in subsequent chapters, this enclosed mall development model is on the decline. An understanding of different types of retail development will help to anchor the discussion in this book. In order to form an understanding of the current retail climate in the United States, this chapter will discuss the beginnings of the enclosed shopping center and chart its growth, saturation and subsequent segmentation.

In 1907, Edward Bouton, president of the Roland Park Company, developed a shopping center in Baltimore that incorporated a singly managed site with architecturally unified buildings, set back from the street to allow space for horse drawn carriages.[3] Unknown to Bouton at the time, his Roland Park shopping center model would eventually become the standard for retail development in the United States, changing the landscape irrevocably. Roland Park Shopping Center endured, although in an updated format with a paved front parking lot, until the early 1970s when the company took actions to tear it down due to the deteriorating structure and lackluster business. The community protested and took measures to save the structure, citing its historical

7

relevance. Because of the community's rescue efforts, one can still experience Bouton's 1907 vision today. Roland Park, as the first shopping center, is an example not only of an new development approach based on parking and centrally managed architecture, but also illustrates the importance of a shopping center to the community.

Prosperity in the 1920s saw the rise of high-quality residential communities just outside the central areas of cities. Communities of this type were made possible by Ford's assembly line methods of automobile production and subsequent availability of automobiles to those that could afford them. The automobile posed accessibility problems for the downtown shopping areas, home of the large department stores. The rise of the automobile and new up-market development on the urban outskirts opened the door for a new shopping model. Country Club Plaza, built on what was at the time the outskirts of Kansas City, was the first architecturally unified suburban shopping center. J.C. Nichols, inspired by Bouton's Roland Park development, set out to design a high-end equivalent. Nichols' Country Club Plaza utilized a themed approach to all the shop treatments and established a strict and over-arching management of the structure to keep uniformity with the environment. Parking for the Country Club Plaza was provided in parking garages and on the street and not directly surrounding the structure. Country Club Plaza was bisected by functional suburban streets and therefore was a more integrated part of the environment than successive models. However, this center can be defined as the first suburban shopping center, as it was the first time a developer had created a centrally controlled space with a themed approach to the shopping environment in the outskirts of the urban area.[4]

Both Bouton and Nichols' shopping centers had adopted a street-facing placement for their establishments that followed the traditional placement of shops on main thoroughfares for the highest visibility and accessibility to foot traffic. In the 1930s, with the establishment of the automobile, developers realized that street-level placement of shop fronts was no longer necessary, as the shopper was more readily lured into the environment by the placement of large signage along the main thoroughfares. Hugh Potter experimented with inward facing shop fronts in his Highland Park shopping center. Built in an up-market residential development of Dallas in 1931, Highland Park was an architecturally unified shopping center built around a courtyard, a site "all in one piece; un-bisected by the street, with on-site parking determined by parking demand."[5] "Highland Park Shopping Village can be called the prototype for subsequent decades of planned shopping centers," notes the ULI.[6] These early shopping center models formed the foundation of the contemporary shopping center model; however, it wasn't until the 1950s that this vision would fully take shape.

The Depression and subsequent entry in the Second World War created a shortage in housing and auto production. These two areas came back into focus at the end of the 1940s, resulting in a mass movement to the auto-dependent suburbs of cities. A vision for shopping in the newly developed auto-dependent suburbs was taken on board by architects and designers of the period. Victor Gruen, one of many designers who escaped war torn Europe for America in the 1930s, was the pioneer in creating an updated shopping center model that would dominate the next fifty years of retail development in the U.S. To solve the problem of auto-accessible shopping in the newly created suburbs of the early 1950s, Gruen envisioned a fully enclosed shopping center that would be the "heart and brain" of the city and its surrounding region.[7] Gruen wanted to create a "utopian experiment,"[8] as he called it. He wanted a space that would be something more than simply a place to buy essentials; his goal was to design a space that would encourage the consumer to linger longer, thus extending the possibilities of socialization and community.

Victor Gruen found inspiration in the medieval European town squares and turn of the century arcades, using them as a guideline for creating a shopping environment that would provide the consumer with a vibrant civic heart. Gruen wanted his modern consumer space to be something more than just a "collection of stores."[9] He visualized the shopping mall as an enclosed city, based on the landscape of European cities, in which consumers could leisurely stroll without the distraction of dodging traffic. Gruen's initial designs were a reflection on the designs of the shopping arcades of his native Vienna and of the design of the iconic Galleria Vittorio Emanuele II in Milan, Italy. The Milan Galleria was essentially an enclosed arcade that linked the two major pedestrian areas of the Duomo and La Scala Opera. The covered pedestrian arcade allowed for a strolling atmosphere where the public could shop and relax in one of the mall's cafes without worrying about dodging traffic or raindrops on the chaotic streets of Milan. By enclosing the center and blocking traffic access, the Galleria had created an effective and attractive public space. Notes Rubenstein, in his book *Pedestrian Malls, Streetscapes and Urban Spaces*, "In 1867, when this galleria opened, it was the center of Milan's public society, the place to see and be seen."[10]

The original suburban shopping center designs that grew out of the post war period closely resembled Bouton's vision. In these developments, department stores were linked to architecturally unified pavilion buildings organized in a linear format fronted by a parallel or angled spaces for parking; the "neighborhood center" format. The suburbs promoted a growing need for car accessible neighborhood-serving retail spaces, and architects responded by pushing the stores to the extreme back of the property, utilizing the rest of the expansive block for parking. Although many of these neighborhood centers included pared-down local branches of large downtown department stores such as J.C. Penney and Sears Roebuck, developers soon realized that they were more ideal for grocery shopping, as they promoted more of an "in-and-out" type experience.

The contemporary regional shopping mall began to take shape in Northgate Mall, on the outskirts of Seattle. Northgate Mall, developed by John Graham, Jr., on behalf of Allied Stores Corporation in 1950, was the starting point for the shopping mall as more than just a "collection of stores."[11] An open-air shopping center, Northgate featured a mute exterior structure surrounded by parking; all of the shops faced inward onto a central pedestrian mall and included an underground service tunnel for seamless distribution of goods. Northgate was also influential in that it was the first regional shopping center to include a full-line branch department store in the suburbs. "Northgate literally transposed the city's main shopping street to the suburbs," explains Wall.[12]

Northgate's main difference compared to previous shopping center models was that it provided the first fully functional internalized pedestrian space; a "pedestrian street" of sorts that allowed the visitor to see both sides of the retail environment without having to cross a major thoroughfare. Northgate's "pedestrian street," however, was far too narrow to allow the visitor to linger, as it lacked ample room for anything but commercial space.[13]

Victor Gruen's original shopping center designs took cues from Northgate and earlier models. It linked the abundant parking aspect of the neighborhood center with Northgate's "pedestrian street" concept. Gruen's design, however, was unique in that it adopted the wide corridor arcades of Europe, therefore creating a hybrid that combined the drivable convenience necessary in suburbia with a pleasant walk-able interior atmosphere. This format was first implemented in the design of Northland Mall on the outskirts of Detroit. In 1954, Northland was the largest regional shopping center ever built. Designed in a pinwheel shape, it encompassed a series of inward facing shopping pavilions all grouped around the Hudson's department store. The placement of Hudson's in the center, meant that the visitor would enter from the parking lot and gravitate towards the department store, passing minor tenants as they walked, thus giving everyone maximum exposure. Covered colonnades linked the stores together, providing a visitor with a pleasant semi-weather controlled environment. "Between department store and tenant-store blocks were courts, malls, terraces and lanes, all with colonnaded walks," remarks Wall. "The absence of vehicular traffic enabled crowds of people to enjoy these public spaces, whose fountains and sculptures were to capture [their] attention."[14]

Gruen improved on his design of Northland by working out a format that would replicate elements of a European covered arcade but one that could also combine something seemingly improbable, the use of two or three competing department stores in one shopping center. Organized in a cruciform pattern, the proposed navigation pattern for his new mall vision encouraged the consumer to enter one of the department or "magnet" stores by placing the largest entrances into these areas from the expansive parking lot surrounding the mall. The natural flow would then be to pass by secondary stores, which would be concentrated around the central core of the space. This layout encouraged the shopper to continue moving into another magnet store, which was bookended on the other side of the mall. The use of the central core, or atrium space, was an effective means to break up the space so that the department store on the other side seemed to be a new destination rather than a repeat of the initial entry point.

Southdale Mall, in Edina, Minnesota, was the first fully enclosed shopping center and represents the first full realization of this vision. The Dayton family, who owned the Minneapolis based department store Daytons, commissioned Southdale in late 1952. Bruce Dayton, project director, had several clearly formed objectives for the shopping center, all of which were based around the center being the "premier shopping center" in drivable suburbia.[15]

For the design of Southdale, Gruen drew on his previous work with Larry Smith and Irving R. Klein Associates for the Montclair Shopping center in Houston, Texas, in 1951. The design had proposed a revolutionary concept of an enclosed center with climate control to combat the hot and sticky Houston weather. The shopping center was to resemble the design of the Milan Galleria with an enclosed pedestrian walkway to "make walking enjoyable."[16] Air-conditioning had become standard in downtown department stores of the period, though it had never been proposed in such a large area. The Montclair project offered an innovative and viable new solution to consumer and public space; however, it was never realized due to Korean War restrictions on building materials at the time. Gruen, armed with the research he had done for the Montclair project, implemented his climate-control concepts in the design of the Southdale mall. He anchored Dayton's department store at the Northern end of the center bookended by Donaldson's department store on the south side. The corridors between the stores led to a central climate controlled public space. Wall explains: "The internal court, bounded by two floors of retail, was reached from the parking areas by six lanes, each lined with smaller shops and services. Six service cores, located within the store blocks, enabled the shops and stores to be serviced from the basement."[17]

Despite John Graham, Donaldson's appointed architect, arguing that creating such a large public area would take away from the true consumer function of the mall, the enclosed, climate controlled central core of the mall became the key to the new design. The central core was a space that would not only function to keep out the unpredictable climate changes, but would be a focal point for the whole center, and, as Gruen noted, it would be a place "where the body and eye can rest."[18]

It was in this central core space that Gruen exerted most of his efforts in designing something similar to an outdoor European town center. Sculptures, water features and potted trees were dotted around colorful striped umbrellas sheltering the faux 'plein air' cafe tables from the simulated sunlight, and a stage was erected in the center of the space for public performances and fashion shows. Gruen designed the lighting in the space to closely resemble the time of day through the use of street lamps and skylights. There was no need for installing powerful lights in the atrium ceiling, as skylights sufficed in lighting the space. In the dimmed evening light, hanging Japanese lanterns were lit, creating a festive and romantic atmosphere. Natural light streaming through the atrium style windows on the roof relayed an element of the outdoors; however, there were no windows on the side of the building to allow the viewer to actually look out at the outdoor environment. Every effort was made to trick the visitor into believing they were really outdoors, instead of enclosed in the synthetic concrete slab structure of the shopping mall.

Gruen, in his article "Winter or Summer" in the March 1953 *Architectural Forum*, noted: "Even though they are protected, they must feel that they are outdoor, because one of the court's chief functions is to provide psychological and visual contrast and relief from indoor shops."[19] The effect of distracting the consumer from the true outdoor environment made the completely fantastical interior atmosphere possible.

Whereas the interior of Southdale evoked all the nostalgic comfort of a traditional town center, the exterior featured two stories of solid concrete punctuated only by the occasional glass entryway opening to the anchor stores. The exterior of Southdale mall exemplified the architectural theory of modernist architects Gropius, Mies van der Rohe and Le Corbusier, who championed styles that dictated functionality and unnecessary ornamentation. Gruen's designs called for expansive, windowless cement exteriors punctuated by "big blocks of color and inviting entrance arcades."[20] There were no frivolous decorative elements on the building, as everything was stripped down to its lowest common denominator. The stark concrete walls were surrounded on all sides by seemingly endless parking lots creating what Margaret Crawford calls "pedestrian islands in an asphalt sea."[21] "Like the suburban house, which rejected the sociability of front porches and sidewalks for private backyards, the malls looked inward, turning their back on the public street."[22] The largely undecorated exterior façade of the shopping mall made no attempt to blend in with the natural space around and appeared as a hulking behemoth in contrast to the planned living spaces around it.

The mute exterior of the mall offered nothing to the sidewalks and parking areas and created a distinct divide between the private shop and the cityscape. Instead, the entire streetscape was brought indoors, into the more easily managed interior mall space. The extreme contrast of exterior and interior space was one of Gruen's major successes; the contrast created an effective navigation pattern from the parking lot to the entry arcade and the emergence from the drab outlines of the parking lot into the colorful consumer space of the mall heightened the sense of fantasy. On entering Southdale on a typical subarctic winter's day in Edina, visitors were confronted with a summer atmosphere complete with tropical palms, ice cream kiosks and bright, bold summer patterns. In other circumstances, this atmosphere would seem completely unbelievable; however, the muteness of the exterior space drew the visitor in and made the paradoxical visual signifiers in the space seem believable. Mall developers would later deem this open surrender of reality for the faux comfort of the introverted shopping mall as "The Retail Drama."[23]

Edina's 1952 Southdale shopping mall design was so successful that it became the standard for retail construction in America for over fifty years. "Southdale is not a copy of downtown. Rather, it is an imaginative distillation of what makes downtowns magnetic, the variety, the individuality, the lights, the color, even the crowds," raved a writer for the *Architectural Forum*.[24] *Time* magazine declared the space "a pleasure dome with parking."[25] At the time, like everything else in the shiny new suburban world, it was regarded as an ideal community space, superior to the declining, congested Main Street areas in the old downtown city centers. The success of Southdale was a catalyst for retail change; it provoked a proliferation of shopping malls across suburban America and contributed to the decline of many inner cities and Main Street areas across the country.

In the early 1960s developers realized that they could play a large role in constructing and controlling the new enclosed shopping mall, as the entire space could be run as a single entity. This led to an increased importance in the role of the developer and mortgage banker in the mall planning process and a decreased importance of the architect. Gruen's utopian vision of a shopping center that would provide unique community and cultural spaces waned. Developers began stripping excess landscaping and purpose built sculptures from the spaces to save money and to produce a more purely commercial space. Subsequently, the structures that evolved had little concern for the local community conditions or the environment around it. This developer-led trend created increasingly formulaic retail spaces that had lost the tailored and personal nature of the ideal community space that Gruen had envisioned.

In 1967, fed up with the abandonment of many of the community aspects of his "utopian experiment," Gruen denounced the shopping mall, retired from his company, Gruen and Associates, and returned to Vienna. "I refused to pay alimony for those bastard developments," Gruen said bitterly in an article in the *Los Angeles Times* ten years later.[26]

Gruen's repatriation as a result of his disillusionment did little to deter further expansion of the concept, and the enclosed mall development model continued. An increase of all types of development in suburbia continued to power on into the 1980s with more and more companies leaving the dying urban cores and decamping to the suburbs. A massive growth in office space in suburbia followed, larger than any other period of U.S. history. "By the late 1980s, the cycle was complete; first residential, then retail, and finally jobs left the center city," explains Leinburger.[27] Suburbia was its own complete entity, now called an "edge city," as it contained all of the essential ingredients once available exclusively in the cities.[28] As more and more varied demographic groups moved out to the suburbs, developers and planners sped up the production of shopping centers. Consumers came in droves; the increased control and lack of many community aspects that had existed in traditional downtown areas did not dissuade them in the least. Developers quickly realized that that people would flock to the mall whether it had social or cultural facilities or not, and that they would travel great distances from their communities to seek it out.

The 1960s and 1970s saw a great surge of mall development and innovation. A significant addition was the adaptation of the mall as a "mixed-use" development with additional spaces for offices and proposed housing. An energy crisis during this period was a catalyst for change, and shopping malls responded by retrofitting their spaces to include increased insulation and more efficient heating and cooling systems. The Environmental Protection Agency placed sanctions on shopping centers in the 1970s in relation to air pollution caused by the buildup of parking and the reliance on automobiles.[29] A failure to quantify the amount of indirect pollution caused by shopping centers, however, allowed for the sanctions to be dropped in the mid–1970s. The 1970s also brought about a realization of the impact that the shopping mall was having on communities and a federal government policy on community conservation was drafted; however, it was never enacted due to a change in administration.[30]

By the late 1970s retail had assumed two distinct categories. The first category included non-enclosed shopping centers and was divided into two subcategories — neighborhood centers and community centers. These centers were essentially "strip malls" built to encompass grocery stores and small department stores with a large amount of frontal parking space. Neighborhood centers, however, served the local area within a two-mile radius whereas community centers serviced a larger radius of three to five miles. Neighborhood centers are anchored with a supermarket whereas the community center was developed around a junior department store or large variety store.[31] Community centers evolved to include hardware, home improvement, warehouse and furniture stores in the late 1970s.[32] The second retail category, the shopping mall, encompasses a less necessity driven type of shopping experience. Shopping malls are categorized as enclosed structures that offer general merchandise, apparel and home furnishings. The shopping mall is further subdivided into regional and super-regional. Regional malls, which include at least two department stores, are placed in areas to attract customers from as far as twenty miles away, whereas super-regional malls, which include at least five department stores, can service customers from a one hundred mile or larger radius.[33]

When malls reached a saturation point in the 1970s, developers began to specialize their regional malls. "[Saturation] led to a multiplication and diversification of retailing and mall types into a broader range of more specialized and flexible forms, which allowed for a more precise match between goods and consumers," says Crawford.[34] The regional mall was segmented into up-market and mid-market models. "Fashion malls" defined the up-market segment and included an upper-end department store or a high-end limited department store as an anchor tenant.[35] Popular with developers were "mid-market malls," those with mid-range anchors such as JCPenney and Sears, which appealed to the middle market. "In the 1970s, the mid-markets were defined as the growth opportunities for regional centers," notes the Urban Land Institute.[36] Super regional malls for the up-market shopper evolved in the late 1970s. The super regional mall offered the same retail options as a "fashion mall" but had a more concentrated focus on the entertainment aspect of shopping. As a result of this specialization, which created a formula for discovering consumer desire and responding to it, the mall was considered the most failsafe investment of the period. Notes Kowinski, "As of 1984, the biggest real estate deal in U.S. history was the sale of 19 shopping malls in eight states for more than $700 million."[37]

Overbuilding and recession brought the construction of shopping malls nearly to a halt in the late 1980s and early 1990s. "The shopping center reached the end of a historic era that transformed the retail landscape of the United States into a decentralized hierarchy of shopping center types and locations," explains Kramer.[38] The vast majority of shopping centers that had been built in the 1950s and 1960s were beginning to age and needed renovation. At the same time, a recession caused by a destabilization of the savings and loan industry forced many developers into bankruptcy.[39] In response, many developers began to position their shopping centers as entertainment centers. Super-regional malls began to cannibalize under-performing regional centers and a number of regional malls were forced to close during this period. In the 1990s some super regional malls evolved into "mega malls" that incorporated theme park type attractions, theaters and themed eateries to draw customers from across the country, overseas and local patrons from as far as one hundred miles away. "Mega malls" such as the West Edmonton Mall in Canada and the Mall of America in Minnesota, offer entertainment and retail on a colossal scale. West Edmonton, opened in 1981, has a total of 3.8 million square feet and includes a full scale theme park, ice skating rink, wave pool, sea life habitat and full miniature golf course.[40] For many of the "fashion" and "mid-market" regional malls, the acceptance of discount department stores and other cut-price stores saved their malls from going under. A rise in factory outlet malls, an aggregation of factory-second and off-season offerings in an open-air center, also occurred. According to the Urban Land Institute, factory outlets were considered the most important retail development of the 1980s. This period also saw the rise of Big Box retailers such Walmart. Most significantly, the ownership of shopping centers changed during this period. Mall ownership was divided into publicly listed and privately listed companies, with innovation mainly generated from the private sector.[41]

Despite the turbulent 1990s, the malls prevailed. In 2002, consumer spending in malls accounted for around 70 percent of the gross national product, equaling an amount greater than what most other industrialized nations spend. By 2003, the malls in the U.S. had a combined turnover of 240 billion dollars. Factory outlets, which had been the most important retail development of the 1980s, peaked in the mid–1990s and are now said to be on the decline. According to the Urban Land Institute, "The number of grand openings [of outlet centers] declined from 22 to 43 per year from 1988–1995 to just three between 2004 and 2005."[42] Mega malls and super-regional malls with a mix of retail and entertainment continued to gain market share in the early 2000s and regional malls continued to offer a mix of mid-range and discount stores. At the dawn of a new millennium, malls were a prominent feature of the American suburban landscape and appeared to be a retail environment destined to continue far into the future.

The enclosed shopping mall failed in being Gruen's ideal utopian retail environment; however, it has succeeded in representing a concentrated expression of American capitalism. Capitalism promotes a continuous flux, an ebb and flow, which defines and gives strength to our economic system. The mall has enjoyed unrivaled success as the premier retail development model of the last five decades. Nonetheless, fifty years later, the cracks in many of the concrete exteriors of these megalithic buildings are a metaphor of what's to come. In early 2006, two years before the dramatic global financial crisis, several prominent shopping center development groups began to lose their grip on the market. New shopping models, online shopping and over saturation of shopping malls had begun to dramatically affect the industry. Post global financial crisis, in April of 2009, one of the largest mall management and development groups in the United States, General Growth Properties, declared bankruptcy. With a total of $27.3 billion of debt, the group's case has been declared the largest real estate bankruptcy case in U.S. history and signaled a decline of the enclosed shopping center model.[43] The last enclosed regional mall built in America was in 2006; subsequent retail developments have taken on new forms, the most popular being the warehouse style Big Box model.

According to *The Wall Street Journal*, Big Box centers anchored by freestanding giants are now the preferred model for suburban development.[44] In a new age of austerity Big Box retailers offer consumers bulk savings and a sense of satisfaction in their thrifty retail choices. These Big Boxes are becoming ever more prevalent in suburbia, replacing the "fashion" and "mid-range" regional malls or turning them into dead spaces. In contrast to the regional malls, Big Boxes have little in the way of viable public space to linger, reflect and feel a part of a community. Online retailing may be said to be another factor in the decline of the regional shopping mall, with increasing broadband speeds, more portable devices for browsing the web and consumer confidence in online shopping at a high. Consumers recognize the value in online shopping and the higher possibilities for "finding a bargain," however; despite the benefits, online shopping doesn't offer the same community aspects of a shopping mall. The British Council of Shopping Centers explains, "E-tailing will never replace the shopping experience. Shopping is a social activity in the main.... Online shopping is very much seen as a complementary tool to support retail activity."[45]

The shopping mall arose as a means to address a need for a retail environment in the post war auto-dependent suburbs of the United States. Victor Gruen, the "father of the mall," recognized the shopping mall as more than a consumer space. His design for Southdale Mall, which became the standard for shopping mall construction for fifty years, was successful in combining drivable convenience with a pleasant interior pedestrian space. As a result of rapid post war development, the regional shopping mall has become an integral part of our landscape and community. *The Economist* reports that the enclosed regional shopping mall is on the decline and Big Box stores such as Walmart and Target have replaced many of these failing centers.[46]

Community is a valuable part of every society and America suffers from a lack of community outlets, which author Ray Oldenburg calls "third places," the first place being home and the second being work. "In the United States, third places rank a weak third with perhaps the majority lacking a third place and denying that it has any real importance," notes Oldenburg.[47] Most importantly, regional shopping malls are one of the few community places left to the American public in suburban areas across the country. The loss of this space may mean a further deterioration of community interaction. American's detachment and lack of community can be traced to the rise of suburbia. The next chapter charts the rise of suburbia in the period directly following the Second World War and relays how the suburban lifestyle has affected retail development and personal interaction.

2. Suburbia and the American Dream

America's contemporary landscape was heavily influenced by post Second World War ideals. A new and powerful "American Dream" emerged during this period that would irrevocably change values and lifestyles. The post war period American Dream offered the average person the possibility for a freedom previously thought unattainable. Suburbs offered a retreat from the dirty and crowded urban areas and seemed an ideal place for the baby boomers to raise their new families. Mass production of automobiles gave returning veterans the possibility to choose their destinations rather than have them dictated by urban trolley lines. Post-war suburban freedom, however, came at a great cost to the community and environment. "Life in the subdivision may have satisfied the combat veteran's longing for a safe, orderly and quiet haven, but it rarely offered the sense of place and belonging that had rooted his parents and grandparents," says Oldenburg.[1]

Sixty years later, America is coming to terms with some of the downsides to this American Dream. In its purest form it is a beautiful dream, but one that has dire environmental and social consequences. Although the American Dream of the fifties promoted a suburban utopia of privacy and independence, it also promoted the segregation of the population into homogenous groups. Dependency on automobiles, while offering new freedoms, produced a culture dependent on fossil fuels and a subsequent carbon pollution level to match. This chapter maps the epic rise of suburban America in an attempt to define how this influential period shaped the country's residential and retail landscape, and its broad ranging effects on the community.

The 1950s vision of the American dream is said to stem from the Norman Bel Geddes designed Futurama exhibit and ride at the 1939-40 New York City World's Fair. The exhibit highlighted a system of "superhighways" that would crisscross the country, outlining the blueprint for what became American suburbia. Bel Geddes explains in his book *Magic Motorways*: "The motorways which stretch across the model are exact replicas, in small scale, of motorways which may be built in America in the near future. They are designed to make collisions impossible and to eliminate completely traffic congestion."[2] While participants sat in comfortable upholstered carriages, the ride ferried them through vast American terrains. Through a speaker built into the back of each carriage, a soft, assuring voice directed the viewer's attention to the main features of the highway models on display. Futuristic motorcars raced over overpasses, high-speed intersections and wide bridges at a hundred miles per hour. Pleasant green spaces dotted with planned and decentralized cities were nestled in-between the intricate networks of highways. The ride conjured up powerful visions of a new suburban way a life, a model that would eventually dominate the next fifty years of development in America. "They saw the world of tomorrow lying there inviting before them — a world that looked like Utopia and that did not seem to have a very close relation to the world they knew," notes Bel Geddes.[3]

Post–Second World War American cities had become crowded and difficult to navigate. Middle class families lived in cramped duplexes or apartment complexes. Due to the close proximity to factories, inner city neighborhoods were often noisy, polluted and smelly. If your family were lucky enough to have a car, they would have to battle the daily pedestrian and trolley traffic, while trying to fight for one of the limited parking spaces downtown. Leinburger, in his book *The Option of Urbanism*, explains: "Americans were ready for a new vision of how to live, work and play; in essence, they were ready for a new version of the American dream."[4] The Futurama exhibit foreshadowed the new drivable American Dream as it promoted an end to the crowded inner-city streets, clogged with people, trolleys and cars. It envisioned a new world were everyone would have their own means of transport, the independence to come and go when they pleased, and the opportunity to have their own little patch of paradise miles from the noise and pollution of 1940s urban America. The 1939-40 New York City World's Fair attracted 45 million people, the all-time record for World's Fair attendance, and Futurama was one of the most popular exhibitions at the fair.[5] Futurama, sponsored by the progressive automobile manufacturer General Motors, planted a seed in the minds of Americans that was to grow into the great suburban movement of the '50s and '60s.

Many urbanites left their apartments, duplexes and small homes to settle at the periphery of older, high-density cities in the decades directly following World War II. The new version of the American Dream, Bel Geddes' Futurama, was facilitated by many connecting factors. During the First World War, domestic car and housing production had been sidelined in favor of production for the war. This, followed by the Depression and subsequent entry into the Second World War, meant that there was a significant shortage of housing after the Second World War. The baby boom exacerbated the situation, causing the government to re-think land use and zoning laws. Communities like Levittown on Long Island led the way by re-purposing farmland with thousands of cookie cutter single-family homes organized in concentric circles. The company Levitt and Sons transformed the way that housing was built in America with a streamlined twenty-seven step building process that produced cheap, single family dwellings on subdivided blocks. By buying building supplies in bulk and using a simple design with concrete slab construction, Levitt was able to produce the first 17,311 houses in the planned development quickly and cheaply.[6] Each quarter acre block in Levittown sported a freshly mown lawn and a car in the garage. A down payment on this American Dream cost just one hundred dollars. "We believe," said Levitt in a promotional film of the period, "that every family in the United States is entitled to decent shelter."[7] Kenneth Jackson, in his book *Crabgrass Frontier: The Suburbanization of the United States*, explains: "Initially limited to veterans, the first Levittown was 25 miles east of Manhattan and particularly attractive to new families that had been formed during and just after the war. Squashed in with their in-laws or in tiny apartments where landlords frowned on children, the GI's looked upon Levittown as the answer to their most pressing need."[8]

A "Cape Cod" house in Levittown.

Houses in Levittown were designed without front porches and featured fenced in yards.

Levittown was the embodiment of the post–Second World War American Dream. It offered the middle class urbanite a new form of freedom — the freedom of living with a nuclear family in increased privacy on one's own plot of land in a detached house. In this suburban paradise, everyone owned a car and therefore had the means to go anywhere that the new superhighways would take them. Housing loan programs of the period, sponsored by the Veterans Administration (VA) and Federal Housing Administration (FHA), favored newly constructed homes in the suburbs. Therefore, the federal programs subsidized the new vision of the American Dream by encouraging single-family housing and auto-dependency. Futurama became a reality and the American public embraced it with open arms.

This vision of society was something entirely new and differed from any other society built in history. For the first residents of Levittown, this was indeed paradise. Helen DiGiovanni moved to Levittown in 1951 and said she fell in love instantly with the place. "We came from Philadelphia, where everything was row houses, and I'd never seen anything like it," she says.[9] The feeling of optimism and excitement extended to all new residents. "We had achieved the American Dream," says Hal Lefcourt, who bought a Cape Cod style house in the first wave of Levittown development.[10] The 1950s American

Dream spread across the nation as developers began to replicate Levittown, a model that is still in practice today.

Prior to the great suburban movement of the 1950s, the downtown and main street areas of cities were vibrant centers of civic life. Despite the negative associations of pollution, crowded accommodations and congestion, prewar American cities offered daily interaction with people from all walks of life. Through a reliance on public transport and common services, they promoted an intermingling of all classes, genders and races. "[Post-war American cities had] vitality of urban life, visual interest, social contact, cultural diversity.... Cities depended on ethnic neighborhoods, familiar landmarks, a mixture of the grand and the small," says Wright.[11] Postwar suburbia shattered this fragile co-existence and created a physical boundary, which was to define American behavior for many years to come. "When the widespread automobile owner-ship liberated the customer from the fixed path of the mass transit lines ... the shopper could be pulled almost anywhere ... by what the downtown district so signally lacked — a place to park the car," observed a writer in a 1950s issue of *Architectural Forum*.[12] Suburban reliance on the car allowed for a type of stratification in society that had not existed before. "Though proclaimed as offering the best of both rural and urban life, the automobile suburb had the effect of fragmenting the individual's world," says Oldenburg.[13]

To this effect, suburbia became a means to segregate and control society. Levittown was not only filled with cookie cutter houses, it was filled with cookie cutter families, a situation supported by the automobile but created mainly by the "redlining" tactics of the federal housing programs. FHA and VA grants incorporated guidelines that effectively created zones, mainly in low-income minority areas, where the grants were not allowed. "If a mixture of user groups is found to exist [in a suburban neighborhood], it must be determined whether the mixture will render the neighborhood less desirable to present and prospective occupants. Protective covenants are essential to the sound development of proposed residential areas, since they regulate the use of the land and provide a basis for the development of harmonious, attractive neighborhoods," explains the 1947 FHA housing manual.[14] These stipulations meant that the dilapidated apartment blocks in the cities were left for lower-income minority families while the newly created suburbs were to be popu-lated with white middle-class families. "The agency refused to underwrite houses in areas threatened by "Negro Invasion," explains Wright. "In the cities, it 'red-lined' huge sections that were 'changing' and refused to guarantee mort-gage loans in those areas, claiming that the influx of blacks made the loans bad risks."[15]

Even if minority families had savings or were somehow found eligible for housing loans, many development companies refused to sell to them. As documented by Kenneth Jackson, "The Levitt organization, which was no more culpable in this regard than any other urban or suburban firm, publicly and officially refused to sell to blacks for two decades after the war."[16] Bill Levitt of the Levitt and Sons development company, explained that this was not a choice but an economic necessity. "As a Jew, I have no room in my mind or heart for racial prejudice," elucidated Levitt in 1954. "But by various means I have come to know that if we sell one house to a Negro family, then 90 to 95 percent of our white customers will not buy into the community. That is their attitude, not ours."[17] New zoning laws also favored commercial and heavy industry in the cities over housing, which further degraded city life and created a more attractive lure to suburbia, for those who were welcome and could afford it. By the late 1950s, "virtually every downtown was in absolute and relative decline, virtually no housing [was] being built in the center city," explains Leinburger.[18] Although some major department stores and offices lingered on in the cities until the early 1980s, the zoning laws and mass migration to the suburbs transformed cities into shabby and dangerous enclaves.

In effect, the 1950s suburban model promoted homogeneity. As the automobile allowed for more freedom, the interdependence that once existed in cities and small communities declined. "After four years here [in the U.S.A], I still feel more of a foreigner than in any other place in the world I have been," laments a European woman who moved to the U.S., "People here are proud to live in a 'good' area, but to us these so-called desirable areas are like prisons. There is no contact between the various households and we rarely see our neighbors."[19] Removed from the urban melting pot, Americans became stratified. "Each [suburb] is designed for families of particular size, incomes and ages. There is little sense of place and even less opportunity to put down roots," says Oldenburg.[20] The automobile further isolated the community into small family groups. Grouped in terms of income, race and age, in the outlying suburbs, developers could now establish homogenous goods, services and ultimately entire landscapes to the like-minded consumers.

As work and commerce existed in the city and family life in the suburbs, the new zoning laws had effectively compartmentalized suburbia. Notes Jackson, "When the initial families arrived [in suburbia] with their baby strollers and play pens, there were no trees, schools, churches or private telephones. Grocery shopping was a planned adventure, and picking up the mail required sloshing through mud" to the nearest town center.[21] Increased desire for private spaces — detached homes, lawns and single-family cars — led to a decrease in the importance of public space. "Open spaces and parks are disappearing. Careless highways and unplanned buildings are destroying the trees and fields.... And if you take away the gift of nature, you erode the finest values of the heart and mind," proclaimed President Lyndon Johnson in 1964.[22]

Developers recognized the postwar desire for independence and privacy; therefore, beyond schools and sporting grounds, suburban developments did not provide a downtown atmosphere or community centers where families could meet and socialize. "The housing development's lack of informal social centers or informal public gathering places puts people too much at the mercy of their closest neighbors," says Oldenburg.[23] Relationships in suburban neighborhoods are difficult to attain and maintain, says Oldenburg, as the isolated nature of suburbia often makes it difficult to casually meet one's neighbor and all contact needs to be formally organized and orchestrated in a synthetic manner. "In time the overtures toward friendship, neighborliness, and a semblance of community hardly seem worth the effort."[24]

A single-family home in the suburbs was important to the housewife. Suburbia represented a retreat from the "dangerous" and "dirty" urban areas and gave them the space and privacy for their families that they craved. "To many Americans, the suburban house seemed the only way to provide a good family life," writes Gwendolyn Wright in her book *Building the Dream*. "This was what the government, the builders, the bankers and the magazines told them, and many believed it — or felt they had to."[25] Women, more so than any other group, felt largely isolated in the newly created suburbia. Within their single-family cookie cutter home, they cleaned, cooked, watched television, cared for the children and waited for their husbands to return from their daily trek to work in the city. "Their isolation from work opportunities and from contact with employed adults led to stifled frustration and deep psychological problems," says Wright.[26] Miles from downtown, women couldn't enjoy the same social interaction they once enjoyed in the city. "The suburban wife without a car to escape in epitomizes the experience of being alone in America," says Oldenburg, "those who could afford it compensated for the loneliness, isolation and lack of community with the 'frantic scheduling syndrome.'"[27] The shopping mall and television entered this environment as a necessary diversion for the bored suburban housewife.

Curvilinear streets and auto-dependency made it difficult to recreate the traditional downtown or Main Street of shops in suburban areas. "Community life amid tract housing is a disappointing experience," says Oldenburg. "The space within the development has been equipped and staged for isolated family living and little else."[28] Devoid of a civic heart, the shopping mall entered as a welcome addition to this environment. "Once trolley lines from all over the city brought thousands of shoppers downtown. Now the interstate makes it possible to speed out of the city, exit the interchange, veer into a giant parking lot, and then stroll along a climate-controlled, indoor Main Street at the mall," remarks Liebs, in his book *Main Street to Miracle Mile*. "To a population rapidly succumbing to the opiate of high-speed travel down manicured high-

The curvilinear street format of Levittown.

ways, driving down Main Street with its stop-and-go traffic and bumpy pave-
ment was becoming an annoyance."[29] Oldenburg explains that many found
the mall interior attractive simply because of its tranquility in contrast to the
tangle of utility wires, signage and fume filled highways of cities. "Merely by
eliminating the urban uglies, the interior of any mall is certain to seem pleasant."[30] The intense desire for privatization and control that was rife in the
period made the enclosed shopping center the ideal replacement for a community center.

   Similar to the suburban housing model, the mall encouraged homogeneity by employing security guards and limited entry to sift out any "bad elements" that might try to come in. The mall served a dual function: it promoted
and sustained consumption along with providing the community with a fantastical diversion from the stark realities of suburban living. Ultimately it provided a sanctuary from reality where one could be wrapped in the security of
a safe and controlled environment.

   The importance of television as a major entertainment medium during
this period also helped to establish and perpetuate the suburban dream. Along
with the automobile, the newly created postwar suburban housing tracts
required a television set to connect postwar Americans to the world and provide the family with nightly entertainment. Television was introduced in the

thirties by the NBC (National Broadcasting Center), CBS (Columbia Broadcasting System) and DuMont networks, which promoted their primitive programming to the homes of upper–middle class families. Though television at that time had mainly been a toy for the wealthy, its value as a highly visual and persuasive medium had been recognized. Television, like cinema, was exploited during the war for use as a propaganda machine, but also as a means to distract the viewer from the atrocities of the war by giving them programs that offered fantastical escapes in the improbable utopia of TV-land.

A disused Cape Cod style house in Levittown, 2010.

It wasn't until the 1939-40 New York World's Fair when television, like the dream of drivable suburbia, became imprinted on the public mind as a key ingredient in the new American Dream. In the exhibit Land of Tomorrow, visitors were given a taste of what programs they could expect to see on the magic box and showed an average family enjoying the entertainment benefits of the television.[31] New prosperity after the war allowed television, like the automobile, to be a necessary fixture in suburbia. Notes Spigel in *Make Room for the TV: Television and the Family Ideal in Postwar America*, "Over the course of the 1950s television was rapidly installed into American homes." Spigel explains that television programming of the period promoted the "white-middle class suburban home as their favored model of family bliss."[32] For women stuck in suburbia with young families, the TV was a lifeline to the world, offering programs and commercials that showed them how they could and should live their lives. "The major networks were intent upon designing programs to suit the content and organization of the housewife's day," says Spigel.[33] The mall's interior illusion mimicked the illusions of space and time piped to TV viewers daily. For the children of this generation, the fantasies that were shown to them on the magic box became a three-dimensional reality in the shopping center. The mall became an extension of the fantasy world offered through television, and it was also an ideal medium in which to promote the products on display in the retail environment, thus encouraging the viewer to consume. As Kowinski observed in 1985, "The mall is a visual experience, it's a TV you walk around in."[34]

From the 1950s onward, suburban housing tracts became the favored method of development. Cities sprawled far beyond their boundaries and retail and office space moved with them, creating newer "edge cities." The immense development of suburbia carried on until the early 1990s when the bubble finally burst. "The 1980s real estate and infrastructure boom, the largest in American history in terms of the amount built until then, had to come to an end. It was predictably followed in the early 1990s by the worst real estate downturn since the 1930s depression," writes Leinburger.[35] The downturn resulted partly from the deregulated savings and loans industry, which encouraged banks and investors to invest in risky real estate deals with minimal down payment. This in turn resulted in a large amount of bad real estate loans and the collapse of many savings and loans, commercial banks and insurance agencies. "The entire U.S. banking system was put in jeopardy, so much so that the federal government was forced to take drastic action," explains Leinburger.[36] The federal government took over a majority of the bad real estate loans and placed a lending ban from 1990 to 1992. To avoid a crisis of this level again, Wall Street investment banks came up with nineteen standard real-estate product types for home, office, industrial, hotel and retail developments.

The nineteen standard real estate products were all based on drivable suburban models and were considered investments that were proven to be profitable and low risk investments.[37] Housing was defined in terms of luxury, move-up for sale and entry level. In each category, the housing was specified to be on suburban residential blocks in planned communities akin to the Levittown model. Although each type of property was built on the same suburban development model, each category allowed the homeowner to strategically work towards a more luxurious home and setting. Entry-level housing was farther from the urban areas, requiring the homeowner to drive a longer distance to work. Offering three to four generic styles, developers positioned these homes on small ⅓ acre blocks and utilized cheap, synthetic building materials and finishes.[38] Move-up for sale housing is built closer to urban and "edge city" offices and offer larger, more opulent home styles; however, it employs the same cheap building materials and methods as the entry-level homes. These homes are unlikely to be in an exclusive gated community but in favorable public school zones. Luxury housing is located in the most favorable parts of the suburban environment and is often sheltered in their own internal gated community, which includes a locked gated entry point. Luxury housing often includes perks such as onsite golf courses with grandiose clubhouses. While still employing a set of generic house styles and cheap building materials, these vast homes offer the finest of interior finishes and appliances as well as Jacuzzis, indoor pools and special home entertainment areas.[39]

The housing types presented by the nineteen standard property types promoted an environment that was replaceable. The models further detached the resident from the community, as the desire to constantly move up to a new housing category made the community superfluous. "There is often more encouragement to leave a given subdivision than to stay in it, for neither the homes nor the neighborhoods are equipped to see families or individuals through the cycle of life," says Oldenburg.[40]

In terms of retail development, the introduction of the nineteen standard property types limited developers to continue replicating Gruen's enclosed regional shopping mall, as any variations on this model would be unlikely to receive funding. Beyond the standard regional shopping mall, the retail model favored by the Wall Street investment banks was the "standard neighborhood retail center." According to the International Council of Shopping Centers, "the standard neighborhood retails center is on twelve to fifteen acres of land on the going-home side of a four to eight lane major arterial road ... twenty percent of the site will be covered by the one-story buildings, which are set back from the street by about 150 feet; the rest of the site will be paved with asphalt for parking in the front."[41] The nineteen standard property types also favored a Big Box model in which retailers such as Walmart, Target and Costco occupy warehouse-like retail spaces on the outskirts of built up areas. The Big Box model came to fruition in the late 1990s and is a model that is taking precedence today. The overall result of the nineteen standard property types was an even more homogenous looking American environment than previously thought possible. "This is the reason why any suburban place in the country looks pretty much the same as any other," says Leinburger.[42]

Television, affordable single-family housing, the shopping mall and the automobile all went hand in hand in realizing the 1950s version of the American Dream. This suburban vision established a new outlook for the future. In this new outlook, individual values override community values. Any sense of community was thus gained through consumption and products defined lifestyles. The shopping mall is the spiritual home for this vision of society. It became a veritable "temple" of consumer culture. As the traditional town center, once home of cultural and civic activities as well as consumer activities, died, the mall became the civic heart and shopping became the major cultural activity for American families. Like the controlled image of suburbia, the mall design conveys an ideal image of America. It gives the illusion of a small controllable environment that is quiet, prosperous and neighborly. In this environment "good citizens keep the streets clean and safe and the shopkeepers take scrupulous care of their shops and customers."[43] To the first residents of Levittown, the American suburban vision seemed like paradise and on the outset, it represented an ideal previously unknown to the world. Suburbia, however, has turned out to be less than perfect. Unforeseen by the optimistic 1950s baby boomers, the contemporary suburban environments that now dominate the American landscape have created dire social and environmental problems.

Films and novels have captured the emotional and psychological consequences of living in suburbia since the beginning of the trend. In the 1955 novel *The Man in a Grey Flannel Suit*, Sloan Wilson deals with the themes of ennui and isolation in suburbia.[44] The novel paints a picture of suburban life as fresh and relevant today as back in the 1950s when it was written. "The trick is to learn to believe that it's a disconnected world, a lunatic world, where what is true now was not then ... for now is the time to raise children and make money, and dress properly and be kind to one's wife and admire one's boss and learn not to worry, and think of oneself as what?... That makes no difference — I'm just a man in a grey flannel suit," says suburban husband Tom Rath, the main character in the novel.[45] Wolfe, in his 1998 novel *A Man in Full*, set in the suburbs of Atlanta, writes: "The only way you could tell you are leaving one community and entering another is when the franchise chains start repeating and you spotted another 7-eleven, another Wendy's, another Costco, another Home Depot.... The new monuments were not office towers or monuments or city halls or libraries or museums, but 7-eleven stores."[46] In the highly acclaimed 1999 film *American Beauty*, characters in an average American neighborhood all deal with psychological issues caused by living in a highly controlled suburban malaise.

Although the reality of the 1950s American Dream has a dark side, in its purest form it is a beautiful dream. It represents so much of what is important and inspirational about America, it represents a unique form of freedom and an overwhelming optimism, which carries on to the present day. "I guess I could be pretty pissed off about what happened to me," says Lester Burham, the main character in *American Beauty*, "but it's hard to stay mad when there's so much beauty in the world. Sometimes I feel like I'm seeing it all at once, and it's too much ... and I can't feel anything but gratitude for every single moment of my stupid little life."[47]

Suburbia has now sprawled farther and farther from the edges of the cities. The highway systems of the 1950s have been extended beyond recognition, creating a web of traffic congestion that stretches across the country. For the last sixty years this suburban development pattern has defined how American public life functions. Suburbia offers the positive aspects of increased privacy and perceived independence through the freedom of self-transport; however, there are many drawbacks to this way of life. The redlining tactics of post Second World War housing grants, which so openly discriminated against minority groups, have been discarded, but the policies themselves set a model for homogenous communities that continue to this day. With the ability to live together with like-minded individuals in small family groups, suburbia has become increasingly segregated and narrow in its perceptions. Whereas the private serenity of individual homes on individual blocks of land defines suburbia, concentrated poverty defines many urban areas of America. In the last sixty years the United States has waged wars over the non-renewable supply of petroleum and has faced environmental devastation in many parts of the country as a result of the pollution from auto-dependency. Television and other forms of passive media promote soporific, unhealthy lifestyles, which has in turn dramatically impacted on the health and well being of the nation. The mall, the new town center, is rife with controversy over the denial of First Amendment rights and increased control. Its construction relies on the destruction of mass amounts of arable land, the suburban locations and moat of accessible parking does little to promote public transportation. The United States is slowly coming to the realization that auto-dependent suburban living is not sustainable. Despite this, the powerful 1950s vision of the American Dream that has shaped the nation's contemporary landscape is very difficult to replace.

The next section will reflect on how suburban shopping malls affected the retail environments of urban communities across the country. Through an understanding of urban renewal efforts from the 1960s to the present, a picture of the dramatic effects that auto-dependent suburban living has had on urban spaces in the United States is drawn.

3. The Decline of Downtown

As a result of rapid post-war suburbanization, by the end of the 1950s many downtown centers across the United States had gone into decline. "Virtually every downtown was in absolute and relative decline," notes Leinburger, "with virtually no housing being built in the center city, office space grown at half the rate required to maintain regional market share, industrial zones being abandoned and retail almost completely deserting the downtown for the suburbs."[1] The decline of downtown was a direct result of the influence of the automobile and the new superhighways that linked the suburbs to the cities. With an automobile, the consumer could be pulled anywhere they desired and thus the use of downtown shopping areas declined due to lack of sufficient parking. Gruen, the father of the suburban shopping mall, recognized the effect that the suburban mall was having on the downtown areas of the country and turned his attention back to the downtown areas to address the growing problem of urban decline. Although Gruen's urban visions were ultimately unsuccessful, they became a model for re-inventing the city center, which was further enhanced by the visionary developer James Rouse. This chapter will discuss the efforts of mall developers and designers to re-vitalize the city center in the early 1960s and the effects of these efforts on recovering the viability of the urban marketplace.

In the early 1960s the Johnson administration launched the "Model Cities" program. Model Cities was an admission by the U.S. government that the urban environments across the country were enclaves of destitution and poverty. Model Cities was a reaction to local, state and federal government urban renewal programs of the 1950s that fostered mass demolition of row-houses in urban slums, replacing them with large modernist style tower blocks. The tower blocks did not curb violence, but instead further centralized the violence, which in turn led to widespread disillusionment with the urban renewal process. Model Cities, as a reaction to previous urban renewal efforts, attempted to revitalize the urban environment through social programs and funding for structures that would foster a community environment. Notes

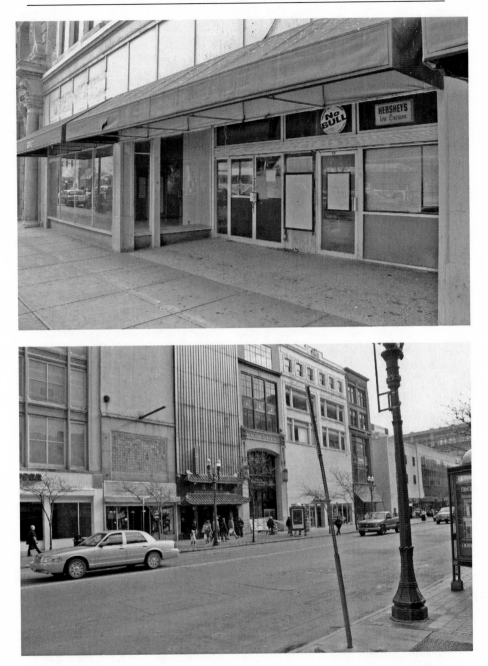

Top: A vacant building in downtown Syracuse. *Bottom:* Salina Street, Syracuse, was once home to many large department stores but it is now home to many vacant and derelict buildings.

Derelict home in downtown Syracuse, New York.

the *Encyclopedia of Chicago*: "The Model Cities initiative created a new program at the Department of Housing and Urban Development (HUD) intended to improve coordination of existing urban programs and provide additional funds for local plans. The program's goals emphasized comprehensive planning, involving not just rebuilding but also rehabilitation, social service delivery, and citizen participation."[2]

Pres. Lyndon Johnson delivered his plan in the impassioned "Great Society" speech, declaring that the great society would be "a place where the city of Man serves not only the needs of the body and the demands of commerce but the desire for beauty and the hunger for community.... It is a place where men are more concerned with the quality of their goals than with the quality of their goods."[3] Johnson found an unlikely recruit for his urban vision to carry out his mission. Victor Gruen, the creator of the suburban shopping mall model that had aided in the destruction of downtown to begin with, was asked to participate in the Model Cities program. In 1956, Gruen was an integral part of Ladybird Johnson's White House Conference on National Beauty, and he took his role seriously. Gruen began to envision the shopping mall as a means to redress the urban decline across the country and started to formulate plans for its effective implantation in American cities.

Victor Gruen's urban vision was spelled out in his 1964 book *The Heart of Our Cities*. "A real city is full of life, with ever-changing moods and patterns;

the morning mood, the bustling day, the softness of evening and the mysteries of night, the city on workdays so different from the city on Sunday and holiday," says Gruen. "In contrast America's 'downtown' areas, those part-time ghost towns, spawned by the one-sided and one-track development of many of our city cores, which are busy eight hours a day on weekdays and deadly silent and unpopulated in the evening, during the night, on Saturdays and Sundays."[4] Gruen's goal was to make a vibrant city center that would encourage urban participation far beyond working hours. What the cities of the 1950s lacked, explained Gruen, was an ability to balance the needs of auto-accessibility with that of the pedestrian environment. To do this he felt that the automobile should be "tamed" to fit within a pedestrian environment. "I insist that the solution to coexistence of the human and automotive population does not lie in the taming and training of people," said Gruen, "but in the taming of the motorcar."[5]

He outlined a three-step process that would "tame" the automobile. The first measure was the inclusion and increase of quality, and convenient public transportation at a reasonable price for commuters. Gruen also suggested a system of underground roads to handle service traffic, thus allowing the loading and unloading of goods to happen under structures instead of at street level. His third suggestion for "taming" the automobile was to create parking structures with "pedestrian transportation systems" attached. These covered "moving sidewalks" would whisk the pedestrian from the covered parking lot to their destination within a climate-controlled tube conducive to walking all year round.[6] Although Gruen had no direct power to fund and control the construction of effective urban public transport systems or a mass system of pedestrian walkways, he was able to fulfill some of his objectives in the construction of urban retail spaces. His suggestions therefore came to fruition in his plans for the revitalization of the downtown shopping areas of urban environments across the country. Although the proposals for downtown areas such as Rochester, New York, and Fresno, California, facilitated some of Gruen's optimistic plans for urban renewal, they ultimately stemmed back to models based on his suburban shopping center designs, thus creating a suburban mall in an urban environment.

Gruen championed the enclosed shopping center as a means to re-develop the congested and disorganized downtown areas of cities. Midtown Plaza, a project developed by Gruen in conjunction with the department stores McCurdy's and Forman's, was a prime example of his initial success in the urban landscape. The mall, which officially opened in 1962, replaced the dying downtown area of Rochester with a vibrant, enclosed consumer fantasy-land with three levels of underground parking and Rochester's first "skyscraper;" a 30 story office block that towered above the mall. Gruen's design utilized similar features of his Southdale plan. Midtown Plaza featured a bland exterior surface area whereby the urban shopping mall was further "enclosed," introverting itself from the city streets, a design flaw that would eventually aid in its demise. In the same manner as Gruen's suburban shopping mall designs, the interior of Midtown Plaza was meant to be a pedestrian fantasy-land of retail pleasure. In Midtown, he heightened the sense of fantasy in the atrium space by commissioning a 28-foot high baroque style clock with rotating puppets in the folk dress of different countries. Deemed the "Clock of Nations," it was meant to evoke the town clocks of old European city centers such as Munich and Prague. Gruen's high kitsch clock became a focal point of the space, a successful gathering point and feature of the atrium. In *The Heart of Our Cities*, Gruen relays fondly, "The 'Clock of Nations,' which we had visualized as a landmark for the plaza, has not only fulfilled this function but has gone beyond that. At the striking of the hour, hundreds and sometimes thousands congregate around it to admire the puppets."[7]

The design of Midtown differed from that of Gruen's suburban designs in that he emphasized the ability of the mall to curb traffic congestion through a system of subterranean tunnels that would seamlessly supply goods to the shops and underground parking which would alleviate the need for an expansive parking system outside the mall. Midtown, unlike his suburban designs, was a multi-purpose space in which people could work, shop and socialize, thus encouraging citizens to utilize the area outside of working hours. In the first 10 years, Midtown was swamped with visitors. At the opening alone, 10,000 people crammed into the hallways and atrium of the mall to witness the festivities. To Gruen, Midtown was the archetypal example of the success of his "utopian experiment." In its first three years it successfully bridged the gap between community and consumer space. The atrium space was constantly booked with dances, art exhibits, historical displays, community fundraisers and concerts. It not only functioned as the cultural heart of the city but also as it's civic heart, as Gruen explains, "Midtown plaza was also the scene of political meetings of both major parties, each attracting more than 10,000 participants."[8] With Midtown Plaza, Gruen believed that he had created a superior model to revitalize the urban core: "What is especially interesting about the pattern of urban participation is that the activities are not concentrated, as in most downtown areas, within the eight-hour working period; cultural, social and recreation functions make the plaza an active, bustling place from early morning to late at night, throughout the week and even on Sundays and public holidays."[9]

Although enclosed shopping centers like Midtown Plaza became the preferred model of urban re-development of the period, especially in cold Northern climates, Gruen pitched another solution to urban renewal, one that drew

The Midtown Plaza Clock (currently held at the Rochester Airport).

more directly from European cities. Central city pedestrian marketplaces and streets were a staple of the urban environment since Greek and Roman times and had existed in New England and Midwestern towns up until the 19th century. By the end of the Second World War, however, the number and availability of automobiles changed the urban environment, making it congested and potentially dangerous to the pedestrian. Gruen was to revitalize the concept of an outdoor pedestrian mall in his designs for the Fulton Mall in Fresno, California. Due to the large

Top left: "Israel" puppet display on the Midtown Plaza Clock. *Top right:* "Puerto Rico" puppet display on the Midtown Plaza Clock. *Bottom:* "United States" puppet display on the Midtown Plaza Clock.

suburban movement of the early 1950s, downtown Fresno had become simply a bypass on the way to the suburbs. With a lack of parking and difficulty in pedestrian movement, many stores closed their downtown outlets and decamped for suburbia. The deterioration of downtown became especially apparent in 1956 when the retail giant Sears Roebuck abandoned its downtown premises and moved to the suburbs.

In 1958, the Fresno Redevelopment Agency hired Gruen and Associates to come up with a plan to revitalize the dying downtown area of Fresno. Instead of creating a totally new central space, like he did in Rochester with Midtown Plaza, Gruen suggested retaining the historic central business district and making it exclusively accessible to pedestrians by closing the roads to traffic. Instead, traffic was diverted around the district to a ring road with ample off-street parking. The increased infrastructure for automobile traffic was the essential ingredient in the model for "taming the motorcar," as Gruen explained that the mall could not function without it. "Introducing one pedestrian mall into a city core area without taking the necessary steps to improve circulation and provide automobile storage space only serves to multiply the troubles instead of eliminating them," explained Gruen.[10] The main pedestrian area featured Gruen's signature festival atmosphere with fountains, trees, public art, streetlamps and a large sculptural clock. The mall opened in 1962 to great fanfare and in its first few years was a viable commercial success, dramatically increasing the retail activity in the area. Bernard Traper, in the October 1966 issue of *Reader's Digest*, wrote: "As I write this, I am sitting contentedly, a cool drink at my elbow, right in the middle of Fulton Street.... Two and a half years ago, I would have been run over, arrested or firmly led away to have my head examined. What I am doing now is simply part of the new pattern of life this bustling city has adopted; one starting from the premise that downtown is for people."[11]

Developments such as Gruen's 1962 Midtown plaza and the Fulton Mall sparked a short period of resurgence in the downtown areas of Rochester and Fresno; however, by the 1970s both Midtown and Fulton, as well as many other urban re-developments, had failed to attract steady numbers and began to decline again. As explained in the previous chapter, by the mid–1980s suburban growth had spurred offices to move to the suburbs, thus creating "edge cities," therefore making traditional downtown areas even more redundant. Gruen's optimistic viewpoint of a vivid urban environment was curbed by the fact that the general population had fully embraced their drivable suburban lives and was unwilling to turn back to dependency on public transport and other shared services. Johnson's Model Cities program and subsequent local government initiatives were not effective in reviving the urban cores of cities across the country.

Top: Urban decay in Rochester, New York. *Bottom:* Rochester's first skyscraper, the Midtown Plaza office tower.

"Over time, these programs were putting billions of dollars into cities, but the cities were offering a kind of lifestyle the market did not want at the time," says Leinburger, "These individual programs could not effectively counteract the transportation policies, subsidies and financial guarantees that over time directed trillions of dollars of infrastructure investment into what most Americans wanted: drivable suburban development."[12] Downtown areas became associated with poverty and crime, factors which discouraged the suburban shopper. Consumers, above all else, valued the perceived safety and convenience of the suburban shopping mall. The downtown shopping centers still proved difficult to navigate and the perception of high crime in these areas effectively killed Gruen's attempts to revitalize them. Another reason for the decline of Gruen's inner-city shopping malls and pedestrian shopping streets was they did not offer enough of a point of difference from the suburban shopping mall to warrant a trip downtown. The concept of a shopping mall as a means to revitalize the urban environment was not totally without success, as another model came to fruition that provided the visitor with the point of difference lacking in Gruen's creations.

Initially inspired by Gruen's urban experiments, the visionary developer James Rouse created a superior version of the enclosed shopping center in the urban environment, a model that would prove to have more permanence than the Fresno or Midtown projects. Rouse studied the success of the re-developed historic 1893 Ghirardelli chocolate factory in San Francisco. William M. Roth acquired the near dilapidated factory in the early '60s and with the visionary support of architects Wurster, Bernadi and Emmons, he turned the rambling factory buildings into an upscale specialty retail center. "When it opened in 1964, Ghirardelli Square demonstrated for the first time almost all of the characteristic features of what was to be christened the 'specialty center' and which differed fundamentally from those of the main regional centers," explains Maitland.[13] A "specialty center," as defined by the Urban Land Institute, is "a non-traditional shopping center" that has "special architectural character or flavor."[14] Ghirardelli Square offered the same festival atmosphere visible in Gruen's Midtown mall; however, the historic building itself added an interesting destination worth traveling to downtown for a visit. "There the mall is the magnet, which draws shoppers to itself through sheer force of character, despite its off-center location and as a focus for a collection of traders which, individually provide a marginal attraction," explains Maitland.[15]

Rouse replicated and enhanced this concept when he took on the project of re-developing the derelict Faneuil Hall marketplace in 1964. The historic Boston icon had functioned as a marketplace and meeting hall since 1742 but had fallen into disrepair during the period of suburban growth in the 1950s and '60s. As Rouse's proposed development for the center was not the standard suburban, enclosed shopping mall model, it posed some risk to investors and despite public support, Rouse had difficulty finding funding. Along with funding difficulties, issues with city planning and traffic flow caused Rouse significant headaches and the project took over ten years to complete. Despite the issues, on completion it became a huge commercial success, attracting a steady 12 million visitors a year.[16] Rouse's vision of urban renewal was a triumph in retail development; Faneuil Hall created a meeting point and social space for local office workers and a tourist destination of international repute that revived the declining city-scape of central Boston. Like the typical enclosed shopping malls in suburbia both Ghirardelli Square and Faneuil Hall are centrally controlled spaces with retail tenants and interior treatments specially selected by developers.

Though both malls exhibit many of the characteristics of the enclosed shopping center, the essential difference is the lack of department stores and more emphasis on specialty shops and food outlets. Because of these characteristics, Rouse deemed this type of development a "festival marketplace." The festival marketplace is more about the experience than the goods for sale. It relies more on impulse buying and tourist trade and often provides the visitor with informal entertainment, such as buskers and street performances, to enhance the "festival" atmosphere.[17] Based on the success of Faneuil Hall, the festival marketplace model was replicated in many urban centers and achieved the longevity that Gruen's urban re-development failed to achieve.

At the height of their success in the 1980s, around 31 festival marketplaces were present in downtown areas across the country. Over the past ten years, however, many of these entertainment based urban retailers have succumbed to a similar fate as Gruen's Midtown Plaza. The main problem with the festival marketplaces is that they do not offer the same genuine community aspects of the historic marketplaces or historic icons they replaced. Essentially the festival marketplace is a consumer space masked by the guise of historical architecture. The festival market works to attract tourists and first time visitors to a city, but as its goods are is based on a "festival" approach, it does not sustain return consumption. Notes Maitland, "It must be said that their activity is not inherent but induced; that they offer goods and services superfluous to daily need; that their environment enthusiastically embraces 'pretence [sic] and fakery'; that their novelty and sense of quality are self-consciously cultivated; and that they have little real meaning in their urban context."[18] New York's South Street Seaport is a prime example of this. "South Sea Port's market proved too narrow, its attractions too weak, to lure New Yorkers," explains Alexandra Lange from the Design Observer. "Locals don't need more café chairs, but a real lawn, they don't need picturesque fruit stands, but a real farmer's market. It needs to feel as if work is still going on, not as if the architecture is merely a false front."[19] Lange explains that what urbanites seek most is a true sense of community, and not a fake. "What the neighborhood needs is the amenities it currently lacks: a green, a school, mundane shopping options. The [festival marketplace] pretends to be a new neighborhood while really trying to create a fancier, more contemporary tourist trap."[20] This sentiment is echoed by the Urban Land Institute, which states that festival marketplaces proved successful in only limited locations with a large population base and influx of tourists. They note that people are searching more for authentically entertaining environments rather than entertainment for the sake of tourists. "The evolution has progressed from entertainment to entertaining environments."[21]

By the late 1980s it became clear that shopping malls could not save the cores of ailing American cities. The drivable suburban model had proved far too attractive to the average American to influence them to return to the declining, crime ridden and congested urban centers. "The selection of a car-based transportation system drove out most other transportation options, such as public transit, bicycles and especially walking and this automobile dependence is at the root of many of the negative consequences [of suburban living]," says Leinburger.[22] Glaeser, in his book *Triumph of the City*, explains that new buildings and infrastructure promoting new traffic patters or retail trade cannot save a city. "Urban renewal may have replaced unattractive slums with shiny new buildings, but it did little to address urban decline."[23] Building a new shopping center in an urban environment, as evidenced by Gruen's Midtown Plaza, may promote a temporary revitalization of an urban core; however, inevitably it will decline again without true investment into the creation of an environment conducive to a sustainable community. "Investing in buildings instead of people in places where prices were already low may have been the biggest mistake of urban policy over the past sixty years," says Glaeser.[24] With the exception of some larger urban centers such as New York, many inner cities across the country are still areas of concentrated poverty and urban decline.

People have abandoned properties in many inner-cities, leaving a blight of empty houses and office and retail spaces in their wake. Present day Detroit is an example of effects of mass suburbanization. Today one-third of the city's population lives in poverty and its median income is roughly half the U.S. average. "In 2008, Detroit had one of the highest murder rates in America, more than ten times higher than New York City's," says Glaeser.[25] Currently, the city of Detroit has more than 90,000 abandoned or vacant homes and residential lots.[26] "Two-hundred-thousand jobs were lost in the space of three years," explains Sudjic, "and left Detroit with a sprawling post-industrial wasteland in the middle."[27] The solution has been to simply demolish buildings and houses in the dead urban cores and leave empty spaces in an attempt to "right-size" declining cities. The city of Detroit is practicing a policy of mass-demolition to rid itself of the urban decline. "More than 28,000 houses have been demolished since 1989–90," notes Wilgoren. "The city spends $80,000 per year maintaining its empty lots."[28] City residents note that when the city demolishes properties, "they don't plant grass, they don't plant trees, it's just a big scar."[29]

In Buffalo, New York, vacant properties in the urban core have reached crisis point. "The planning and zoning codes of the 1950s were based around the automobile. Planners saw cars as the cure-all for urban problems," explains Chuck Banas of the American Institute of Architects, "and so they destroyed neighborhoods, displaced people, and used valuable waterfront property to make automobile travel easier."[30] Mayor Byron Brown instituted a "5 in 5" plan to address the problem of vacant housing in the city core. "The idea was to take down 5,000 homes in five years," explains Sondel. "The city has demolished more than 4,000 homes at a cost of more than $61 million since 2006."[31] The plan is turning out to be very costly for the city and as such the mayor has since proposed a new goal to refurbish 500 houses in five years. "The path back for declining industrial towns is long and hard," says Glaeser. "Apart from investing in education and maintaining core public services with moderate taxes and regulations, governments can do little to speed this process."[32]

The benefits of suburban living, as outlined by Leinburger are terrestrial affiliation (having a piece of land to call one's own), lower costs, due to inherently cheaper construction and infrastructure subsidies, more land, lower community taxes, improved public schools, privacy, perceived safety and abundant free parking.[33] The suburban vision of the future, as conceived in the late 1930s, is still the visible American Dream today. "It seemed at the end of the 1980s that the pendulum simply couldn't swing any further toward drivable sub-urbanism," says Leinburger, "but it did, now with the financial power of Wall Street behind it. The spread continues, despite the increasingly apparent negative consequences of building this one development form to the exclusion of all others."[34] The urban shopping malls of the 1960s, '70s and '80s did little to curb the decline of the inner cities that they populated, and in some cases it proved to accelerate the decline by killing off smaller retailers. With the perception of crime and traffic congestion, urban shopping malls failed to attract the suburban consumer.

The festival marketplace, while initially a more viable concept than downtown shopping malls, have also proved to be a failure in revitalizing the city core. As noted by Glaeser, buildings alone cannot save cities, the cities must make an authentic community by investing in the creative economy of a city in order to pull the population back to these centers. Despite trillions of dollars spent on creating new infrastructure in cities over the past sixty years, the urban environment will continue to suffer unless the mindset of the average American can be converted from a reliance on the automobile to a reliance on public transport and shared services. Walk-able urbanism has yet to take on mass appeal, cities across the country still exhibit mass sprawl, and the average citizen still prefers drivable suburban living.

As discussed in this chapter and the previous, with the mass suburbanization of America, the regional shopping mall emerged as the visible "heart" of suburban communities, replacing the downtown areas of cities. The next section will look at the symbolism of the shopping mall. In a reflection on the concept of "the religion of the market" and how the suburban shopping mall model fills the role of "a temple of consumerism," as well as the underlying signifiers of Main Street America, an understanding of the importance of this model in contemporary American society is reached.

4. The Mall and Religion

It has been argued that the mall represents a replacement for the church in contemporary society. This chapter explores the concept of the "religion of the market" through an understanding of the Protestant ethic and its relationship to capitalism. In the context of the "religion of the market" the mall can be defined as a "temple of consumerism." The individual nature of a capitalist value system, however, conflicts with the necessary communal aspects of society. A discussion of the negative effects of the "religion of the market" establishes the problems inherent in the capitalist system. The visual signifiers in the shopping mall relate to traditional temples of worship. An understanding of the embedded religious symbolism inherent in this space establishes a framework, which will be utilized in future chapters, to discuss retail models that have replaced the regional mall. From a historical and contemporary perspective, the following explains why the mall can be considered more than simply a consumer space and how this model offers a connection to spiritualism in an increasingly secular environment.

According to David R. Loy, in many countries around the world, consumerism has surpassed all other belief systems, becoming the most popular value-system.[1] Economists and theologians have asserted that capitalism shares many of the same beliefs and structures as traditional religions. Max Weber, in his book, *The Protestant Ethic and the Spirit of Capitalism*, explains that although we believe the capitalist system to be secular, it is firmly rooted in a religious structure based on the Protestant ethos.[2] "Weber's arguments imply that although we think of the modern world as secular, its values (e.g., economic rationalization) are not only derived from religious ones (salvation by injecting a revolutionary new promise into daily life), they are largely the same values," says Loy in his paper "Religion and the Market."[3] Market capitalism promotes an ideal, similar to the promise of life after death, that by an absolute faith to the system of profits one will find "salvation" in the attainment of worldly goods. Capitalism and the Protestant religion share "the same values," says Loy, although capitalism is "transformed by the loss of reference to an other-worldly dimension."[4] "Sixteenth-Century Protestants trusted in grace to get them to heaven; modern capitalists trust in the market to get them prosperity. The logic is an identical future-oriented hope," explains Pahl in his analysis of Weber's work.[5]

Capitalism and its popularity as a value system can be traced back to the rise of the middle classes in industrial England and Germany. It was during this time that the idea of working your way up in the world became a reality and the middle classes began to define the nature of the "capitalist spirit." "Even in the nineteenth century its [capitalism] classical representatives were not the elegant gentleman of Liverpool and Hamburg, with their commercial fortunes handed down for generations, but the self-made parvenus of Manchester and Westphalia, who often rose from very modest circumstances," writes Weber.[6] Previously European societies functioned on a strict class-based system, which favored a traditionalist approach of passing wealth among small dominant family groups, thus the attainment of a better life was impossible for many of the lower classes.

Polanyi, in his definitive work *The Great Transformation: The Political and Economic Origins of our Time*, explains that in all economic systems prior to the Industrial Revolution, labor and land remained separate from commerce. These two entities followed a strict class process, allowing the landed gentry to rule over those without land and thus establish a strict social hierarchy. "Under the guild system, as under every other economic system in previous history, the motive and circumstances of productive activities were embedded in the general organization of society," explains Polanyi.[7] "The relations of a master, journeyman, and apprentice; the terms of the craft; the number of apprentices; the wages of the workers were all regulated by the custom and rule of the guild and the town."[8]

The guild system gave religion a very powerful role in society as it fulfilled the function of "salvation" or a sense of looking forward to a future paradise in the afterlife. Pre-Reformation, the Catholic Church was also dominated by class hierarchy; assuming that piety was reserved for the upper classes and therefore the lower classes could participate in church activities but would never reach the church hierarchies. According to Weber, the Reformation was in itself a rationalization of the church and resulted in a more logical and universal system that mirrors the capitalist spirit. "To the Catholic, the absolution of his church was a compensation for his own imperfection," notes Weber, "The priest was a magician who performed the miracle of transubstantiation, and who held the key to eternal life in his hand."[9]

Protestant religions that arose after the Reformation took the "magic" out of the equation and rationalized the role of the church. Instead of an ambiguous magic quality that was difficult to define, the Reformed church replaced this with the concept that "a life guided by constant thought could achieve conquest over the state of nature."[10] According to Weber, "It was this rationalization which gave the Reformed faith its peculiar ascetic tendency, and is the basis both of its relationship to and its conflict with Catholicism."[11] Catholicism held fast to the class system while the Reformed church allowed "broader groups of religiously inclined people a positive incentive to asceticism."[12] Instead of focusing on a narrow and special class of the devout, it allowed every man to be a monk in his daily life. Essentially the Reformed church, by breaking down the class structures, provided the foundation for a value system embodied in the "capitalist spirit."

The Industrial Revolution of the late 18th and 19th centuries built on some of the significant social changes that the Reformation had brought about three hundred years prior. Fundamentally, the Industrial Revolution encouraged a further transformation of the role of common man in society. As Polanyi explains, a great change occurred in the nature of the market at the end of the 18th century — it moved from a regulated market to a self-regulated market. This change was significant in that it re-defined the rigid structure of pre-industrial society.[13] Polanyi discusses that the change to a self-regulated market meant "human society had become an accessory of the economic system."[14] Thus the market itself informed man's hierarchy and as a result, a value system arose from this movement and was called a "capitalist spirit." A "capitalist spirit" defined that "salvation" could be attained in this life as long one adhered to the capitalism ethic. The true spirit of capitalism, as explained by Ben Franklin, can be understood as an attitude, one which seeks profit rationally and systematically.[15]

Embedded within this "capitalist spirit" are moral values that relate to the logical and rational system of gaining capital. "All of Franklin's moral attitudes are colored with utilitarianism," says Weber. "Honesty is useful because it assures credit; so are punctuality, industry, frugality and that is the reason they are virtues."[16] This strengthens the argument that capitalism itself is a religion, based on a set of rules and virtues, which aid in attaining a higher goal. In the capitalism system, "man is dominated by the making of money, by acquisition as the ultimate purpose of his life," explains Weber, "Economic acquisition is no longer subordinated to man as the means for the satisfaction of his material needs."[17] Weber explains that as a result of the powerful spirit of capitalist values, the recruitment of labor in industrial countries can be done with comparative ease. This ease, notes Weber, is strongly rooted in the religious foundations of the Protestant ethic on which the United States was founded and the adherence of the capitalist model to certain universal values.[18] Similar to the Protestant ethic that provided with thought and constant devotion, any man can become a monk in his daily life; capitalism promoted that with hard work any man can attain financial freedom. "This provides the most favorable foundation for the conception of labor as an end in itself," notes Weber, "as a calling which is necessary to capitalism: the chances of overcoming traditionalism are greatest on account of the religious upbringing."[19]

Although the "capitalist spirit" is underpinned by the Protestant ethic, Weber's theories suggest that the capitalist spirit has become a religion in its own right and therefore can affect someone without a traditional religious upbringing. "In fact, it [capitalism] no longer needs the support of any religious forces and feels the attempts of religion to influence economic life, in so far as they can still be felt at all, to be as much an unjustified interference as its regulation by the State."[20] Loy argues that in our contemporary market driven economy, the power of traditional religions and the role they play in people's assessment of their values has waned. "Traditional religions have failed to offer a meaningful challenge to the aggressive proselytizing of market capitalism," says Loy, "which has already become the most successful religion of all time, winning more converts more quickly than any previous belief system or value-system in history."[21] The validity of Loy's theory is further supported by the collapse of communism in many parts of the world, resulting in the rapid adoption of market capitalism and its ascendancy as the dominant economic force. "The Market is becoming the first truly world religion, binding all corners of the globe into a world-view and set of values whose religious role we overlook only because we insist on seeing them as secular," says Loy.[22]

In correlation to Weber's definition of the capitalist spirit, the shopping mall can be described as a "temple of consumerism." Similarly, just as the capitalist spirit was influenced by the Protestant ethic, the physical structure of the shopping mall arose from design principles based on houses of worship. Pahl and Zepp use this framework when speaking of the mall as a sacred space. "The malls religious symbolism and the ritual life found in them imply that for many people they are 'real' places — places where there is a certain sense of reality about the sacred and the humanly meaningful experiences found there," explains Zepp.[23] Pahl supports this and states, "Malls communicate the 'spirit' of the market." He goes on to say, "Malls have become sacred spaces because traditional churches, synagogues, temples and mosques have failed."[24] As evidenced by mall developer James Rouse's revelation that his original mall designs were based on the design of Catholic cathedrals, the mall is full of visual signifiers that can be directly correlated with the church.[25] Zepp dissects the visual signifiers in the mall and discusses the use of water, bodies, nature and the concept of "the center."

The use of water features in malls is commonplace and can be linked to the biblical concept of "water of life." "Apart from using it to quench thirst, the main human experience of water is restoration, re-creation and healing," says Zepp.[26] "Mall developers have attempted ingeniously to satisfy this human longing to be near water."[27] Nature is utilized in a similar biblical fashion, as it is often positioned near water features creating a sense of the Garden of Eden. "When water is united with vegetation," says Zepp, "we are reminded of Eden, the prototypical garden, the enchanted glade — the place from which life sprang."[28] Nature is also used to evoke a feeling of kinship with the earth and an organic harmony. Zepp explains that the use of trees in the mall provide the visitor with a visual connection to the Tree of Life. "The tree is the classic symbol of vegetative life ... the budding of trees in the spring represents the re-constitution of all life," says Zepp.[29] In an effort to promote the idea of a constant vitality, developers fill the mall with foliage, plants and trees that seem to be ever blooming and green.

According to Zepp, the center of the mall, the atrium space, is one of its most powerful spiritual spaces. Gruen designed the atrium to be a space where "the body and eye can rest," and it was this space that Gruen and subsequent mall developers have spent significant effort facilitating a comfortable environment. "Almost every shopping mall has a center court ... the heart of the mall.... This is the space which uniquely says that the mall is "more than" a marketplace," says Zepp.[30] Swiss psychologist Carl Jung explained that the concept of a "center" is important in human existence, and the circle as a symbol of a center is represented in every world religion throughout the ages.[31] Religious orders have based their temples on the concept of a pathway to a large central space and this can be observed in the structures of ancient Catholic cathedrals, Islamic mosques, Buddhist stupas, and Jewish temples and synagogues. This central space helps to balance humans and is essential in creating harmony and direction in their lives. "When we are at the center, we can get our bearing, orient ourselves again, and find ways out of life's disorders. We discover at the center a source of power; this mirror of the universe concentrates the generally available dynamism," explains Zepp.[32] The mall, with its central atrium space, fulfills the need for the center and provides a sense of renewal and energy. Zepp says, "Malls at their centers, strive to be places of vitality and energy."[33] Therefore, the mall in this sense is a substitute for a traditional religious space, as it offers one of the key elements of religious space — centeredness.

The use of lighting and the placement of words and phrases in the mall promote a spiritual state of mind akin to the use of lighting and words in a church or mosque. "Light of many kinds is featured in shopping malls, but each light is strategically placed to draw the senses in and toward one attraction or another," notes Pahl.[34] Zepp compares the use of lighting in the atrium space to the use of lighting in the Roman Pantheon and the clerestory of a cathedral. "The opening in the dome of the Pantheon give us the same perception of expansiveness as the skylight in the mall and the clerestory of a cathedral. This sense of expansion provides us with a feeling of freedom and openness, even though we are in the midst of a highly organized space," explains Zepp.[35] Beyond providing the shopper with a view of the products on display, lighting is used to generate both a feeling of calm and excitement.

In the atrium, the central core, the lighting is usually subdued; often the primary source is the skylight. In other areas, specifically the game and arcade areas positioned to teenagers, bright signs and flashing lights proposition the visitor. "Neon light is used to beckon with its peculiar glow, especially in the signs above the entries to mall attractions, casting an aura that entices with its soft yet vibrant colors," Pahl explains. "Natural light is also a prominent feature of most mall designs."[36] This positioning can be compared to areas of a church which have dimly lit areas for quiet prayer and reflection as well as brightly lit areas for community activities, sermons and public lectures. "Light, of course," explains Pahl, "is our primary experience of energy."[37]

Similar to the religious prose, which is placed around cathedrals at the base of statues, on the walls or in sacred texts, the mall is filled with symbolic phrases and words. These words and phrases, which can also be compared to mantras or prayers, are prevalent in the advertising and signage in the mall. They promote ideas of love, happiness and devotion, all of which promise us a connection to a spiritual state of mind. "Malls advertise themselves in words that promise us unity, devotion, love, happiness, and other phenomena that were once the benefits of traditional religious practices," explains Pahl. "The words are there with unmistakable religious meanings when we start to think about them."[38]

It can be argued that traditional religion continues to have an established and healthy presence in contemporary American society. According to Gruber and Hungerman (2008), "Religious service attendance is one of the most popular activities in the United States. In a typical week, 20 percent of the U.S. population attends religious services, and half of the population attends religious services at least once per month."[39] The prevalence of religious orders and rhetoric in the United States may be, however, more firmly focused in the "capitalist spirit" than in the traditional views present in those orders. "Many so-called houses of prayer in fact have become temples to mammon," explains Pahl.[40] "One of the most famous speeches in the history of American religion, in fact, delivered over six thousand times, is [Baptist Preacher] Russell H. Conwell's 'Acres of Diamonds,'" says Pahl. "In it Christianity was clearly being tailored to the religion of the market."[41] In the speech Conwell states, "To make money honestly is to preach the gospel."[42] He returns to the importance of applying oneself to the market: "Apply yourselves, all you Christian people, as manufacturers or merchants or workmen to supply that human need. It is a great principle as broad as humanity and deep as the scripture itself."[43]

The prevalence of this belief system is widespread, explains Pahl. "This same gospel is now marketed at some 'mega-churches' across the United States, whose architecture increasingly mimics mall designs and at smaller churches that are not-so-mega but are wanna-bes."[44] Whereas devout businessmen and housewives alike may go to a church once a week, they will frequent a mall and participate in the market daily, thus making it more important to them as a temple of worship. "They may go to church on Sundays, but on Monday through Saturday the true orientation in their lives — and their true 'god' becomes apparent," notes Pahl.[45]

The confluence of religion and the market is also evident in the placement of churches in the mall space. Churches in malls may be attributed to the revocation of "blue laws" in many states. Blue laws restrict commercial activity on Sundays in a mind to promote religious activities. "By the end of the 19th Century nearly every state had a least some law prohibiting certain activities on Sunday," say Gruber and Hungerman. "Laws prohibiting general retail activity on Sundays were fairly widespread as of the middle of the twentieth century."[46] Many states have now repealed these laws while attendance at religious services has waned. Gruber and Hungerman created a model to measure church attendance and sponsorship in relation to the revocation of blue laws and found that church attendance and sponsorship is greatly affected by the retail competition on a Sunday. Ultimately, Gruber and Hungerman's study shows, that given the choice, the general population will choose to worship at the "temple of consumerism" rather than at a traditional religious venue. "The repeal of these laws in cities and state substantially increases the opportunity cost of religious attendance by offering alternatives for work, leisure and consumption," explain Gruber and Hungerman.[47]

The study also ascertained that traditional religions struggle to compete with the "religion of the market." "Religious participation clearly is affected by competitive forces, secular opportunities do compete with religious opportunities for temporal and monetary resources."[48] Therefore, as a result of this direct competition, church groups began to work out methods to position themselves in the mall.

In the 1980s, religious groups began to see the importance and dominance of the mall; they especially recognized a shift from the church to the mall as the center of a community. The Mall Area Religious Council (MARC), formed in 1987 to assess the relationship between religious groups and the Mall of America, is an example of how religious groups began to position and integrate themselves in the marketplace.[49] In fact, since opening, the Mall of America has incorporated space for a non-denominational "Chapel of Love Wedding Chapel." Although it can be argued that the site functions more as a commercial venue than a religious one, as it sells wedding services and paraphernalia, it opened a door for more purely religious spaces, such as churches for prayer and reflection, to enter mall spaces across the country. Mall management has traditionally frowned upon the placement of a church in the space of the mall, as it potentially interferes with the consumer function. As a result of the global financial crisis, which has caused declining property values and a decrease in mall occupancy, there has been an influx of religious groups populating the consumer space of the mall. "As retailers slipped away, lost to the recession, mall owners have become increasingly willing to consider non-traditional tenants such as churches," says Jesse Tron, a spokesperson for the International Council of Shopping Centers.[50] Within a mall space, the church functions as a service vying for the consumers' attention in a similar manner to a retailer. "Pastors say they like to locate in shopping malls for the same reason retailers do — ample parking, high visibility and synergy with neighboring businesses." says Dietz.[51] Although a church in the mall may work to promote a resurgence of religious participation, it is ultimately a sign of the dominance of the "religion of the market" and the effects it has had on influencing the religious tendencies of the general public in many parts of the country. "People in the Northwest are un-churched, the vast majority of folks, so we've had to really change how we approach people," says Pastor John Bishop of Living Hope Church in the Westfield Mall.[52] "This fusion of commerce and religion at the shopping mall is a sign of the economic times," says Dietz.[53] Like Conwell's "Acres of Diamonds," the church in the mall is an indicator of a market-driven approach to religion. When positioned in this manner, Pahl's theory, which relays that traditional religion has failed to inspire the general public, is supported, as it shows that many churches now rely on adapting to the "religion of the market" to re-position themselves to the community.

A major fault of the "religion of the market" is that it does not provide us with the same moral grounding as traditional religions. Polanyi explains that when the market moved from a regulated to a self-regulated one, humans became commodities. At its rational heart, capitalism dictates that humanity, as in labor, can be boiled down to a commodity that is bought and sold.[54] In effect, the "humanity as commodity" dictum takes all morality out of the equation. Adam Smith notes this in his *Theory of Moral Sentiments*: "The market is a dangerous system because it corrodes the very shared community values it needs to restrain its excesses."[55] When divorced from any moral foundations, the "religion of the market" can represent something quite dire for humanity. "Our collective moral capital has become so exhausted that our communities (or rather, our collections of now-atomized individuals each looking out for number one) are less able to regenerate it, with disturbing social consequences apparent all around us."[56]

Gruber and Hungerman uncovered, in their survey of religious attendance after the revocation of blue laws, that a lack of traditional religion with its emphasis on moral behavior leads to a deterioration of community values. "When individuals attend church less, they undertake activities that may be privately optimal but socially costly."[57] The biggest issue with a value system based purely on the market is that it has no reliance on a moral fabric to function and therefore promotes a very individualist perspective. "A basic contradiction of the market is that it requires character traits such as trust in order to work efficiently, but its own workings tend to erode such personal responsibility for others," explains Loy."[58] The "salvation" aspect of the capitalist spirit, which promotes a worldly paradise, requires an individual, rather than community, focus. In the long run, individualism can erode the community functions of society that make it bearable. French philosopher Tocqueville observed the effects of individualism on community when he visited the United States in 1831. "Individualism at first only saps the virtues of public life; but in the long run it attacks and destroys all others and is at length absorbed in selfishness."[59]

A new stage of economic rationalism has arisen in retail that threatens the community and spiritual aspects currently visible in the shopping mall. This shift will be further discussed in later chapters when we explore the following question: If the visual signifiers that make the mall a religious space are stripped away to make way for a more purely commercial space, where does one find a spiritual connection in their communities? The use of vacant retail space for churches may be seen as an indicator that the retail models replacing the mall are not fulfilling a spiritual connection. Churches in vacant retail spaces show a confluence of religion and the market and relay that traditional religion needs to emulate the religion of the market to appeal to the community. Although there may be negative connotations relating to the worship of money and capitalist sentiments, conversely it may be seen as a positive return to some of the moral values lacking in capitalist society that are represented and reiterated in traditional religions.

As a commercial venue, however, the mall cannot support the largely unprofitable churches that have begun to enter them post global financial crisis. "Churches don't pay market rate for the space that they're in," says shopping mall manager Paige Allen. "Any kind of nontraditional use is not going to pay retail rents. It's a trade-off."[60] The mall, a space generally larger than a traditional church, cannot survive simply with church patronage. "Mall managers can tap their retail tenants for contributions to the general upkeep and some tenant pay a percentage of their sales to the landlord, but not so with churches ... malls don't want churches — period," says Carol Grey of International Church Realty.[61] While the mall displays powerful symbols that imbue it with a spiritual character, Pahl identifies that capitalism as a religion and subsequently the mall as its temple can only deal shallowly with this spiritual character. "All the mall can give us are very finite experiences of consuming whatever commodity that happens to strike our current fancy," says Pahl. "The promises of unity and happiness and love are lies.... But today the system is packaged in such a way that souls continue to climb this stairway to heaven, when it is really an escalator, leading nowhere."[62]

The values of capitalism embodied in the concept of the "religion of the market" have in many ways surpassed the relevance of traditional religion in many countries throughout the world. Founded on the Protestant ethic, the "capitalist spirit" is a value system firmly based on a utilitarian mindset. Although we are prone to believe that the capitalist system is secular, Loy argues that it is firmly rooted in a spiritual system. As such the "capitalist spirit," defined by Ben Franklin, forms the basis for an understanding of the "religion of the market." If defined as a religion with an attached value system, the natural conclusion is that the mall is the place of worship for this religion; the "temple of consumerism." The overarching premise in Zepp's work is that the enclosed mall, as a replacement for our religious space, is an essential element of our contemporary society. "Mall architecture unmistakably re-creates the center by use of colossal crosses, squares, and circles," says Zepp. "This integrating form directs human movement and attempts to give the visitor a sense of stability, unity and meaning."[63]

Pahl's theories support this and suggest that the mall, and not the church, provides a far greater breadth of Americans with a "spiritual" connection. "If churches aren't connecting people to true happiness, how can we blame people for seeking happiness in a place that promises it to them accompanied by powerful experiences of water, light, trees and bodies?" says Pahl.[64] Through the use of powerful visual signifiers, the mall connects us to feelings of centeredness, unity, community, energy and vitality. "When something has imposed itself on our personal consciousness and social fabric with as much force as the malls, it is worthy of attention by culture watchers and academics," notes Zepp.[65]

To further the argument that the mall is an important symbolic space, the next chapter will explore the importance of Main Street U.S.A in American culture and how this has been reconstructed in the shopping mall.

5. Main Street

Main Street is simply the "built-up commercial area or downtown" of a community; however, this row of commercial shops facing a central thoroughfare has come to be a powerful symbol of American identity.[1] "Architecturally, Main Street is characterized by a repetition of individual buildings that have faces or 'personalities,' explains Francaviglia in his book *Main Street Revisited*.[2] These architectural personalities made American small towns unique and gave a strong sense of place to the people in the community. In pre-industrial America, Main Street played an important role providing essential goods and services to the residents of small towns. As America evolved into an industrial nation, Main Streets expanded to become downtown areas servicing larger urban populations. However much the model grew, the repetition of architecturally diverse buildings along a major thoroughfare continued to mimic the original Main Street concept and imbued a sense of the familiar.

The post–Second World War suburbanization and auto dependence changed this construction pattern with the creation of the auto-accessible shopping mall. Although the mute concrete exterior of the fully enclosed retail environment had little semblance to the traditional American Main Street, the interior is rife with symbols of this historic model. Due to mass suburbanization, many Americans have now grown up without actually experiencing a true Main Street. The concept of Main Street, however, is one that is embedded into the fabric of the country's collective conscious. This chapter will explore the concept of "Main Street" and its application in the shopping mall environment.

The ideal Main Street is immortalized in Walt Disney's Main Street U.S.A in theme parks all over the world. Disney's Main Street is based on Walt Disney's hometown of Marceline, Missouri. The real Marceline, Missouri, however, is far from the ideal Main Street. It was constructed in 1888 as a stop off point on the Atchison, Topeka, and Santa Fe Railway between Kansas City and Chicago. Beyond the richly decorated Santa Fe station, the

Top: A typical Northeastern Victorian-style Main Street in Cohoes, New York. *Bottom:* Main Street in Kinderhook, New York, displays Dutch architectural influences.

A Victorian-style shop front in Kinderhook.

Main Street was a muddy central thoroughfare that passed functional brick and mortar buildings. "To the dismay of some merchants in 1905, Marceline's streets ... were a quagmire of mud in wet weather, dusty in dry weather and what one critic called an 'equine latrine' throughout much of the year as horses left piles of droppings in the streets as they plodded along pulling wagons," says Francaviglia.[3] The discovery of a coal seam in the 1900s helped boost industry in the area; however, the town essentially was a junction servicing the needs of people passing between Kansas City and Chicago.

When Disney moved here as a boy in the early 1900s, Marceline was still the picture of a bustling small town community. It had all the accouterments of a turn of the century town — a dry goods store, meat market, department store and ice cream parlor. To Disney, Marceline was more than a commercial thoroughfare; it represented the heart of a true community, a community where everyone knew each other, cared for each other, was tolerant of one another and was willing to lend a hand when needed. Main Street U.S.A, based on his childhood vision of Marceline, was the starting point of Disney's grand theme park vision. In Disney's version, Main Street was skewed by the innocence of youth, it was transformed into a perpetually coal dust and graffiti free environment untouched by the poverty and malice that was present in the industrial-age Main Street of Marceline.

In Walt Disney theme parks, the shop fronts of Main Street U.S.A are always freshly painted, window boxes brim with ever-blooming flowers and starched lace curtains poke out from false second story windows. Ornate street lamps and perfectly sculpted trees stand in front of buildings with vintage characteristics. Wood and brick cladding and Victorian style moldings mask the squat concrete understructures of the buildings. Faux "Ma and Pa" shops selling Disney-branded trinkets, horse-drawn carriages and an imposing brick steam-train depot with "Disneyland Railroad" emblazoned on the side of the mechanized miniature engines are the features of this utopian re-creation. In the center of Disney's Main Street is an idealized town square, with Victorian-era park benches, a cannon and well sculpted trees and bushes. "The square created in Disneyland possesses an aura of magic," says Francaviglia.[4]

There are now generations of Americans who have grown up in subdivisions detached from any real Main Street; however, they can connect immediately to this false reality. "Significantly, the public square in Disneyland has become one of the most sacrosanct places in America," says Francaviglia.[5] Many real Main Streets that still exist in small towns across the country have been stripped of any viable consumer function. They were eclipsed years ago by the shopping mall, the neighborhood center, the Big Box center and other retail models. In many post war developments around the country that never had a Main Street, Disney's utopian vision of Main Street and the visual evocations of Main Street in the shopping mall are the only connection to this environment. Despite the fact that historic Main Streets are no longer a functional reality in many parts of the country, the symbolism of Main Street has continued to be a very powerful part of American identity.

Main Street is America's first manifestation of free-market capitalism and perhaps this is why it is so revered as a national icon. While Main Street is known primarily as a commercial strip, the origins of many Main Streets can be traced to purely residential spaces that evolved into commercial spaces. "Early historic photographs of Main Street often reveal a streetscape consisting of both houses and commercial buildings," explains Francaviglia.[6] "By the mid–eighteenth century, the majority of colonial port cities contained some form of primordial Main Street that served as a corridor for trade," notes Liebs in his book *Main Street to Miracle Mile*.[7] In New York State along the Erie Canal, for example, small towns flourished along the trade route that led the great port of New York City. The main streets along the canal provided goods and services to the transient workers and tradesmen. Churches, stores, stagecoach inns, stables and rooming houses populated the clapboard buildings in towns throughout the state. The railroad further expanded this corridor, advancing trade in villages and connecting people and goods across the country. Towns serviced by rail lines began to erect more substantial two and three story brick buildings, replacing the older and more impermanent wooden structures of Main Street. With the advent of the railroad, Main Streets across the country, whether it a bustling city shopping district or a tiny strip of shop fronts strung along a railroad track, became magnets for trade. In shops from Albany to St. Louis, counters brimmed with the products of the Industrial Revolution; the wares of New England factories and mechanized Midwestern farms sat side by side. "Time and development had transformed embryonic thoroughfares ... into the principal places of exchange for the industrial revolution," says Liebs.[8]

Francaviglia explains that the origins of American Main Street architecture, while deep and prolific, can be traced back to a few cultural traditions. American frontier architecture was influenced by the styles of northwestern Europe and Hispanic Mexico, while northeastern American Main Streets are heavily influenced by the architectural styles of northern Europe, countries such as France, England and the Netherlands.[9] French building styles are evident in many northwestern and central communities, such as Detroit and St. Louis. Dutch style gabled "false-front" shops are particularly noticeable in New York and New Jersey, while German architectural styles can be seen in Pennsylvania and Texas. Architectural styles of the British Isles, however, had the greatest impact on American northeastern towns. "In parts of northern Europe, but especially in the British Isles, one type of town that appears to be a prototype for American communities consists of a series of formerly individual houses with rooflines paralleling the street," explains Francaviglia. "These were joined together to form a continuous built up commercial streetscape that actually consisted of individual buildings."[10] This type of streetscape became known as the "row house." The buildings were not only residential but served commercial purposes as well. Row houses were placed directly at street level, and not set back like rural homes, so that the street became an integral part of the overall construction. These buildings were placed "end to end" on either side of the road, creating a continuous flow of commercial and residential space. The early American "Federal" style, as this type of construction came to be known, is what ultimately formed the blueprint for the American Main Street.

The southwestern United States had evolved differently from the northeast, with distinct influence from the Spanish, therefore the Main Streets of these areas are distinctly different. "From Florida to Texas to California, the Spanish or Mexican 'borderlands' area of cultural influence produced very different buildings by the eighteenth century," explains Francaviglia.[11] Flat-roofed, single story buildings with sparse decoration were more common in these areas and reflected the Mexican adobe style architecture. Construction features such as tiled roofing lent a unique characteristic to the structures; however, their cubic shapes remained quite sparsely decorated in comparison to the Federal style buildings of the northeast. "Simple porches with Spanish Colonial–era trim were often added to shade people from the rays of the sun, but these buildings are usually striking in their simplicity," says Francaviglia.[12] As the streetscape of the southwest evolved to meet the new commercial demands of the early 1880s, the window and door openings were expanded, though the style of the structures remained essentially unchanged.

In the 1850s, with an influx of Anglo influences, the southwestern street-scapes began to take on more characteristics of their northern counterparts. Although the Anglo-influenced Main Streets had now become more of a unified streetscape, reflective of the "row houses" by adjoining buildings from end to end of the street, they retained their Spanish-inspired appearance. "Using both Hispanic and Anglo techniques, southwestern Main Streets achieved a unique form."[13] The Southwestern style, still evident in Main Streets from Texas to Arizona, relays a unique contrast to the architectural styles adopted in the northeast.

As the United States evolved, many new architectural forms entered Main Street. In the mid–1800s Greek Revival styles, with Greek and Roman style columns and classical proportions, were employed in Main Street façades to show wealth and stature. The Greek Revival movement followed the political events of the period, when the country moved from being a protectorate of the British to a self-governed republic. Cities that were founded in this period, such as Syracuse, Rome, Corinth, and Carthage, borrowed names from Greek and Roman towns and displayed a reverence for the democratic principles on which the constitution was founded. "On Main Street, Greek Revival style buildings were popular as banks, land offices, and stores, for they helped to generate a sense of confidence in their enterprises," notes Francaviglia.[14] By the 1840s Main Streets across the nascent nation had taken on a more fully formed commercial character. Buildings that had been purely residential took on a "two-part commercial" character. The lower levels were dedicated to commercial enterprise, with the upper floors dedicated to residential space. The windows on the lower floors were extended to allow for proper retail displays. "Main Street began to be recognized by its distinctive buildings: two-part commercial buildings with parapet walls that rose above the roofline and in effect 'capped' the façade," explains Francaviglia. "These buildings were readily identified as 'business houses' along Main Street by their style alone."[15] During this period, American streetscapes were also heavily influenced by Victorian styles. Victorian Main Street shop fronts applied false fronts with ornate trimmings that reflected a mixture of Italianate and classic styling to invite entry. This period promoted the façade of the building as the most important part of the structure, as it faced street level. "The Victorian street-scape dramatizes the relationship between commerce and architecture but it is always operative on Main Streets of any era," says Francaviglia.[16]

At the turn of the century, the American Main Street had come of age, as its commercial and stylistic character was now fully formed. Victorian styles dominated the Main Streets across the country, creating a more standardized format. "As earlier building types were remodeled to match new construction, American small town streetscapes took on a very stylized, and highly standardized, appearance by the 1880s," notes Francaviglia.[17] The Victorian shopfront façade was replicated throughout the country, creating the nation's first uniform national architectural style. "Although it's design roots are European," explains Francaviglia, "in the hands of American entrepreneurs, it became a characteristically American form: attractive, affordable, easily constructed, easily installed and most importantly, standardized."[18] The technological advancements of the late 1800s and early 1900s also helped to shape the Victorian era Main Street vision. Electrified street lamps replaced gas lamps in the late 1880s and electrified trolleys appeared in the 1890s. Telephone and electric tramlines stretched the length of Main Street by the end of the 1880s, creating a tangle of wires that obscured the street view. Main Streets, which had primarily been dirt or cobblestone thoroughfares, also began employing concrete and vitrified paving bricks during this period. With the rise of the automobile in the early 1900s, Main Streets across the country were paved to allow for a smooth driving surface and to link them to outer highways.

When mass production of the automobile became a reality in the 1920s, the idyllic Disney-type Main Street essentially changed. City planners began to realize that Main Street was a relic of the past, not suitable for the new traffic conditions. Lack of parking was the main reason for a gradual decline of the Disney-type Main Street. With trains no longer the main means of transport, the car allowed the shopper more mobility to go wherever they pleased rather than settle for what was available in walking distance to a station. "Municipal government took stopgap measures to accommodate the auto ... they pushed back curbs, widened streets, installed directional signs, lights and traffic controls.... Private businesses demolished occasional structures to make way for parking lots," says Liebs.[19] Shops began to sprawl beyond the edges of the Main Street, in undeveloped land where it was possible to incorporate parking. This further shattered the cohesion of elements and styles that existed along Main Street. An increase of "tax-payer" strips, squat, single story retail outlets along major truck routes, caused more businesses to leave the Main Street areas altogether.[20] Although the buildings on "tax-payer strips" were meant to be temporary development, designed to produce tax revenue for the short term that would help to fund long-term investment in more permanent structures, they ended up becoming the permanent development solution for roadside retail.

The slowing production of automobiles and retail development during World War II allowed Main Streets across the country some temporary relief. And as a result it took some time for Disney's version of Main Street to completely disappear. Diners, drug stores, soda fountains and drive-in theaters characterized the Main Street of the 1930s and '40s; options that began to cater towards auto-dependence without totally succumbing to it in general. Oldenburg describes a scene from a typical 1940s small town Main Street in River Park, MI: "[Bertram's Drug Store] was centrally located and equally accessible to all; important functions were located in or near it.... Motorists passing through stopped to purchased small gifts, magazines and newspapers.... Youngsters played cribbage and canasta by the hour in booths opposite the soda fountain.... Men played poker in a small back room. Without question, the drugstore was the most preferred third place or hangout of the youth of River Park."[21] Small town America of the '30s and '40s exhibited a close connection between the home and the community. The homes of this era had wide front porches that looked out onto the street. Elms bordered the narrow roads and the scarcity of automobiles allowed for children to safely play along the streets and boulevards without fear. Although gripped by the terror of one of the most horrific wars the modern world has ever known, the sense of community that existed in these small towns helped to ease the blow and to establish a spirit of interdependence that is very difficult to find today. "Awareness and respect were not viewed as a threat to individual identity but as necessary for the production of amenity, charm and beauty," says Kunstler. "These concepts are now absent from our civilization. We have become accustomed to living in places where nothing relates to anything else ... and the absence of respect remains unchecked."[22]

Main Streets across the country were not just commercially driven venues; they were the center of town life and community. "Main Street was the home not only of stores and offices, but also of imposing churches, theaters, banks, hotels, courthouses, city halls, war memorials, libraries and other banners of community well-being," explains Liebs.[23] More than simply a collection of buildings, Main Street represents an American ideal. It represents the human connection to community. In the small towns of America at the turn of the century, everyone knew everyone else on sight, by voice, by reputation and by the reputation of the individual's family. The people of a town were interwoven in a multi-generational and binding connection to home and place. Prior to the advancement of the automobile, one purchased everything from their town, and trusted their local grocer, dressmaker or small goods proprietor to provide them with quality goods. In the typical small town Main Street, nearly everyone could access the town by walking to it. In his book *The Great Good Place*, Ray Oldenburg relays the history of a typical Midwestern Main Street: "No resident had to walk more than four blocks to reach Main Street. Everything the town had to offer was accessible on foot. Main Street was not too long to exceed the capacity of the eyes to recognize human beings along its fullest extent."[24]

Prior to the introduction of television, people in small towns relied on each other for sources of novelty, diversity and entertainment. Thus physical conversation and connection to other human beings was necessary and colored the everyday lives of people in small towns and cities alike. In this sense public buildings took on an importance unknown to our generation, which is more familiar with the mutable and bland concrete structures of contemporary shopping malls, post offices and town halls. Kunstler states in his book *Geography of Nowhere* that "earlier American building types were set in a different landscape, characterized by respect for the human scale and a desire to embellish nature, not eradicate it."[25]

Although in its purest form, Main Street is simply a commercial row of shops, it has come to represent a utopian ideal of American life. "In a perceptual/geographical sense, Main Street is both mundane (typographic) and paradoxically 'utopian.' It is both an imaginary place (literally no place) and also an ideal (or perfect) place," says Francaviglia.[26] Main Street captures the American imagination in a way no other architectural structures have been able to replicate. "Main Street and other idealized place images may be the points of refuge for Americans who would just as soon turn back the clock if it meant recapturing lost innocence and simplifying their lives."[27]

Main Street, as imagined by Walt Disney, can be both a commercial space and a physical commodity in and of itself. Americans buy into the 'image' of Main Street, and in this space the values of innocence, simplicity, refuge and community are manifested through the late–Victorian style buildings on the faux Main Street. The space itself is a much a commodity as the objects available for purchase in the souvenir shops. Agger notes: "Postmodern capitalism creates capital out of images and images out of commodities, utterly blurring the boundaries between the real and imaginary."[28] Therefore, when the real Main Streets, which were sites of historic and functional commercial architecture, were replaced by the shopping malls, the shopping malls borrowed images from our deteriorating Victorian and Hispanic style Main Streets to link the visitor to values of innocence, community, and refuge.

"The memory and example of the pre-war small town and its Main Street have become sufficiently dim, such than many now claim that it has been reborn in the form of the shopping mall," says Oldenburg.[29] Main Street is evoked in the mall in many ways. The shopping mall, as a retail environment that is central to the suburban community around it, re-creates the functionality of pre-war American Main Street. The bland modernist outer shell has little exterior semblance to the architectural variety of post-war Main Street; however, the interior of the space is rife with symbolic references. "In malls, as in Disney's Main Streets, every aspect of design and circulation is carefully orchestrated," says Francaviglia.[30] With its facing rows of shops and central town squares, the interior layout of a shopping mall also evokes the layout of historic Main Streets. The food, courts, shop fronts and hallways of shopping malls borrow visual clues from historical Main Streets to create a feeling of familiarity and attachment to the visitor.

In describing the Fairfax Corner Mall in Virginia, the Urban Land Institute relays the structure's Greek Revival characteristics. "The 'Main Street' corner of one building is reinforced by a cylindrical form supporting a dome that rises above the cornice with a deep entablature detailed with brackets and modillions, while another 'main street' corner of the other building is reinforced by a hexagonal form."[31] The surface treatment of the buildings is a direct reference to the historical Greek Revival architecture of the area and reflect the development trend to re-create Main Street indicators. In the design of the Bell Tower Plaza in Lee, County Florida, the Spanish/Hispanic style of stucco walls and tile roofs is replicated. "The center is designed in the style

A Main Street re-creation in Hampshire Mall, Massachusetts.

Top: Sangertown Square Mall "Main Street," Utica, New York. *Bottom:* A typical small town American Main Street in Auburn, New York.

of a Spanish Mission and presents an aura of tradition, durability and quality," cites the ULI. "Design features include light colored stucco walls, barrel tile roofs, clay paver tiles, timber details and graceful arches.... Bells in the tower strike the quarter hours and provide carillon music."[32] In both centers, a reference to styles entrenched in the historical Main Streets of these areas connects to the nostalgia and community sentiment of yesteryear.

The community sentiment that the mall is attempting to relay with its Main Street signifiers, however, never really comes to fruition. This is because the mall is a centrally controlled commercial space, less reliant on the symbiotic relationship between shopkeepers and townspeople than the real Main Street. "Whatever one may say about the typical shopping center, it is an abstracted reincarnation of Main Street, where all of the merchants agree to maintain regular hours and carefully control their signage and sales pitches — techniques which avoid the appearance of haphazard or eccentric individualism," notes Francaviglia.[33] In the turn of the century American Main Street, individual shopkeepers invested in their trade and were willing to go to all efforts to generate a personal connection, spirit and feeling of community. The mall draws from a much larger radius than the Main Streets of yesteryear, people from communities 100 miles away and farther will travel to a shopping mall. Therefore people we will only have a momentary connection with populate the shopping mall and that connection may simply be passing someone in the vast corridors of the retail environment. The jobs on offer in the mall — cashiers, janitors, food-stall workers, retail assistants and baristas — are considered temporary, transitional jobs, and therefore even the people who work there will continually change.

On the strength of the replication of certain elements of a Main Street, park benches, fountains, faux shop-fronts, the mall attempts to fabricate the sentiment of a Main Street community. It misses the mark, however, as community of small town America before World War II was created by a continual interaction and an interdependence that no longer exists in the staunchly independent and isolated suburban mentality of contemporary Americans. The mall is a meeting place; however, one normally meets at the mall people they already know such as family, schoolmates or friends and colleagues from work. Unless one actually works at the mall, thus furthering the potential to form a temporary community among the people they work with, it is rare to form a community by simply visiting the shops everyday. "Today, unlike Main Street, the shopping mall is populated by strangers," says Oldenburg.[34]

Geographer Alan Baker describes Main Street as an integral element in the "collective consciousness" of Americans.[35] The pre-war American Main Street has become a powerful visual symbol linking the viewer to concepts of community, innocence and refuge. The shopping mall, like Disney's Main

Street U.S.A, took visual clues from the Main Streets of yesteryear and remixed them to suit the commercial nature of the space. Main Street is most often evoked in historic Victorian styles in the northeast and Hispanic styles in the Southwest and Western areas of the United States. In any contemporary shopping mall, it is possible to pick out multiple visual signifiers that represent the changing Main Street of pre-suburban America. From Federal style windowed shop fronts, Victorian moldings and Greek Revival pillars to the Southwestern white-washed walls and tiles, the mall is a kaleidoscope of styles all meant to evoke the deep connection to community that is at the core of the Main Street vision. "Main Street persists because we instinctively believe that architecture and design affect behavior and can enable us to keep a sense of our roots, a valuable asset in times of great social and economic change," says Francaviglia.[36] "Main Street is, in fact, one our most important and persistent statements about America in time and space."[37]

Although abstracted, the mall represents an American Main Street vision, one that roots us to historic connotations of the community. Because many suburbanites grew up without a true connection to Main Street, the mall is their Main Street and presents them with an environment that links them to visions of historical American Main Streets. This is why people that have no real connection to a traditional Main Street still have a strong idea of what American Main Street represents. In this sense, the mall perpetuates some of the ideals of pre-war American Main Street that are at the heart of the American collective conscience. Thus, although the mall is a highly controlled and synthetic space, which lacks some of the true community aspects that the Main Street of yesteryear provided, it is a very relevant site of American cultural identity. The shopping mall inspires the visitor in a way that the Big Box discount warehouse stores, with their lack of historic Main Street symbolism, fall short.

The mall is not an ideal community center; however, it does serve as a primary site for community interaction for some demographic groups. The next chapter will further reflect on how the shopping mall replicates the community aspects of a traditional Main Street through a discussion on how primary user groups, elderly and teenagers, use the regional mall for community interaction and social needs.

6. Teens and the Mall

Since its creation, the enclosed shopping mall has proven to be a particularly relevant space for teenagers. For suburban teenagers the mall is an essential place for community and an important tool for teaching the consumer culture that permeates many levels of society. "All ages tend to come to malls," notes Zepp, "but teenagers and the elderly are most in evidence ... the mall provides the strongest sense of community for teenagers and older persons."[1] The mall may not be an ideal space for everyone; however, for teenagers it has proven to be a very important social and formative space. Notes Devlin: "Research in the 1980s indicated that teenagers typically went to the mall with friends, but not often with their parents. And a survey indicated that 63 percent considered themselves users of the mall and spent from 1 to 5 hours there at a time."[2] Devlin continues: "Shopping was a reason for being there among only about half of the teenagers interviewed."[3] Teenagers use the mall not only as a place to shop, meet friends and find temporary employment, but also to alleviate social and intimate loneliness. Parents, assured of the "safety" of the enclosed mall, often use this space as a de facto babysitter for their children. The mall gives the teenager a sense of freedom unknown in the more overtly supervised school environment.

Recent extensions of the "mall escort policy" and the decline of teen employment threaten contemporary teens' opportunities for monetary and social freedoms. The closure of many regional malls post global financial crisis has given rise to a longing for these spaces as echoed on social media sites. The following chapter will reflect on the importance of the mall to teenagers and how the loss of mall spaces has led to powerful feelings of nostalgia in this group.

The mall has been recognized a social space for teens from the early '60s, as reflected in popular culture. The mall is now the civic heart of most regional areas in the United States, and as such it has become an important site for the documentation of the American condition. Since the 1960s, the mall has been used as an allegorical backdrop in films and television for relaying the

American experience. In the 1960s retrospective sitcom *The Wonder Years*, teen Kevin is perturbed that his older brother has his license, as now his lift to the mall — his primary social space — is in jeopardy since his brother refused to take him when he had use of the family car. A 1969 episode of *The Brady Bunch* entitled "Voice of Christmas," hinges on youngest daughter Cindy going to see Santa at the mall so she can ask him to give her mother's laryngitis affected voice back. The popular 1980s sitcom *Full House* uses the mall as a backdrop for many situations involving teenager DJ and her best friend Kimmy. Framed within the context of the shopping mall, the story of America has been transported across the globe through the medium of film and television. The mall provides the world with a window into the teenage American's psyche; it gives a portrait of the collective desires, beliefs, behaviors and dreams inherent in this group.

At the height of mall culture, in the mid '80s to early '90s, groups of individuals began labeling themselves "mall rats." The term "mall rat" has entered the contemporary vernacular and is defined by the *Cambridge Dictionary* as "a young person who goes to shopping malls (large covered shopping areas) to spend time with their friends."[4] Kevin Smith's cult classic 1995 film *Mallrats,* in which suburban teens find solace from their problems in the mall, popularized the term.[5] Previously the term had more of a negative connotation, as suggested by Kowinski in his 1985 book *The Malling of America*. Kowinski says it refers to "people who seem to do nothing else but hang out at the mall. [They are] young men who may have been regulars as teenagers but somehow never graduated from the mall.... The classic mall rat is unable to hold a job and simply comes to the mall as something to do everyday."[6]

The *Mallrats* film, however, made the connotation something less pathetic, as it portrayed attractive, American suburban males and females interacting in an acceptable social space. The mall is viewed in a similar light in Amy Heckerling's 1995 film *Clueless*. In this film, a group of attractive and wealthy California teens use the mall as a consumer space and an important social space. Home, school and the mall are all shown as the centers of teenage life. Apart from home and school, which are both portrayed as being dominated by adult rules, the mall is shown as a respite from this structure, a third space that is both welcoming and calming. "I felt impotent and out of control. Which I really, really hate. I had to find sanctuary in a place where I could gather my thoughts and regain my strength," says Cher, the main character in the film, as she is shown entering a mall.[7]

As reflected in these films, many suburban Americans strongly relate their childhoods to the mall. Explains Underhill, in his book *The Call of the Mall*, "There's a whole generation who got their first wild taste of independence at the mall. It's where they were dropped off on Friday nights by Mom and permitted to run free — to shop, blow their allowance, and socialize themselves into adulthood. For these guys, the connotations of the mall are mostly positive. For them, the mall is real."[8]

Devlin refers to two subgroups of youth, "pre-teens" (ages 9 to 12) and "teens" (those between 13 and 19). Devlin notes: "'Pre-teens' are more easily stimulated and persuaded by the mall environment, whereas the 'teens' can be more critical of overt methods to persuade them to buy."[9] She says different attitudes to the mall arise from different ethnic groups. "White teens are more likely than non-white teens to be drawn to the mall for eating, whereas the opportunity for social contact and sensory stimulation attracted non-white teens."[10] The most current teen segmentation, compiled in 2009 by advertising giant Euro RSCG Worldwide, groups teens in five categories related to social and behavioral tendencies. "Its analysis identified five female segments and six male. Females segmented into In-Style Socialites, Jockettes, Most Likely to Succeed, Style Meets Thrift and Traditionalists. The male segments are Big Man on Campus, Red-Blooded Boys, Technosapiens, Tuned Inward, Under Construction and Young Metrosexuals," says Kuchinskas.[11] The Euro RSCG segmentation, although a means to show social stratification in this group, was created primarily to allow marketers to target specific product categories to each group.

Teen segmentation, whether by ethnicity, age, or behavior, all shows a common link to consumer culture and subsequently the shopping mall. Teenagers are perceived as being a valuable market for consumer spending. According to Devlin, "One market research estimate is that in 2006 teens had $153 billion of spending power."[12] Devlin states that American teenagers, taken as a single demographic group, make up the core of mall users.[13] American teenagers, seen as a powerful consumer group, use the mall as a place to buy consumer goods; however, the mall represents much more than simply a place to shop. Teens have an affinity to the space that goes beyond the simple buyer transaction.

Due to the enclosed nature of the space and the use of security guards and cameras, the mall promotes a feeling of safety. Parents, therefore, feel assured that they can leave their teenagers to wander on their own in this perceived "safe zone." Kowinski notes that parents feel comfortable with the mall because "the mall is safe, it doesn't seem to harbor any unsavory activities and there is adult supervision [security guards]; it is after all a controlled environment."[14] In lieu of a community center, the mall is the primary social space for adolescents age 12 to 15 and kids age 8 to 12.[15] In a growing number of broken and working families, the mall has become a default babysitter for adolescents. Andra Case, marketing director of Pyramid Companies, supports this, stating that children as young as ten years old have been spotted in groups without adult supervision in Pyramid Malls.[16]

In response to the deficient home situations of many American adolescents, the local mall, as a third space, gives a feeling of group attachment not possible at home or school. "Kids spend so much time at a mall partly because their parents allow it and even encourage it," explains Kowinski.[17] As the mall is one of the few spaces in a highly controlled society where youths are often allowed to wander without supervision, the mall offers them a sense of freedom from adults not possible in the home or at school. Farrell, author of *One Nation Under Goods: Malls and the Seductions of American Shopping*, explains: "Even at an early age, we depend on the consumption economy for the signs of our independence, even as we've apprenticed to the pattern of work and spend that characterizes so much of American life."[18] The safety of the mall space, as perceived by adults, therefore gives the mall high significance to the teenager. The mall is a place where, unfettered from the overt control of adults, teens can work out their identity and place in society.

For a teenager, the mall is more than a place to shop; it is a primary place of socialization and also functions as a salve for social issues that can affect suburban adolescents such as depression and loneliness. "The mall appears to meet any number of social needs teenagers have and may in fact address two different aspects of loneliness, intimate and social," explains Devlin.[19] Devlin defines intimate loneliness as the feeling of isolation that occurs when teens feel "different" from others, whereas social loneliness relates to teens that don't have anyone to talk to or interact with. The mall is an important venue for adolescents to form an understanding of themselves while staving off the loneliness and boredom inherent in many suburban American settings. Kim, Kim and Kang reiterate this in a 2003 *Family and Consumer Sciences Research Journal* article entitled "Teens' Mall Shopping Motivations": "The venue through which teens can fulfill their unique needs seems to be a shopping mall where they can socialize with friends, enjoy entertainment, or solve their loneliness or other psychological stresses."[20] The mall space is bright and vibrant with constant upbeat music playing in the background. It therefore offers a positive and exciting visual stimulation for the bored and lonely teen. "Shopping malls can function as a positive venue for teens to alleviate their loneliness via multiple means such as socializing, browsing, entertaining, or simply buying what they want," explains Kim, et al.[21] For teens on their own, the shopping mall also functions to provide a feeling of social interaction simply by being in a public space with other people of a similar age.

The mall also offers a means to play with and discover one's identities. Through the mannequins in shop windows and the pedestrians walking the mall corridors, visions of how to act, dress and think are all presented to the receptive teenage brain. "The mall is an important place for American adolescents to work out their identity and community ... the mall allows teens to play with their attractiveness and sexuality," says Farrell.[22] Larry Elkin of *Business Insider* agrees, stating that teens can thrive in a number of social spaces such as summer camps, sports events, and classrooms, but that few of these places have the same nurturing effect on them as the shopping mall.[23] "Elements of the mall supply kids with things they'd like to get from their families; warmth, old-fashioned mothering and home cooking," says Kowinski.[24] Kimberly Schonert-Reichl, professor of psychology at the University of British Columbia, says that many communities around the country lack appropriate youth centers or similar places for adolescent interaction. "Hanging out at the mall may be a developmental necessity. At this age peer relationships are so important. A mall is a public space, so it's a safe spot to meet the opposite sex or to get together with friends."[25]

Particularly in this stage of human development, individuals encounter decreases in family influence and increases in peer and media influences. As reflected in popular culture, the mall was a highly relevant public space for the teens from the early '60s, and it continues to be an important space for today's youth. There is a general misconception that the Internet has replaced many forms of social interaction and shopping for contemporary teens. Although on-line means of socialization have dramatically increased in the last decade, social analysts assert that TV is still a dominant media for contemporary teens and that online shopping and socialization have not replaced the mall. "While they [teens] indeed use the Internet heavily to relax, socialize, be entertained and stay informed, they are also heavy TV users," explains Kuchinskas on *MediaPost.com*.[26] TV has a stronger real-time social aspect than the Internet, as it allows groups to congregate around it and therefore becomes a part of group culture. As reported in a 2000 study by Lee, Lennon and Rudd, television viewing is related to increased desire for compulsive consumption, thus prompting teens to go to the shopping mall.[27]

Despite a fluency and comfort level with the Internet among contemporary teens, research by Baker and Haytko in 2000 shows that Internet shopping is not likely to replace mall patronage.[28] Andra Case, marketing director of Pyramid Companies, one of the largest mall development groups in the Northeast, backs this up saying that online shopping habits of teens presents no real threat to malls. Malls have responded to teens' online presence by using "push marketing" strategies. In push marketing, the mall utilizes its Web site to encourage mall entry by sending coupons and other special offers directly to a subscriber's cell phone on detecting entry to the mall. Regardless of the possibilities of online communication, people still have a need to meet and communicate in person. "One of the reasons why electronic versions of shopping, online and through home shopping networks on television do not offer the same forms of interaction and stimulation as being in a shopping place, is because of the lack of diversion and social interaction," says Moss.[29] In essence, the individualist form of shopping available on the Internet cannot replace the social aspects of the mall.

Despite an increase in digital forms of social interaction, the mall continues to be a very popular meeting place for teenagers in contemporary society. Although an escort policy existed in the Mall of America since 1996, escort policies were limited elsewhere to select shopping malls.[30] Since 2000, shopping malls across the country have rapidly adopted "escort policies." In an attempt to crack down on large groups of adolescents wandering the malls, many now stipulate that a guardian must accompany underage teens. The policies vary per mall development group. At Pyramid Companies malls, an adult must accompany teens under 18 Friday through Sunday after 4 P.M. At the Eastfield Mall in Springfield, Mass., teens under 16 are banned from the mall in the evenings unless accompanied by an adult. Like an exclusive nightclub, adolescents must present an ID card when prompted by a mall security guard. Sarah Miller from the *Christian Science Monitor* explains that mall managers are no longer as accepting of being a de facto babysitter for adolescents. Miller states, "Parents, they say, no matter how frazzled and frenzied, should not be dropping off their kids unsupervised in such an unstructured setting for so long."[31]

Andra Case, of Pyramid Companies, admits that the mall is a community hub and the only form of public space in many suburban areas. Case explains, however, that groups of unaccompanied youths are intimidating to older shoppers and families. "Malls with such escort policies have experienced increases in sales, decreases in retail fraud, as well as a reduction in loitering," says Devlin.[32] The Mall of America released data that showed a decrease in retail fraud from 300 cases in 1995 to only 2 in 1996 with the adoption of the escort policy.[33] While this data clearly shows the benefit of adopting his policy for the mall management, the policy discriminates against some of the people that need it the most, adolescents from time-poor, single-parent situations whose parents do not have the time or leisure to accompany them. "There are not that many places where teenagers can go and socialize," says 15-year-old Mike Lemme, of Chicopee, Mass., in the *Christian Science Monitor.* "Instead of banning all teenagers, they should find a way to get the people causing the trouble out."[34]

As a consumer space, the mall promotes consumption, but unlike other suburban spaces for this group, it is possible to use the space without paying. Notes 13-year-old Alexis Deighton in *Today's Parent*, "I don't have to pay to go to the mall; if I want to go swimming with my friends, it costs money."[35]

This is a benefit to the space, although the mall as a privatized commercial space depends on a steady flow of income to stay afloat. Mall managers recognize that teenagers alone cannot sustain the mall. Teens have traditionally offered a larger amount of disposable time and income than other demographic groups; however, the recent economic climate is decreasing their power as a buying force. The escort policy, which appears to target groups of teens using the mall as a social space without intent to purchase, is a necessity in the eyes of mall management, as it placates the older patrons who currently have the expendable income to sustain the space.

With the increasing frugality of many American households after the global financial crisis, teens have less disposable income. "I used to spend $100 a week, and now I spend like nothing," says California teen Ali Ghassemi in a 2009 *New York Times* article.[36] Teens, like the majority of Americans affected by the crisis, are making more frugal retail choices. Euro RSCG's teenage segmentation index relays that the largest percentage of American teenage girls fall into the "style-meets-thrift" category.[37] This group, which encompasses the highest earners and spenders, imitate fashion trends with value-priced purchases from discount stores such as Target or Walmart. Although they continue to use the mall as a social space, they are less likely to make major purchases there.

The need for a social space is compounded by the fact that many teens are now out of work. The traditional teen-exclusive temporary jobs are going to the middle-aged unemployed or recent university graduates for whom more lucrative work is increasingly scarce. A decrease of teen work opportunities is resulting in a decline of teens as a major consumer group. During the 2010 peak summer season, the unemployment rate for teens was 26.1 percent, the worst since 1949.[38] John Challenger, CEO of outplacement group Challenger, Gray and Christmas, says that this can be attributed to an increase in competition from "millions of older workers."[39] Malls have traditionally been places where teens could get their first experience in the world of work. "Now," explains Challenger, "teens are facing heavy competition from people in their early 20s particularly, who are taking some of those better teen jobs that usually they leave alone."[40] Idle teens will therefore use the mall as an outlet for their boredom during times when they would normally be gainfully employed. Without any income to spend in the stores they become a disadvantage to the consumer-friendly mall, intent on increasing lagging sales. For the teens, the dearth of job opportunities in the mall means important job skills such as flexibility, responsibility, customer interaction, and ability to take direction will not be reiterated outside the home and school environments.

As explained in-depth in Chapter Ten, *Dawn of the Dead Mall*, the viability of the regional mall is on the decline. This is significant to the teenagers who once used the space as their primary "third place." In early 2000, several Web sites emerged that recognized the loss of a mall as quite personal and important to this group. On sites such as *DeadMalls.com* and *Labelscar*, users relay stories, videos and images of their favorite "dead malls" for public comment in an attempt to informally catalogue malls across the country that have gone the way of the dinosaurs. The sites reflect the ownership and sense of place that adolescents growing up in the early 1980s and 1990s and today associate with their local mall. Damas and Schendel, creators of *Labelscar*, have explained that a mall is not simply a mutable consumer space. They note that malls represent an essential part of the formative years of American teenagers. Regardless of the fact that many downtown areas in America have declined, many have never been removed or demolished and ultimately have the ability to resurrect themselves. Malls, as private property, can be fully redeveloped or removed from the landscape completely, erasing spaces that had once been crucial to many people's lives.[41]

Deadmalls.com and *Labelscar* offer a window into the relevance of the mall as a public space for many young Americans. The dreams and experiences of these individuals show how malls have helped shape identities and visualize dreams. J.J. Buechenr writes: "The Mohawk Mall has a special place in my heart. There are so many memories there including my first trip to the mall without any supervision and my first date in the 7th grade."[42] Writes Brett Castleberry: "I remember the somewhat scary escalator to the second floor [of the Colonial Plaza Mall], with its corrugated, slinky-like handrails.... Belk's [department store] sold Scout uniforms and accessories, and seeing them on display made me dream of joining the Cub Scouts, which I did when I was old enough."[43] Writes Erica Hayes: "As a child, my Dad used to take all of his kids there [to the Rainbow Mall] on weekends. He grew up in the area but lived out of town (or state) for much of our lives, and so when he came to visit, he'd pick up me and my brothers and sister and we'd all go to the Rainbow Mall for lunch, Haagen Daas [*sic*] ice cream, and toys. I'd ride the cool-shaped elevator up and down while my brothers tried to hold the sides of the 'up' escalator. We made every trip an event — there are pictures and movies of us there, just eating ice cream and acting goofy.... I'm heartbroken that a place that housed so many of my childhood memories could fall so quickly."[44]

The stories repeated here are followed by countless more; memories of sharing a quiet moment on one of the mall's park benches with a parent or grandparent now deceased; a laugh and a burger at a café with a good friend; the excitement and anticipation of twirling in front of the mirror in a prom gown; stealing a first kiss in the mall movie theater. Many who have grown up in the United States can relate to these stories and can generate countless stories of their own mall experiences. Woven together these stories of small but precious moments generate a tapestry of American life and illustrate that the mall is an important part of the identity of young Americans.

In many cases people failed to recognize the mall as an important place until it was long gone. On Web sites such as *Labelscar, Deadmalls.com,* and *Remembering the Penn Can Mall,* the words "sadness" and "love" as well as the phrase "only place to be" are recurrent in user-generated content describing dead retail spaces. The overwhelming sentiment is that many spaces that once defined people's lives are gone. Many malls that operated in the '70s, '80s and '90s have ceased to exist and among the ones that remain, the possibilities for social experience have declined.

To conclude, for the last sixty years the mall has proved to be an important social and formative space for American teenagers. The regional mall often functions as the only public space for this group. The mall has been shown to relieve the intimate and social loneliness endemic in this group, as well as to provide opportunities for identity construction and socialization. For this generation and the next, however, the perceived freedom from adults in the mall and opportunities for part-time work are not as transparent in the lingering super-regional centers, which show an increase in the use of controlling escort policies and a decrease of teen employment opportunities. With the regional enclosed mall on the decline, many accessible social spaces for teenagers have been erased from the environment. This has led to feelings of nostalgia for the space among this group as echoed in such Web sites recording the history of lost malls.

The next chapter will explore the importance of the mall space to the other primary user group, the elderly, in an attempt to understand the similarities and differences in the importance of the space to both groups.

7. Senior Citizens
and the Mall

The mall has represented an ideal form of public space for American senior citizens since it was first established. Active and even the less-mobile senior citizens use the mall for social interaction, exercise and community. In an otherwise isolated suburban existence, the mall is a place where they can relax, exercise and meet friends all in the perceived safety of the enclosed shopping center. "Rather than driving to the local donut shop for coffee and conversation, many seniors head to the shopping malls, do some walking and then congregate in the food courts or interaction areas where comfortable chairs provide a good place to talk about the latest medications, the "good ol' days," or just plain gossip," explains Pittsburgh physician David Lindburg.[1] Sociologist George Lewis supports this statement: "The mall is a central life setting for many elderly persons who frequent it on a regular basis."[2] Senior citizens feel less alone and isolated in the mall space as it allows them to feel a sense of community and security not possible in many introverted suburban communities. "Many of these persons are retired, many widowed. They feel they have little else to fill their days," says Lewis.[3] "Without the daily concerns of work and family," relays sociologist Frascone, "the elderly derive meaning from the personal relationships they develop at the mall."[4]

Senior citizens are defined as those in the age group of 65 and older. According to recent census data, the 65 and older demographic represents 13 percent, or 1 in 8 people, of the U.S. population. This number is estimated to double in size by the 2030, where the population is expected to rise to 19 percent or 72 million people.[5] More than half of the population (57 percent) are females. In terms of ethnicity, the group is mainly white, with 80 percent of the population falling in the category of white and 10 percent comprised of Hispanic, Asian and black.[6] The group can also be divided into the sub-groups of Oldest Old, Greatest Generation and the Silent Generation. The Oldest Old are at the highest end of the age scale and represent the portion of the population that lived through the Great Depression. This group was the first to experience Social Security, is often thrifty with spending and accrued large savings as a result of their experiences. The Greatest Generation represents the mid-section of this population, the group that lived through World War II. This group was the first to experience suburban housing and the consumer culture that emerged post-war. The final group, the Silent Generation, is representative of the lower end of the age spectrum. This group represents the generation that gave birth to the populous "baby boomers." It is also referred to as the "lucky few" due to their financial stability as a result of their small numbers.

Financial stability varies in these sub-groups and has a relationship with consumer spending. The population among the silent generation (age 65–74) relies less on social security and public funding (50 percent) whereas the Oldest Old and Greatest Generation depend on this funding more frequently (66 percent).[7] Senior citizens represent a spectrum of life experiences and economic prosperity, which inform their purchases. Despite differences in experience and disparity in income, studies have shown that the group as a whole uses the consumer space of the shopping mall for communal and consumption purposes.

A 1985 study entitled "The Shopping Orientation Segmentation of the Elderly Consumer" by Lumpkin shows that senior citizens can be sub-segmented into three primary groups in relation to their consumption tendencies. Lumpkin took opinions from a sampling of 373 participants age 65 and older. Lumpkin then grouped the participants' responses in terms of Shopping Specific (relating to responses to shopping in general), Financial (price motivations), Activity (socially active), and Fashion (level of fashion consciousness). The three groups that were formed from the study informed a pattern of shopping inactivity (group 1), economic consciousness (group 2), and socially active (group 3). While participants from group 3 and 2 tend to go shopping for necessity, group 3 participants were also found to use the space for social interaction and entertainment. Group 2 used the space for both purposes, but also widely for fashion reasons. Group 2 were positioned as "active apparel shoppers."[8] Group 2 and 3 represented the largest number of participants, suggesting that shopping is a highly relevant activity for this group for both entertainment and consumption.

According to Lumpkin, the most influential group in the segment was group 2. "They enjoy shopping, probably due to their interest in fashion and active life style, as well as for the social interaction, and have a propensity to shop around. They like to shop where they are known, which is likely due to the interaction this familiarity encourages," says Lumpkin.[9] The findings of Lumpkin's study supports research by Anderson, Zepp, Lewis, and Devlin, which shows that the mall is a highly relevant and important community space for this group. The following chapter will explain why the shopping mall is a relevant community space for this group.

Anderson argues that the shopping mall has become a significant means for enhancing the quality of life of senior citizens. In a 1992 quality of life study, Anderson found that the typical elderly person that utilizes the mall is a male who views the mall as a means to satisfy needs for social activity, health, happiness, and overall morale.[10] In a 1999 study entitled "Going to the Mall: A Leisure Activity of Urban Elderly People," Graham, Graham and MacLean found that in interviewing 300 elderly Montréal residents, 67 percent of them used shopping malls to fulfill their social and leisure needs.[11] In a two-month observation of a New England shopping mall in 1988, sociologist George Lewis found that while the mall was not an ideal space for all demographic groups, it did represent an essential public space for senior citizens. "Some [senior citizens] visit the mall every day, arriving when the doors are opened in the morning. Many stay all day, leaving in mid to late afternoon. A few will have a light dinner at one of the mall eateries before going home to bed," observed Lewis.[12] Lewis says the mall is used as a place of exercise and a general meeting space, but it also fills the gap in the lives of senior citizens formerly occupied by their career. "Retired and living alone, many of these senior citizens seek the mall as a safe and neutral ground to keep up old job contacts — not just the more surface relationships with old customers, but more primary ties with workmates themselves."[13]

Due to the lack of true community spaces in suburbia, American culture puts an emphasis on the work and domestic environment as the main points for social contact and interaction. These relationships therefore struggle to supply a third level of social interaction that is offered in a more community minded society. In America's work-driven culture, social life is often tied to job contacts and interaction at the workplace, and on retirement senior citizens can feel quite distanced from society. The mall offers this group a replacement for the work-environment, a place to go everyday where they can socialize outside of the home.

"The elderly, once they are retired especially, are cut off from the familiar and fulfilling world of work," says Lewis. "Their income drops sharply and they are likely to be treated more and more as children by both their families and their non-senior citizens acquaintances."[14] Says Zepp, "Both young and old are at the shopping center to escape their respective worlds of loneliness."[15] Whereas the young are afraid of not being part of a "group," the senior citizens fear boredom and lack of companionship.[16] Devlin notes that senior citizens use the mall for two distinct purposes. "One involves consumption (and the value and service related to purchases) and the other involves the experience itself."[17] Zepp observed that older Americans use the mall in the same manner as they once did a traditional main street or town square. "Women in small groups will window shop or browse, while men, often their husbands, will gather around tables or on circular benches near the fountain, to chat or play cards…. It's all reminiscent of the male bonding and socializing that took place around the cracker barrel and pot-bellied stove in the old country store or in the park in Bel Air."[18] This behavior shows that the mall has become a replacement for the social spaces previously available to this group. It provides the entertainment factors needed for both men and women of this demographic, a group that adhered to a more strict code of gender separation in their social activities. With a lack of the small town community environments where many senior citizens grew up, "the mall is the only real place for a lot of American people to meet other people."[19]

The mall, as opposed to a downtown area, gives the senior citizens a sense of security. "The mall is perceived as a serene, crime-free environment," says Zepp.[20] In the same manner that parents feel safe leaving their teens at the shopping mall, the senior citizens feel that the mall is a safe place due to its enclosed spaces and the presence of patrols. "Malls provide a place we [senior citizens] can feel safe. You don't have to worry about a dog slipping out. You always have a bathroom, and most malls have security. Even if you have a heart issue, they have defibrillators," says Donovan.[21] "My wife died two years ago. I haven't had much to do. Now on Sunday after church, I go down to the mall, spend the afternoon, have supper. I look forward to it all week," says a senior citizen in Boston.[22] A senior mall-goer in Florida repeats this sentiment: "My wife and I come here three times a week. I sit on the bench, watch people and read a lot. It's weather-protected and always clean."[23] "If they [senior citizens] are widowed and live at home," says Lewis, "they have lost most of the primary face to face support they have relied on for most of their adult lives."[24]

In his book *The Great Good Place*, Ray Oldenburg says that senior citizens can become irrationally fearful if they are "starved for association." Younger people often do not find the value in simple everyday interactions with store clerks or cleaners; however, the senior citizens "often pursue these relationships eagerly." "Not being able to count on human association, having to exert themselves to maintain it, the senior citizens recognize the importance of association and communication more clearly and urgently than the rest of us," says Oldenburg.[25] The mall provides an inviting second home for this group, a place where they can attain social interaction and daily entertainment that they desperately need.

When the seniors reach an age where they can no longer drive, they can become further extracted from the car-dependent society of suburbia. Thus close access to a local shopping mall can become a lifeline to the elderly individual living alone. Notes Oldenburg, "unable to get about as they once did, unable to keep contacts afar, they take a renewed interest in those living and working close by."[26] In many suburban areas across the country there is no safe and reliable allocation of public transport, thus the senior citizen that is unable to drive for long distances will feel an increased dependence to the areas close by their home. The Center for American Progress quantifies that for the entire U.S. population 65 and older, only one-half have access to basic public transportation.[27] The regional mall, which services a radius of 20 to 30 miles, is therefore essential to this group, offering a more commutable social space in areas that have little else in the way of community space. Significantly, in some communities the shopping mall is one of the few places that offers free mass-transportation. "There is regularly scheduled mass transportation available for the benefit of the shoppers," explains Lewis, "[however] it [a free shuttle bus] would most likely not be available on a regular basis for say, transport to a non-economically oriented center or meeting place such as a park or activities center."[28] Although this is primarily for the economic benefit of the shopping mall, it does provide some relief for senior citizens that can no longer drive.

From a purely economic perspective, the shopping mall can provide the struggling senior citizen with some relief. According to the Center for American Progress, poverty among senior citizens is on the rise in the U.S., particularly in certain areas. The center says 3.4 million seniors age 65 and older live below the poverty line in the United States.[29] Factors in the rise of senior citizens in poverty are the weak economy, an increase in electricity and fuel costs, and rising health care costs. "Rural senior citizens have higher rates of poverty than the urban senior citizens, and rural areas tend to have a higher percentage of senior citizens in their total population than their urban counterparts," explains Alexandra Cawthorne. She says, "Rural people are less likely than their urban counterparts to leave their homes when they retire. Senior citizens residents of rural areas may have less access to necessary services and rely more heavily on private transportation."[30]

Although seniors may not have the purchasing power for the consumables at the mall, the space itself with its perceived public areas for lingering and opportunities for interaction can provide them with a sense of comfort and ease their economic woes. The mall is "in you and you are in it," explains Zepp. "There are no clear-cut lines drawn between shoppers, conversationalists, strollers and diners. This special use of space is not threatening, but rather gives a patron the sense of ease and welcome."[31] The regional mall is one of the few places available to suburban senior citizens; it gives them a place to go during the day and offers respite from the expense of heating and cooling their homes. As many malls offer a free shuttle bus, it also gives the senior citizen a transportation option. The mall shuttle bus is limited and economically motivated; however, it extends the opportunities for public interaction.

One result of the global financial crisis has been an increase in unemployment across the U.S. While this may not seem overtly relevant to senior citizens on pensions, recent data shows that this group has suffered from an increase in poverty and a decrease of part-time employment options, including regional mall jobs. Many economists had anticipated a rise in employment options when the baby boomers reached retirement age; however, the 2008 economic crisis and subsequent recession has led to the opposite. "Economists and demographers expected a large exodus from the workforce as the first baby boomers reached 60 in 2006, yet the weakened economy and rising health care costs are causing many aging Americans to delay retirement," states the Center for American Progress.[32] The percentage of U.S. residents ages 55 to 64 continuing in the workforce rose from 63.3 percent in 2007 to 64.8 percent in February 2008, an increase of more than 1 million workers.[33] The economic crisis has also caused many retired senior citizens to consider re-entering the work force as they struggle to pay their medical, housing and daily living expenses. In 2009, Experience Works completed a survey of 2000 low-income people over 55, and found that 46 percent needed to find work in order to keep their homes. "These people are at the age where they understandably thought their job-searching years were behind them," said Cynthia Metzler, president and CEO of Experience Works, "But here they are, many in their 60s, 70s and beyond, desperate to find work so they can keep a roof over their heads and food on the table."[34] The Experience Works survey also revealed that senior citizens were sometimes forced to choose between paying rent, buying food or medication. As the primary commercial hub in many regional areas, the shopping mall often provides this group with employment options for part-time and temporary jobs. These jobs can be essential to relieve the economic pressures on senior citizens that are struggling to make do.

A unique benefit of the enclosed mall, particularly relevant to this group, is the opportunity to exercise in the space. "Mall walking" was conceived as early as 1956 at Gruen's first enclosed shopping center, Southdale, on the outskirts of Minneapolis. The phenomenon of mall walking among groups of senior citizens emerged as a way to exercise in a climate controlled environment in which seniors could reasonably blend in, pass the time and feel safe all in the same space. As icy winter climates made it difficult for seniors to safely exercise outdoors, cardiologists began to prescribe their patients to walk the mall's climate controlled corridors for exercise and the trend grew. In the absence of other suitable public spaces for exercise, mall walking, or ambling around a shopping center for exercise, has become a major fitness option in the United States. Currently most malls offer mall walking as an activity and allow "walking groups" access for up to three hours earlier than the shops open.

Pensioner Elayne Gilhousen finds this very beneficial to her daily life. "The mall has furnished us with an area where we can hang our coats.... We walk at 9 A.M., from 45 minutes to an hour, depending on how many people we stop and talk to ... my husband has had a series of illnesses and, for us, mall walking is essential, not only for the exercise but for the social activity, being able to say hello to someone, and smiling at them," says Gilhousen.[35] Mall walking doesn't cost anything and is therefore accessible to senior citizens functioning on subsistence level pensions. In *Get a Life: You Don't Need a Million to Retire,* author Ralph E. Warner suggests that mall walking "may be weird but it works!"[36] He suggests that mall walking is a relatively cost-free and engaging way to spend time in retirement: "It has lots going for it simultaneously allowing retired people to visit old friends and make new ones while enjoying several hours of fairly strenuous exercise. And when the walking is done, many stick around to socialize over tea or coffee."[37]

Mall walking may seem a beneficial activity for malls as it promotes community interaction and gives the mall a populated appearance during low foot-traffic periods, such as early mornings and weekdays. The fact that this group often lingers for hours without purchasing and uses the space for social rather than purely economic reasons presents a problem for mall management. "We really don't want them to come here if they're not going to shop," complains a mall manager. "They take up seats we would like to have available for shoppers."[38] Mall walking is often initiated by the community and not by mall management. This activity does little to stimulate the commercial purpose of the environment and can be a detriment to the shopping mall as it creates a "focus in the mall that is not economic in nature."[39]

Management finds it difficult, however, from a public relations standpoint to ban this activity. Unlike the "teen escort" policy described in the previous chapter, it is difficult for management to put similar constraints on this group. "Politically, however, it is hard — especially with the elderly — to ban or even to overtly discourage their presence," says Lewis, "but it can be contained and monitored by security personnel."[40] At the Jefferson Valley Mall in Yorktown Heights, NY, in 2008, mall management changed the opening hours as well as denying the walkers access to the entire second level. This caused a community uproar and backlash against the mall, which gave a further allocation of space for the walkers but did not change their hours. "The conflict illustrates a paradox of life in suburbia, where much of the commerce has moved into big shopping centers," explains Lombardi.[41] This event, labeled "the cane mutiny" by local newspapers, shows the mall's vulnerability in terms of its need for public approval; however, it also relays inability of the privatized mall space to provide true public space for the community. "People consider malls public space, where they have the same rights and privileges as they would on a public street," says Lombardi. "But malls, in fact, are private property and their owners have a legal right to restrict not only entry to the premises, but also the First Amendment rights of those inside."[42]

Despite its deficiencies, the regional mall plays an essential role in the lives of senior citizens in the United States. It provides this group with a social environment beyond their homes with the benefit of controlled heating and cooling to allow exercise and the ability to reduce the costs of heating and cooling their own home during the day. Moreover, the mall is an essential place of community for senior citizens. The regional mall is often the only place for daily social interaction for this group. "To be sure, the community mentioned is to a large extent fabricated, artificial and contrived," notes Zepp. Nonetheless, "it may be the only working and workable expression of community for a sizable segment of our population."[43]

The decline of regional mall spaces will greatly affect this portion of the population. Without an environment that allows for a space to linger and to feel a part of society, this group will be greatly disadvantaged. Big Box centers have little to offer in terms of public space to linger and reflect. They also do not offer the same opportunities for exercise, socializing and visual variety. Significant to the elderly poor who rely on part-time jobs to subsidize their existence, Big Boxes represent a decrease in the number of job opportunities available for part-time employment in the community as they force competitive companies out of business.[44] Lifestyle centers (discussed in-depth in Chapter 10) bring the enclosed mall "outdoors," but lack the climate controlled ambience that is essential for mall walking in harsher climates. There has been some thought, however, on how current "dead mall" spaces can be re-developed to suit this group.

The reincarnation of a shopping mall as a "medical mall" is one of the ways developers have addressed the usage of empty mall space. According to a recent study by Hunter Industries, the medical mall concept has been around since the late 1980s. "However, they did not come into vogue until health care became more consumer driven in the face of rising health insurance premiums and rising health care costs," the report states.[45] This situation caused health insurers to put pressure on health care reimbursements and led hospitals to offer increased outpatient services. Medical malls are a way for medical practitioners to diversify and therefore court more health care dollars. "Medical malls offer the convenience of being close to where patients live, and they provide an alternative to inpatient care at a major hospital," says Hunter Industries.[46]

U.S. hospitals have been traditionally built in higher density urban areas, therefore, the medical mall brings senior citizens living in more distant suburbs the opportunity to have close access to inpatient care. Hunter cites many examples of where the regional mall has been re-purposed as a medical mall. The University of Mississippi Medical Center in Jackson re-purposed an 850,000 square foot shopping mall into a medical mall. In Poughkeepsie, New York, the Vassar Brothers Medical Center opened their Fishkill medical mall in a space adjacent to the defunct Duchess Mall. In the still viable Dixie Manor Shopping Center, in Louisville, Kentucky, the Jewish Hospital and St. Mary's Health Care have set up a medical mall in space once leased by a clothing retailer. Similar to regular malls, medical malls offer a consumer experience, which includes public space along with "a one-stop shop concept of medical services."[47] These services can include anything from pediatrics, family practice and primary care, to cardiology, ear, nose, and throat specialists, diagnostic and laboratory specialists, hearing aid shops, and fitness centers.

One can get an idea of how this model could work to replace the retail shopping mall in many regional areas where it is failing. "The aging of the Baby Boom generation and their demand for state-of-the-art medical care will likely increase demand for creation of medical malls," notes the Hunter Industries report.[48] The reincarnation of shopping malls as medical facilities may work to sustain the social purpose of the space for senior citizens. As a place where medicines are dispensed and aliments treated, however, it can provide an experience akin to a nursing home and remind the older person of the inevitable rather than distract them from thoughts of dying. Currently, only 50 medical malls are in operation in the United States, so this model is not, as yet, prevalent.

According to Zepp, communities that are formed within a mall can be limited and synthetic; the shopping mall does not evoke a feeling of primary community among all of the general population. This chapter and the previous, however, have shown that the mall is a relevant and essential space for community among the demographic of senior citizens and teenagers. "These groups form the mall's closest approximation to a primary community," Zepp explains.[49] Adds Lewis, "These economic monoliths are now about far more than shopping."[50] The elderly use the shopping mall to exercise, socialize and form the community needed to stave off the isolation that can occur in this group. Similarly, teens use the space for socialization but also in order to fulfill the need for group association. The loss of this space, as evidenced in both this chapter and the previous, will lead to the loss of a primary interaction zone for the young and old in America.

Although the enclosed shopping mall space provides a beneficial social experience for teens and senior citizens, issues with control and environmental destruction are also associated with this environment. The following chapters will look at the social problems inherent in the mall development model as a basis for discussion on the overall effectiveness of this model as a form of public space.

8. The Mall
as "Public" Space

"Most Western theories of democracy posit a public sphere of some sort in which citizens or members of a community can participate in deliberation and decision-making regarding the way the community is organized and governed," says Staeheli and Mitchell.[1] One must remember that although a shopping mall replicates and mimics the public town squares and Main Streets of previous eras, it is a fully privatized space. In her 2009 documentary *Malls R Us*, Helene Klodawsky asks: "Is there only one true language at the mall — the one where money talks?"[2] The mall as a form of public space has always been problematic. In theory the concept of a democratic space, unfettered by the noise, frustration and pollution of traffic, covered from the unpredictable elements, where all can come together in the joint pursuit of consumer objects seems utopian. The mall, however, is far from being democratic.

Naomi Klein, in her book *No Logo*, explains, "The conflation of shopping and entertainment found at the superstores and theme-park malls has created a vast gray area of pseudo-public private space."[3] Klein goes on to say that public figures such as politicians, police, social workers and even religious leaders have all recognized that malls have become our contemporary replacement for the town square. "Unlike the old town squares," says Klein, "which were and still are sites for community discussion, protests and political rallies, the only type of speech that is welcome here is marketing and other consumer patter."[4] At the expense of First Amendment rights, the mall provides us with the feeling of safety, due to its enclosed and closely monitored environment. Despite this, however, the mall is not immune to the crime and violence that have come to be characterized with the declining town centers. The privatization of public space across America has led to an overarching quality control of the social environment, which in turn, created a unique form of social space for teens and the elderly. The mall, however, also represents a decline in certain constitutional rights that had previously been offered in the town squares, old city centers and Main Street areas. This chapter looks at the issues with the mall as a public space and how the overt control of this space is both assuring and unsettling to the American public.

In 1939, Justice Owen Roberts asserted that "wherever the title of streets and parks may rest, they have immemorially been held in trust for the use of the public and, time out of mind, have been used for purposes of assembly, communicating thoughts between citizens and discussing public questions.... The privilege of a citizen of the United States to use the streets and parks for communication must not be abridged or denied."[5] In the absence of parks and Main Streets across the suburban landscape, the mall has been quantified a public space. As demonstrated by cases processed by the Supreme Court from the late 60s onward, however, picket lines and peaceful protests are continually disallowed in mall spaces by mall management.

"The mall stands as a powerful embodiment of privatization an commercialization of space," notes Barber.[6] In general, mall management frowns upon any activity that might detract or interfere with the consumer purpose of the space. "The mall can provide a 'free' space, where even the most intimate and human behaviors can be celebrated and remembered," says Pahl, "although of course most users of the space need to pay for it."[7] The mall aims to create a feeling of community, however, the main goal of this community is to facilitate consumption and not to foster a genuine sense of public space for the general use of the community. Although one may perceive "their" mall as being part of the community and a place for social interaction, it is simply a privatized commercial space with a central management structure that can allow the public to use it — on their terms. In this sense, the mall blurs the lines between public and private space.

Since the creation of the enclosed shopping center, several legal battles have been fought over the right to use the shopping mall as a public space to mixed success. Mall owners frequently cite that their spaces are privately owned and therefore they have the right to dictate what activities occur. As a result, First Amendment rights are frequently denied at shopping malls. In 1972, The United States Supreme Court sided with the shopping mall in the case *Lloyd Corporation v. Tanner*. The case, which pitched an Oregon shopping center against anti–Vietnam War activists distributing pamphlets, was ruled in favor of the shopping center. The court cited that hand billing had no relation to any purpose for which the mall was being used. Another example of the denial of First Amendment rights in shopping malls extends across the country in the annual "Buy Nothing Day," an event sponsored by the Media Foundation. "Buy Nothing Day" is a movement that originated in Vancouver in 1992, which protests the destructive effects of over-consumption on the environment. In 1999, advocates for "Buy Nothing Day" attempted to peaceably assemble at shopping malls across the United States to promote their cause; they were all denied access.[8] Writing in 1974, Peter J. Kane lamented that shopping centers "prohibit virtually all First Amendment activity taking place without the shopping center owner's permission. The owner is free to grant access for the purpose of First Amendment activity on a limited and selective basis to whatever groups he sees fit."[9]

Gradually, in California, mall management companies had to come to terms with their spaces being used as legitimate forums for public protest or speech. In the benchmark case *PruneYard Shopping Center v. Robins, et al.*, the Supreme Court of California favored First Amendment rights over the mall developer's rights. In the 1980 PruneYard case, student protesters were denied the rights to peaceable protest on the grounds of the upscale PruneYard mall in Campbell, California. The Supreme Court claimed that the mall offered, through a vigorous advertising campaign, a populated and "congenial" public atmosphere. This space was in fact the only atmosphere in the area that represented any semblance to viable public space. PruneYard was quantified as having around 25,000 people present cumulatively on weekends. As such, the court states, "A handful of additional orderly persons soliciting signatures and distributing handbills in connection therewith, under reasonable regulations adopted by defendant to assure that these activities do not interfere with normal business operations would not markedly dilute defendant's property rights."[10] Although reviled by shopping centers across the nation, this case set a clear argument for the shopping center to be seen more as a public, rather than private, property. The PruneYard case by no means validates the use of shopping centers across the country as fully public environments open to the presence of picketers and protesters. In fact, many states reject the California Supreme Court ruling and continue to see the mall as a privatized space, capable of creating its own rules and regulations.

Covert segregation of mall spaces is identified as another issue in the legitimacy of the mall as a public space. As evidenced by the teen escort policy and mall walking bans, discussed in the previous chapters, shopping centers have the ability to police who comes in and out of their malls and to dictate how welcome visitors will function in the space. Often shopping centers are a direct reflection of the segregated environments created by mass-planned suburban housing. "Heavily patrolled malls now provide a safe urban space with a clientele as homogenous as that of their suburban counterparts," explains Crawford.[11] Underhill explains that the shopping mall, although seen to be "wholesome" and "all–American," is often the opposite. "[Malls can be] snobbish, xenophobic, elitist, and hateful."[12]

In the 1990s several cases of discrimination were brought against various shopping malls. The paper "Race Is Not the Issue" discusses a discrimination case in Boston against the Copley Place shopping center which actively excluded minority tenants.[13] The NAACP (National Association for the Advancement of Colored People) accused a mall in Columbia, South Carolina, of utilizing discriminatory hiring practices in 1991.[14] The University of Legal Services (ULS) program for the District of Columbia cites a 2003 case of discrimination against the mentally disabled in the City Place Mall, Maryland. National Children's Center (NCC) is a group that provides services for adults with mental retardation and developmental disabilities. When using the shopping mall food court for a social outing, the NCC was approached by mall management and asked to leave. The ULS brought a complaint to the United States District Court in Maryland and reached a federal consent decree for the NCC to use the space.[15] For years, the shopping mall has been able to position itself as the "new Main Street," however, unlike the "old" Main Street, writes Kowinski, it "maintains strict control over who gets into the mall and who doesn't."[16]

Although the relinquishment of some democratic rights in the pseudo-public space of the mall seems like a high price to pay for a happy shopping experience, this form of control alleviates a deep seated fear of violence and crime present in the American psyche. The feeling of security is often more about perception than reality and the mall, which is so good at engineering fantasy, has no problem relaying an overt sense of control. According to a 2007 Gallup Poll on homeland security, 67 percent of participants believed that there was more crime in the U.S. than the year before and 38 percent responded that they feared walking alone in their own neighborhood.[17]

"Violence, crime and fear are endemic to American life," states Dempsey.[18] The mall works to combat this fear by placing 24 hour closed circuit TV cameras in obvious places throughout the space. In addition to security cameras, a small army of security guards patrols the area in uniforms with a styling similar to state and federal police. In post 9/11 America, many malls across the country prefer use of armed security guards or off duty policemen as security. Due to a state law legitimizing it, security guards in North Carolina share some of the privileges of the state and local police; they are empowered to make arrests and issue citations.[19] Many malls let out retail space to local police substations, thus fully enforcing an idea of control. "Perception is perhaps even more important than reality," explains Hazel. "In a business that is as dependent as film or theater on appearances, the illusion of safety is as vital, or even more so, than its reality."[20]

Aristotle wrote, "The goal of the city is to make man feel happy and safe."[21] A veritable fantasy city unto itself, the mall works to position itself in this light. The shopping mall sets its own rules, regulations, and security measures, most of which work to protect the commercial nature of the property and feed into the psyche of the consumer who is looking for a safe and secure environment. The use of security guards in the mall is one of the most visual and personal signs of this illusion. Guards can create a feeling of safety but may also work to visually dispel the aura of a "safe" environment. "Many academic scholars view private security as a 'second rate service compared to the police,'" says Steden and Nalla. "In everyday understanding of private security, its workers are at best depicted as somewhat shady 'watchmen,' and at worst represent 'corrupt gangsters' or 'hired guns,' unscrupulous and devoid of conventional ethics."[22] Cinema and television often show the security guard as an uneducated and comic character. In the 2009 film *Paul Blart: Mall Cop*, the profession of the mall security guard is seen as second-rate to "real" policing.[23]

The film portrays the job as being mundane and available to those with limited education. The disturbing element of this portrayal is that if the shopping mall is considered the "new town center," then the private security guard replaces the traditional role of the policeman. To achieve a look of authority, mall management often has private security guards in uniforms that mimic the look of local police officers. This act of "disguising" the private security as a local authority may actually backfire. The confusion of private security uniforms with police uniforms can result in an officer being perceived as the "lowlier" and often less respected profession of private security guard. "Citizens may find it increasingly difficult to tell public and private agents of social control apart, not only because they engage in some similar functions but also because many of their observable behaviors are identical," explains Steden and Nalla.[24] When placed in the realm of the privatized security guard, therefore, the genuine police authority may not elicit the same respect.

While the portrayal of private security guards as "shady watchmen" in popular media may be exaggerated, there are issues with control and regulation among this sector that give genuine reason for concern. "Private security is perceived as an ambiguous occupation worldwide — a conclusion that demands further attention in the light of extant literature on public policing," states Steden and Nalla. "Unlike the police, the massive presence of private security is a relatively recent and under-researched development in modern society."[25] In a 2003 study, J.R. Roberts security consultants found that there are more than 3 times the numbers of private security guards than police officers in the United States. "The presence of private, uniformed security guards has become a ubiquitous feature of the American landscape, seen at shopping malls, hospitals, parking lots, offices, and more," notes Roberts.[26]

The worrying aspect of this is, unlike police officers who are bound to the legal structure set out in the U.S. Constitution, the provisions of the U.S. Constitution do not restrict security guards. "Security officers do not have to give suspects the Miranda warnings before questioning and the exclusionary rule does not apply to the evidence they seize," explains John Dempsey in his book *Introduction to Private Security*.[27] There are no established federal guidelines governing private security, therefore, each state individually determines training and background checks in their licensing requirements. As such, standards can deviate dramatically from state to state. "Only a small percentage of guard companies go to the expense of administering pre-employment screening tests to identify suitability for the job," says Roberts. "They often employ people who may have behavioral issues which places clients at a risk."[28] In Pennsylvania, unarmed security guards do not require a license and armed security guards only need to take a 40-hour weapons safety course to qualify. "Under the current system," warns Roberts, "citizens are well advised to wonder whether the sight of a security guard should trigger relief or concern."[29]

Another, more recent, manifestation of control in the mall space is the overt presence of army recruiters, often in full military dress. In the 1990s the mall was shown to be a place of solace for teens in films *Clueless* and *MallRats*. In the year 2010, the placement of recruiters in the mall corrupts this fantasy. Recruiters target the idle teens, youths who are already feeling pressured by the economic downturn to find gainful employment. The Army has created special game arcades with simulated battle scenes in a method to target the teens in the mall. "The U.S. Army, struggling to ensure it has enough manpower ... is wooing young Americans with videogames, Google maps and simulated attacks on enemy positions," says John Hurdle in a 2009 article.[30] In the recruitment centers in the mall, teens can "hang out on couches and listen to rock music" while they play the video games. For unemployed, idle teens, this is an enticing area.[31] Compared to the traditional recruitment centers, "It's a more relaxed environment, you don't feel like you're being pressured," says 20-year-old Eddie Abuali.[32]

Apparently this method is working; since the implementation of the arcades the Army recorded the highest number of recruits since the post 9/11 patriotic fervor. This increase also relates directly to the scarcity of jobs since the economic downturn. "Recruitment was more difficult about two years ago when the U.S. was struggling in Iraq and jobs at home were easier to get," states Maj. Larry Dillard, who continues, "Now [that] we are in an economic downturn it will be easier."[33]

Because of their enclosed nature and the security measures set up by mall management companies, one may perceive the mall to be safe; however, the mall can be vulnerable to the same crime and violence that occur in the downtown areas of cities. Since their creation, documented cases of theft, rape, and harassment in shopping malls fill police blotters across the country. On a sunny December day in 2007, at a peaceful Omaha, Nebraska, shopping mall, a 19-year-old gunman walked into the mall and opened fire. Nine people, including the gunman, who shot himself, perished in the incident and four other people were critically injured. The teenager responsible was a gawky looking white male, with dark curly hair and glasses, who had been recently fired from his part-time job at the McDonalds in the mall for stealing $17 from the cash register.[34] In his suicide note he said that he loved his family and friends, however, he explained, "my whole life I've been a piece of shit; now I'll be famous."[35]

Shocking as this may be, it is not an isolated incident. Eleven months prior to the Nebraska shooting, at an affluent Salt Lake City mall, an 18-year-old male armed with both a handgun and shotgun wandered the mall's corridors shooting at will. When the smoke cleared, five people lay dead and four critically injured. "I've worked here for 28 years, it's been the safest place to be," recounted a sales manager, in total disbelief at the extent of the carnage.[36] According to the National Retail Federation, "From 2004 through 2008 there were 17 shooting incidents at U.S. shopping malls and retail stores, with 34 killed and 33 wounded."[37] In over 71 percent of these incidents, the shooter was between the ages of 15 and 25; in 100 percent of the incidents the shooter was identified as male.[38] In most cases the shooter was acting alone and looked like an average American teenager, thus very difficult for any security official to pick them out from a crowd.

In October 2008, the National Retail Federation and the International Council of Shopping Centers created the Active Shooter emergency response guidelines for retail staff. The guide attempts to explain the shooter's agenda, stating, "A shooter may be a troubled current or former employee, or related to an associate with domestic problems." The guide concludes more broadly, however, that it is very difficult to quantify why people are driven to these acts. "We live in a dangerous world and the stakes keep getting higher," explains the guide.[39]

The trepidation of mall visitors and management and the need for overt control and protection in this space is understandable. In this sense the presence of armed security and the teen escort policy makes complete sense. However, the consequences of increased security and a tightening control on our public spaces seem to dispel some of the basic freedoms that the American population holds dear. Citizens are willing to submit to the rules of a shopping mall, to give up some of their constitutional rights, if it means a safe and violence-free space. What is next in this grueling cycle of violence and mistrust? How much more freedom must the American population give up for the perception of safety? And is one ever really, truly safe? "We are an open and free country, and we don't want guards at every doorway," says FBI director Robert Muller.[40] A Kansas City security consultant group states that it is almost impossible to prevent mall shootings without turning shopping centers into armed camps.[41]

In a post 9/11 article discussing increasing security measures in shopping malls, the suggestion of metal detectors and armed guards at the entries is discussed. "Metal detectors are anathema to malls and stores, which do everything they can to invite shoppers in. Going through a checkpoint at a mall; leaving it to beep at shopper's belt buckles and loose change, is enough to drive people to QVC," notes *U.S.A Today*.[42] The use of increased security and the perception of threat could further turn people away. In a 2008 CNN article, independent security consultant Chris McGoey explains that "rising unemployment in a recessionary environment facilitates all types of crime such as robberies and burglaries and drug use among young people."[43] This downward cycle can draw people away from the mall and back into the perceived security of their own homes, purchasing what they need via online retailers. "For one thing," notes McGoey, "retailers will lose sales if people become fearful about shopping at a particular mall."[44] McGoey also explains that mall shootings and other violent acts cause expensive lawsuits, which could potentially bankrupt a developer already on shaky ground.

In an economic downturn with the threat of more violence and crime, a fortified mall with metal detectors and armed guards at the door might serve as an ample barrier; however, it hardly seems to represent America's brand of freedom. On the flip side, a vision of a world without any form of public space is more frightening; without it citizens could become confined to their homes and cars making them further withdrawn, petrified and paranoid of external dangers, thus extending the mistrust and violence.

"Without even meaning to the mall has transformed our country and not always for the good," says Underhill.[45] The shopping mall is now the only form of viable public space in many communities across the United States, even though it is not truly a "public space" in the purest form. Mall management reserves the right to control what happens in this privately owned environment. As disputes in many Supreme Court cases suggest, the mall functions as and is utilized by the public in the same way as public spaces such as town squares and therefore is essential in the public life of the community. However, the issues of denying certain activities in this legally defined private space become difficult to overrule. "The debate over public access to the mall, its function as a de facto public space and over the kind of speech rights that pertained to the mall, points to the importance of space in allowing public debate and, ultimately, to sustaining a sense of 'public-ness' in the context of the perceived incivility of the contemporary city," say Staeheli and Mitchell.[46]

Some Americans experience a high level of fear and anxiety in relation to violence and crime, therefore, the shopping mall's provision of a controlled and safe environment is perceived as a welcome refuge from the "dangerous" outside world. In this sense, Americans are willing to relinquish some basic constitutional rights to experience a safe community environment. The space, patrolled by security guards that are often armed and populated by army recruiters in full military dress, gives the illusion of being a controlled environment. However, the mall is as susceptible, if not more so, than the downtown urban areas that are perceived as dangerous. Documented cases of mall shootings and other violent acts are a testament to this. Creating a more "fortified" shopping mall with metal detectors and random bag checks is an answer to securing the space; however, these measures could promote further discrimination and alienation, thus diminishing public freedoms and possibilities for social and public interaction in the space.

Overall, the issues of public space presented by the privatized mall are all the more poignant in light of this demise in many areas. While the mall, as represented in this chapter, is by no means the utopian community environment Gruen imagined it to be, it has come to replace the civic centers that once existed across the country. As the primary "town center," it is therefore a very important and essential space for public interaction. Perhaps a decline of the space may give rise to new models that will address the "public-private" debate in a better light; however, its decline could also lead to a suburban environment devoid of public space. The next section will look at the impact that the shopping mall has had on the environment, as a means of reflecting on how this space has irrevocably changed ecosystems.

9. The Mall
and the Environment

The first few chapters have addressed the meteoric rise of the enclosed shopping center model and its importance as a space for young and old. The shopping mall, however, can be argued as influencing widespread destruction of the environment through its development process and auto-dependency. "Ironically, the creation of a natural environment in the mall is often accompanied by the destruction of the natural environment outside the mall," notes Zepp.[1] Taking up large tracts of land once used as rural space, many shopping malls have disrupted the natural balance of the environment around them.

Gruen recognized the destructive effect that shopping centers could have on the environment, noting in 1955: "Just as landscape was an environment in which nature predominated and of which there were many different varieties so too were there many types of city-scapes, including traditional buildings, blocks, avenues and squares. But, unfortunately many other new-scapes ... transportation-scape; the tinny surfaces of miles of cars and acres of parking lots ... are becoming even more prevalent."[2] As the expansive parking lots of shopping centers attest, they are reliant on personal transport, and are rarely made fully accessible to mass transit.

The Environmental Protection Agency has pointed out that malls cause a significant amount of pollution through the excessive use of automobiles as well as through the widening of roads and the creation of new ones to service these centers. The over-development of suburbia, the reliance on personal transport and the vast oceans of asphalt and concrete that define the public space of the American mall are not a sustainable way of constructing public space. "Suburbia, the way we're doing it now," says Dunham-Jones, "it's not sustainable, affordable or particularly 'green.'"[3] While many have researched the effects that the stark exterior space of the mall have on the psyche, it is often less obvious that the synthetic natural environment created inside the shopping mall can have negative physical effects on the average American.

"We now have generations of Americans who have never walked for any length of time in cities or even towns," notes Underhill.[4] The following chapter will reflect on the shopping mall and its degenerating effect on the natural environment around it. It will also look at how replacing the natural environment with a synthetic environment has affected the health and well-being of the general public.

According to the Urban Land Institute, by 1984, an estimated 25,508 shopping malls, encompassing super-regional, regional and community centers, existed in the United States.[5] Data from the same source notes that in 1950 only 100 such centers existed across the country. This rapid growth pattern mirrored suburban growth over the same period. In the 1970s a realization that the enclosed shopping mall model, with its reliance on the destruction of large tracts of land and its reliance on the automobile, caused a shift in policy. "Severe restrictions and regulations were established," notes the Shopping Center Development Handbook, "to protect the environment and to save energy."[6] Beginning in the mid–1970s, land development was restricted to curb undirected and rampant destruction of the environment. "Measures were taken to legislate national land use policy and to enact nation and state controls over sensitive ecological areas such as wetlands, scenic areas, and costal zones," explains the Shopping Center Development Handbook.[7]

In the Clean Air Act of 1970, the Environmental Protection Agency (EPA) focused on shopping centers as an "indirect source" of air quality deterioration. The EPA argued that while the shopping mall itself does not represent a direct threat to clean air, indirectly the large concentrations of parking at shopping malls causes a significant source of air pollution. The energy crisis of the 1970s was a catalyst for shopping centers to enact several conservation controls on the amount of energy used. "Centers have been retrofitted by increasing insulation, installing automatic climate controls and altering heating, ventilating, and air-conditioning (HVAC) systems to make operations more efficient," notes the Retail Development Handbook.[8] These measures, which effectively help the shopping center to save money, are standard development practice today.

In July of 1979, on the back of the EPA recommendations and reforms, the U.S. Department of Housing and Urban Development released the draft of "a Regional Shopping Center Policy." This policy was later re-labeled "Community Conservation Guidance," as the goal of the policy was to control the over-development of regional shopping centers in order to curb the destructive effects that development was having on communities, both ecologically and socially. The policy was a realization that the current development models were un-sustainable. It recognized that if unchecked, the rapid development of shopping centers would lead to the further deterioration of urban and suburban environments. In the report, a series of guidelines for assessing "community impact analysis" were generated to determine the potential effects of proposed shopping centers. If enacted, the American suburban and urban environments might be greatly different today; however, the policy was discontinued when the federal administration changed in 1980 and thus shopping center development continued to follow the same patterns set up in the 1950s.[9]

As evidenced by the Clean Air Act of 1970, the shopping mall itself cannot be directly blamed for the increase in air pollution. The shopping center industry also enacts environmental quality control on the interior heating and cooling of its structures. The shopping center is culpable in environmental destruction, however, in the fact that it is a structure that supports mass-production of automobiles by promoting an auto-dependent public. As evidenced by the Community Conservation Guidance, it is also highly culpable in the destruction of social environments in communities. Moreover, structurally, following the principles of Modernist design, it has influenced ecosystems by covering them with physical structures and parking lots that have caused direct and indirect pollution.

When reflecting on the suburban American landscape, the Modernist movement has been most influential in shaping this space. The Modernist movement began with the opening of the Bauhaus design school in the early 1930s. It was a reactionary movement which condemned the fanciful styles and decadent tastes of the Art Nouveau and Beaux Arts styles. Modernism, championed by Walter Gropius, head of the Bauhaus school, took its inspiration from the Industrial-age utilitarian buildings such as factories and grain silos. It shunned previous styles that encouraged a return to classical design motives and promoted a "utopian-revolutionary" outlook, which assumed that everyone deserved a clean and functional space from the lowliest factory worker to the high-powered executive. Although borne out of utopian constructs, Modernism, which lowered everything to its lowest common denominator, de-humanized architecture by equating it to nothing more than the functional pieces of a large economic machine.

Kunstler, in his book *The Geography of Nowhere*, blames much of the eventual environmental and social decline inherent in contemporary American communities on the Modernist architectural movement. "Modernism did its immense damage in these ways: by divorcing the practice of building from the history and traditional meaning of building; by promoting a species of urbanism that destroyed age-old social arrangements and, with them, urban life as a general preposition; and by creating a physical setting for man that failed to respect the limits of scale, growth and the consumption of natural resources, or to respect the lives of other living things."[10]

An exemplar of the urban environment championed by the Modernist

movement is Le Corbusier's famous "Plan Voisin" for the Marais district in
Paris. Plan Voisin called for the destruction of the entire historical Marais district in order to lay the foundations for twenty-four concrete and steel, sixty-
story high-rises. The cruciform buildings, while offering great potential for
mass-housing, had no exterior decoration or character and presented nothing
to the street-level.[11] Plan Voisin (also know as "Radiant City") was ultimately
discarded and as a result, the contemporary district of le Marais still retains
the characteristics of historical beauty and community that have existed there
for hundreds of years.

Compared to France, the United States was a new country lacking a
powerful attachment to the past. It was thus far easier for Americans to accept
the Modernist ideal and as such the city planners in the United States succumbed to the Modernist movement. "Le Corbusier's particular brand of
urbanism came to exert over the planning profession," explains Kunstler. "His
"Radiant City scheme became the only model for urban postwar development
in America."[12] Thus the contemporary landscapes of urban and suburban
America closely models the Plan Voisin and has ultimately resulted in dire
community and environmental consequences. The great failure of this model
is the de-humanization of the environment and community. "In their effort
to promote a liberated and classless society," explains Kunster, "the Modernists
and their successors tried to stamp out history and tradition.... They failed
to create a social utopia, but they did tremendous damage to the physical settings for civilization."[13]

In the original shopping mall designs, Gruen took clues from the Modernist designers in creating his functional exterior structure. Gruen felt that
the regional shopping center was a successful concept because it compartmentalized traffic, keeping it out of the pedestrian environment. "The regional
shopping center has actually implemented the concept of separation of utilitarian and human activities, and through the general popularity and economic
success of the arrangement has proved that the concept is feasible and prac-
tical," says Gruen.[14] He notes that the mall's interior replicates "superior environmental qualities" such as weather protection and the use of skylights to
provide adequate lighting without strain on the environment.[15]

While creating a pleasant interior atmosphere and evoking a natural setting with its name and interior elements, the shopping mall is at odds with
the external atmosphere. "Malls, composed of rows of basic boxes enlivened
with porch like overhangs, shared the design logic of the suburban tract," says
Crawford, "economics rather than aesthetics prevailed."[16] Similar to the Modernist Plan Voisin of Le Corbusier, the shopping mall promotes a separation
from the natural and an emphasis on the structural. Like suburban housing
tracts, it compartmentalizes society. And despite the efforts of the interior to

mimic nature through the use of water, plants and natural light, the mall has in fact destroyed entire ecosystems and rural environments.

Says Kunstler, "The suburban developments of today and the shopping smarm that clutters up so much of the landscape in between them arose from the idea, rather peculiar to America, that neither the city nor the country was really a suitable place to live."[17] Americans had turned to suburbia for a respite from the dense urbanism of post World War II. Suburbia at that time represented a serene, safe and natural environment. By the late 1960s, however, most urban and suburban areas across the country had lost touch with the natural environment and synthetic and controlled environments became the standard. "Environmentalists have worried about the disturbance of rural areas, the disorientation of small communities and the exploiting of prime farmland [created by the mall]," says Zepp.[18] "The natural amenities, one of the attractions of the suburban dream, became threatened as more people moved away from the city," explains Wall. "As one subdivision joined another—filling valley floors, climbing up the slopes of foothills, or eating into forestland—open spaces disappeared."[19] Robbins relates that suburban America has become a shadow of the 1950s utopian vision of a bright future. "Efforts to accommodate the automobile based rules of the suburb created seas of surface parking anchored by a mere handful of significant, if isolated, towers."[20]

The innate need for a human connection to nature, however, remained. It is evident in the naming of shopping centers and office parks in the urban sprawl. Malls often use names like "Brookfield," "East Lake," and "Clifton Country Mall." "Often these malls may not be near any of the natural environments suggested by their names," says Zepp. "The possibility of being reunited with nature, while ostensibly shopping, still continues to attract us."[21] The naming of synthetic structures to reflect a natural setting was a reaction to the fact that many natural environments began to disappear.

Suburban housing and especially the shopping mall, with its sheer size and scale, have irrecoverably affected ecosystems across the country. "By covering acres of ground they [malls] effect the characters of biotic activity, creating space with little species diversity and few organic interactions," explains Farrell.[22] An example of ecosystems that have been depleted as a result of the shopping mall is Crossgates Mall in Albany, NY, and the Karner blue butterfly. The Karner blue butterfly is a species that thrives in savanna and barren ecosystems in the northeastern areas of the United States and parts of Ontario. Due to loss of habitat, the butterfly is now considered endangered and has been extirpated from the ecosystems of five U.S. states and the Canadian province of Ontario, where it once thrived.[23] Karner blues are dependent on wild lupine, which requires suitable sunlight for growth. When habitats are shaded by large-scale developments, lupine growth becomes difficult and thus the species dies out.

An existing Karner blue population was identified in the Pine Bush scrub directly next to the Crossgates Mall development in Colonie, NY. State building approval of the development plans in the 1980s required the Pyramid Companies to acknowledge the butterfly population. Based on this, the development company was asked to set aside a five acre site to enable the butterflies to survive. When the shopping mall proposed an expansion in the 1990s, the state required the allocation of 10 acres of land to be cultivated to sustain the existence of the species. These measures, however, have not aided in curbing the overall decline of the species in the area. According to Save the Pine Bush lobby group, "Prior to construction of the mall in 1984, the largest known colony of Karner blue butterflies based in the largest single patch of blue lupine known in the world was discovered on a hill of approximately five acres on the site of the proposed mall."[24] The original mall development and subsequent additions have had significant effect on the butterfly population in this area, depleting it greatly. "In 1979, there were only about 80,000 Karner Blues in the Pine Bush (as opposed to the millions that lived there earlier this century)," notes Save the Pine Bush. "By 1990, the population had crashed to 500 to 1000 and by 1995, only 100 to 200 butterflies remain in the Pine Bush."[25]

Kowinski theorizes that the destruction of the true natural environment for the fabricated environment of the mall has had a great effect on the American psyche. He explains that by simultaneously destroying the natural environment and then distorting the very idea of what it is by re-creating a version of it in the mall creates a false consciousness of nature. "By faking the only stream that people see on a regular basis ... people learn from the false idea and they may not understand the real streams that they see."[26] A poignant example of this is the case of Thornton Creek and the Northgate Mall. In the design of Northgate Mall in Seattle the shopping mall was built on top of Thornton Creek, which had to be diverted through an underground pipe. Trapping the stream in this way has caused significant environmental damage.

Dan Mahler, president of Thornton Creek Alliance, explains: "As Northgate and Shoreline have developed, more paved surfaces give storm water fewer places to naturally sink into the ground."[27] The runoff, which carries pesticides, oils and other pollutants, was being released into the stream several miles from the site, causing the demise of local populations of salmon. For many years the fountains and foliage, integrated into the interior of the Northgate Mall, replaced the true natural environment that once existed on the site. "What happens when the chief community center of our time are such willfully artificial distortions of reality?" questions Kowinski. "Don't they then have the power to derange our sense of the world and ourselves?"[28]

Thornton Creek remained trapped under the mall for nearly 50 years until lobby groups successfully released it by removing some of the mall's parking lots in 2009. "The final outcome is acceptable for most supporters of Thornton Creek's restoration," says Michelle Ma of *The Seattle Times*.[29] Although the release of the creek signals a positive step in the health of the ecosystem, it may take years for it to fully rejuvenate. "Years of development have encroached and narrowed the stream, causing faster water flow and more stream-bank erosion," says Ma.[30]

Although the synthetic natural environment that is created inside of the shopping mall is meant to replicate the benefits of the natural environment that it has taken over, it has the tendency to affect the visitor in negative ways. In Langrehr's study on "Retail Shopping Mall Semiotics and Hedonic Consumption," he classified the retail environment as having a negative effect on individuals due to the tendency of the interior space to be crowded. According to Langrehr, in crowded interior environments people experience higher levels of anxiety, hostility, and are less likely to socialize or seek contact with others than in similarly crowded outdoor spaces. "Crowding has universally negative impacts on individuals."[31]

A 1994 study on the ambient noise inside a mega-mall suggested that noise plays a role in the physical well-being of the visitor. The noise in the shopping mall is varied and often pitched at different tonal levels that induce confusion, anxiety and stress. "Although malls were originally hailed as the quiet retreat from the sonic congestion of downtown streets," says Hopkins, "sound levels in some mall corridors may now, paradoxically, exceed those of a downtown city sidewalk."[32] Hopkins describes the sounds that permeate a shopping mall as its "acoustic perfume." He says the sounds in shopping malls, from the Musak piped into the corridor to the individual tracks played in single stores, are all carefully constructed by the mall management to "produce and sustain the owner's social and political relationship of domination over patrons."[33] "Unless people leave the sound field," explains Hopkins, "they have little choice but to experience its ideological effects; the ideas and values of consumerism that may influence thought and action."[34] Hopkins' study showed that in a test shopping mall, serious health implications are created as a direct result of the "acoustic perfume." Exposure to the shopping mall's sounds caused increases in breathing, blood pressure, heart rate, muscle tension and stress.

Underhill asserts that the shopping mall has caused significant harm to human sight and distance perception: "The mall has had a huge effect on American life; it has actually taught us to walk differently than we once did."[35]

Because we are so dependent on driving everywhere, often the only place that Americans walk is in the synthetic and highly controlled shopping mall environment. "Mall surfaces are reliable, no obstacles, or surprises," says Underhill, "when entering the mall your eye is immediately drawn way up ahead to the heart of the place."[36] In this sense, the mall has changed the depth perception, reaction time and ability to deal with uneven surfaces and hazards in other environments.

Gruen, culpable for the creation of the Modernist-style shopping mall design, eventually turned his attention to the regeneration of the urban environment. Towards the end of his career he formed the Victor Gruen Foundation for Environmental Planning and took the initiative to work with Ladybird Johnson in redressing the suburban sprawl that had invaded the American landscape.[37] Gruen had recognized the negative effects that rapid industrialization and modernism had on the environment. "The last chapter of Gruen's life is the most surprising," says Wall. "The 'mall-maker'— the so-called eviscerator of the old cities — is one of the earliest to plead for the sustainable cities."[38] In his book *The Heart of Our Cities*, Gruen tried to redress the rapid destruction that modernism had created in urban and suburban environments. "Nature exists today, in industrially developed countries, only where it is so hostile to human activities that it is permitted to remain undisturbed, or where it has been artificially protected by legislation as in the case of our state and national parks," explains Gruen.[39] "Those who have fled from the congested city realize by now that they have gained nothing. A Freudian giveaway of the fact that their dream wish is that of living in the country is to be found in the way they name their places.... Shopping centers are referred to as villages, and everywhere one finds Town and Country markets, Town and Country shops and Country clubs."[40]

Gruen dissects the industrialized city into a multitude of "scapes," all of which are unrelenting to the natural environment once surrounding them. "We have technoscape, an environment shaped predominantly by the complex apparatus of technology.... It is an area dotted with oil wells, refineries, high-voltage lines, chimneys ... and auto cemeteries," says Gruen. "Then there is transportationscape: millions of square miles covered with tinny surfaces of automobiles; the concrete bands of highways ... all trimmed with traffic signs, billboards and dangling wires."[41] Gruen criticizes the exterior environment of the shopping mall, stating the exterior "appears like an asphalt desert occupied fully or partially by thousands of automobiles."[42] Writing in the early 1960s, Gruen recognized the banal environment around the shopping mall. Although parking was a necessity for the auto-dependent suburbanite, Gruen's statements relay that it was largely the weakest point of the design: "The walk from the parked car to the building core, which might be as long as 600 feet, is not an enjoyable one. The parking lot makes it undesirable to approach the shopping center on foot from the outside — even for those who might be living or working nearby."[43]

Despite Gruen's criticism of the shopping malls' innate design flaws, it continued to thrive for nearly thirty years after his treatise on sustainable urban environments. Gruen's ideal city models were not taken on in the same manner as his shopping mall concept and as a result, America is now left with a multitude of spaces that cannot be classified as city or country. Subsequently, hundreds of shopping malls were built across the suburban environment replacing former fields of wheat or grain with acres of tarmac and concrete structures. The distaste that Gruen later exhibited towards the shopping mall and his dream for sustainable environments has resurfaced in the current economic setting of the United States. The shopping mall, serving as the physical "heart" of America's constructed realities, is starting to deteriorate.

Like the idea of suburbia, which depends on a constant moving-up to a better location or home, the shopping mall was always positioned as a temporary structure. "[Malls] have been designed to be serviceable, nothing more," explains Underhill, "and once they no longer serve they'll have to be razed and replaced with ... I don't know. Maybe something even worse."[44] Kunstler acknowledges that shopping malls, as a model for urban development, have passed their prime. "It remains to be seen how the shopping malls of American might evolve. The conditions under which they flourished — cheap energy, cars for everyone, a credit-driven consumer economy, special tax breaks for big real estate ventures — may be viewed as abnormal and transitory, a fragile equation that could fall apart like a house of cards."[45] Most shopping malls are banal and ugly in their design, says Underhill, and no one will find cause to save them when they fall into disuse.[46] "Only one thing is certain," notes Kunstler, "the malls will not be forever. And none of them were built for the ages."[47]

According to the International Council of Shopping Centers, of the 1,100 enclosed regional malls in the United States, only about one third are viable. "While a third are doing fine, a third have experienced reduced sales and increased vacancies and the rest are in financial distress," says Stabiner.[48] Malls may even be more harmful to the environment when they are in a state of decline. The owners have often left the sites to deteriorate. The hulking empty expanses of concrete and tarmac have become a potentially dangerous blight on the surrounding neighborhood. "The mall's site can rapidly turn into a wasteland of overgrown weeds, cracked concrete, and stray animals, with looters picking sites clean of copper tubing, light fixtures and anything else that can be sold for scrap," says Mok.[49] Unchecked, these dead shopping malls can cause further destruction to the environment as the disused infrastructure leaks effluent and chemicals into the ecosystem.

Once a shopping mall has reached its demise, not only does the physical structure decline, it can affect the very fabric of the community. "Abandoned, boarded up, or still in their death throes, these malls no longer generate profits, no longer service their communities, and worse, drain the financial based and social spirit from their neighborhood," says Smiley.[50] Developer Donald R. Zuchelli says the death of a shopping mall can have grave consequences on community infrastructure such as public services and parks. "As much as 70 % of public services such as police, fire, education and parks are supported by nonresidential entities. The lost revenue from declining shopping centers become a serious problem for local governments."[51]

According to Oldenburg, for some groups the mall is "a habitat that discourages association, one in which people withdraw to privacy as turtles into their shells, denies community and leaves people lonely in the midst of many."[52] Although conceived with a utopian outlook, the shopping mall as a setting for human interaction is not ideal. Not only has it created a habitat that discourages association with others, it has also created a disassociation with the natural environment. Often the only human interaction with nature is in the faux environment offered in a shopping mall. Therefore, the respect and understanding of the true natural environment is skewed. Although the shopping malls built since the 1970s have employed energy saving methods in heating and cooling, the physical structures have much to answer for in their destruction of ecosystems. The shopping mall, as a modernist style structure, dominates and destroys the natural environment around it. The cases of the Crossgates Mall and the Karner blue butterfly as well as Northlands Mall and Thornton Creek show how the shopping mall can have a negative effect on ecosystems.

As evidenced by the EPA reports of the 1970s, the shopping mall is also culpable in the destruction of the environment in its reliance on individual auto-transport and therefore causes an in-direct source of air pollution. The interior environment of the shopping mall has proven to cause stress and anxiety, as concluded in research by Langrehr and Hopkins. As Underhill's research relays, it has also changed human sight, reaction time and depth perception. Kunstler has theorized that the shopping mall was never positioned for longevity as its construction relied on "abnormal" factors that are coming to an end. In a new age of climate change and an increasing scarcity of fossil fuels, the enclosed shopping malls' ability to adapt and change to new conditions is questionable.

In an effort to fully understand the decline of the regional shopping mall, the next section will investigate its current state. Case studies and documented evidence provide a picture of the current viability of this model with a goal of assessing its future. While the decline of the regional shopping mall may have dramatic effects on the availability of public space for the groups identified in chapters 6 and 7, conversely, it may offer some opportunities for addressing the environmental and social concerns raised in this chapter and the previous.

10. Dawn of the Dead Mall

The construction of enclosed shopping malls in the U.S. has ground to a halt, with only one enclosed shopping center opened since 2006. "In the year 2007, not a single new mall opened in the United States, the first time that had happened since the 1950s," notes Devlin.[1] The International Council of Shopping Centers quantify that only a third of a total 1,100 enclosed regional shopping malls in the United States are currently viable.[2] Economists attribute the decline of this model to a change in attitude towards consumption as a result of the 2008 global financial crisis. "The severity of the recession is turning some malls that were once viewed as viable into potential casualties," says Hudson and O'Connell.[3] As Americans have become more pocket conscious, Big Box chain stores, Internet shopping and several alternative development models have risen in popularity.

Besides the global financial crisis, social changes such as demographic shifts and changes in consumer preferences have been identified as factors in the decline of the regional shopping mall. Rendell explains: "A driving force in the decline of the American shopping mall as we know it is a realization that the model is not sustainable, either economically or environmentally."[4] This chapter explores the factors in the decline of the regional shopping mall and maps the severity of its downfall. Through case studies of shopping malls in Upstate New York, a vivid picture is drawn of the situation facing many regional shopping malls in the United States.

As outlined in the first chapter, regional shopping malls can be defined as those that include at least two department stores and are placed in areas to attract customers from as far as twenty to thirty miles away. Super-regional malls, which include at least five department stores, can service customers from a one hundred mile or larger radius. Regional malls also differ from super-regional malls in the area that they encompass, notably a regional mall will encompass 45 acres whereas a super-regional encompasses at least 70 acres of land. Because of their scale and age, regional malls are often highly integrated into the communities where they are located. "Many greyfields (dead malls) are located in established neighborhoods and shopping districts," explains Pricewaterhouse Cooper.[5]

The first section of the book relayed the importance of the regional shopping center to the community, specifically to the defined demographic groups of teens and elderly. Research presented by the International Council of Shopping Centers (ICSC) states that super-regional malls have retained their viability in the marketplace although regional malls face major difficulties. According to the ICSC, "The number of super-regional malls has increased by 9% since 2001, amounting to the addition of roughly five new properties per year," says Martha Peyton.[6] While the super-regional shopping center has been able to remain viable in the current economic climate, it has done so at the expense of the smaller regional center. The bulk of new super-regional malls are created by the consolidation of regional malls to create a single super-regional mall in a viable area. According to Howard Davidowitz, chairman of Davidowitz and Associates, Inc., a national retail consulting and investment banking firm: "There are 300 or 400 malls that are golden; the problem is the rest of them, upscale stores with five or six anchors are going to be fine. If you're a two-anchor, dumpy mall, there are going to be problems when Target builds a store next door and suddenly you're overpriced."[7] The consolidation of regional malls into one large super-regional center relays a decline in the construction of new shopping malls and thus a smaller percentage of regional malls.

Since the year 2006, the total number of viable enclosed shopping malls in the United States has declined dramatically. The ICSC predicted this in a 2003 report entitled "Keeping Track of the Mall Count." "Mall closures and redevelopments will likely outnumber new mall openings for the foreseeable future. There simply are not many construction projects for new malls in the pipeline," explains the ICSC.[8] Stevan Buxbaum, executive vice president of the Buxbaum Group, an Agoura Hills, California, based retail liquidator and consulting firm explains the decline of the mall:

> Across the U.S., we follow about 1,000 regional malls, about 200 are classed as A-class, which indicated that their owners are willing to make significant investments in them to keep them fresh and relevant. Those malls, and the 200 other "Class A" malls are likely to be able to adapt to shopper changes. But there are about another 300 Class B malls and 300 more Class C malls that either don't have deep-pockets owners, or do but the owners have determined that the location does not warrant the significant investment necessary to update the centers. Those malls are more likely to experience more hardships going forwards.[9]

Shopping malls that are not re-generated into super-regional centers are either demolished or left to deteriorate. These malls are called "greyfields" or "dead malls." The term greyfield is defined as "developed sites that are economically and physically ripe for major redevelopment."[10] Pricewaterhouse-Coopers (PwC) estimates that there are 200 to 250 malls approaching the status of greyfields, note that currently 140 regional shopping malls are already considered greyfields or dead malls.[11] The current economic climate is making it difficult to re-habilitate greyfields as viable retail space. "A face-lift isn't going to do much to help," says Mark Eppli. "A new anchor may not do much either."[12]

Major factors in the decline of the regional shopping mall are the tightening of consumer spending and the de-valuation of commercial real estate in the United States as a result of the global financial crisis. Disposable incomes of the average American have been on a decline for years, explains Martha Peyton of TIAA-CREF Asset Management. "This is vividly illustrated by the paltry 1.4 percent growth in per capita disposable personal income after inflation over the ten-year period between 2000 and 2009," notes Peyton.[13] The global financial crisis exacerbated this with an increase in unemployment, which in turn caused a further decline in disposable income. Roy Black, a professor in the practice of finance at Goizeuta, explains that due to the nature of the current recession, expendable incomes are unlikely to recover swiftly. "Unlike the recessions of the 1970s and 1980s, which were generally confined to certain sectors of the economy, the current slowdown is linked to the general economy so its effects are much more pervasive."[14] Lower expendable incomes have driven Americans to seek out more economical choices, and thus the popularity of cut-price, bulk and bargain retailers have become popular options. "A limited number of consumer dollars cannot support all mall models," says Devlin, "Big box power centers have substantially impacted the viability of older neighboring malls."[15]

Shopping malls may be on the decline due to a decrease in stability and investments in real estate investment trusts (REITs). REITs, such as the Simon Group, were launched in 1993 as part of the federal government restructuring post–1990s real estate crash (see Chapter 2) and control the bulk of the shopping malls in the United States. "[They] were launched with IPOs [initial public offerings of stocks] in an effort to raise money against giant bundles of bankrupt, illiquid assets," explains Lindsey. "The trading of commercial mortgage-based securities soon followed; by 2007 they were nearly a trillion dollar market, while the market caps of American's publicly-traded REITs approached half-a-trillion dollars."[16] In a 2005 report the ICSC concludes: "Real estate and the capital markets have become closely aligned over the past decade. This convergence has been healthy for the real estate market and has provided access to greater capital flows than would have been possible in a more segregated market setting."[17] The 2005 ISIC report, however, predicted that REITs would face sobering changes in the future. "While creating a windfall for current owners [of shopping malls], it is clear that this dramatic influx of capital is not sustainable over the long-term."[18] ICSC's 2005 prediction was validated by the global financial crisis, which has seen property prices level, a major cause in the downfall of some REITs and a cause for other REITs to pull back on spending. "The REITs that financed our landscape continue to lurch toward Armageddon," notes Lindsey. "The volume of CMBS (commercial mortgage backed securities) issued annually fell from $230 billion in 2007 to $3 million last year (2009)."[19] Lindsey cites a 2010 Congressional Oversight Panel report that states: "A significant wave of commercial mortgage defaults would trigger economic damage that could touch the lives of nearly every American."[20]

An example in the effect of the global financial crisis on REITs is the case of General Growth Properties. On April 14, 2009 General Growth Properties, Inc., the second-largest mall development group (after the Simon Property Group) in the United States, declared bankruptcy. GGP started out as a small grocery business run by the Bucksbaum family in Iowa. In the 1950s, the company invested in the development of one of the first shopping malls in the Midwest, the Town and Country Center. Their property portfolio continued to grow and by 1989 the company was the second largest mall owner in the United States. The company continued to be largely successful into the 1990s, buying up Center Cos and later the Rouse Company. The downfall of GGP has been attributed to the debt accrued from the company's purchase of the development company Rouse and Co., a development company responsible for creating some of the most iconic "festival marketplace" type of shopping malls, such as Faneuil Hall in Boston and the South Street Seaport in New York. With a total of $27 million in debt, the GGP case has been called the largest real estate bankruptcy in U.S. history. According to Dan Fasulo of Real Capital Analytics: "This is the beginning of the end. This bankruptcy will drive down the values of mall assets in the United States."[21]

GGP managed to pull itself out of bankruptcy 19 months later by securing investments, closing some of their less profitable centers and by agreeing to form a spinoff company, the Howard Hughes Corp., to take on the groups' riskier assets. The company has emerged more compact, a move which places them in a more favorable position in the changing retail environment. The future for GGP, however, still remains uncertain. "General Growth Properties still have challenges facing them," says Kris Hudson of the *Wall Street Journal*.[22] The GGP case represents a turning point in the viability of the enclosed shopping center model, as it has caused investors to speculate on the future sustainability of this model. Notes Crawford, "In their first twenty-five years, less than one percent of shopping malls failed."[23] A model that was once assured profitably is now on shaky ground. The current financial situation aside, many experts believe that the enclosed shopping malls were doomed for extinction regardless.

According to the Urban Land Institute (ULI), the regional enclosed shopping mall is failing due to a shift in the conditions that made the mall a favorable development model to begin with. In the 1950s when the enclosed mall emerged, large tracts of land were readily available for development. Now, says the ULI, "large sites that are suitable for mall construction are difficult to secure, if they can be found at all."[24] Due to the oversaturation of retail in built up suburban areas, "public approvals are increasingly difficult to get; and, except in certain very high growth exurban areas, new markets are limited," says the ULI.[25] *The Economist Online* asserts that the model is on the decline due to a distinct change in the nature of the suburbs: "Although Gruen could not bear to admit it, his invention appealed to those who wanted downtown's shops without its purported dangers.... The suburbs are becoming much more racially mixed while the cities fill up with hip, affluent whites. As a result, suburban malls no longer provide a refuge from diversity."[26] The ULI supports this and explains that the shopping malls built in the 1950s and '60s are now decades old. Since this time period, areas that had once been primarily white suburban communities have become dense urban sprawl with a vivid mix of demographic groups. Shopping malls in these areas have become difficult to sustain due to "limited ability to expand because demographics in their trade areas have become less favorable for reinvestment."[27]

The built-up suburban areas and the increased traffic have made formerly "convenient" shopping malls a traffic nightmare. "As traffic congestion reaches crisis proportions in many places," notes the ULI, "the vaunted convenience of mall shopping is disappearing."[28] Consumers also have less time for shopping than they once did. "We are spending less time in malls, down to 2.9 hours/month in 2003 from 4 hours in 2000," cites Devlin.[29] "While it's probably true that most customers will always drive to the mall," says the ULI, "their busy lives are reducing the time they are willing to spend shopping." Traffic congestion and time commitments mean that increasingly, consumers are looking for "in-and-out" and "one-stop-shop" type of experiences. "As choices increase closer to home in smaller, more convenient shopping environments that offer many of the same stores, customer preferences will continue to shift," notes the ULI.[30]

Family demographics and shopping preferences are also cited as reasons for a shift away from the enclosed shopping center model. "Demographically, families in which one parent works and the other stays at home (and has time to shop) no longer dominate," says the ULI. "Non-traditional households of all types are ascendant and often have very different, and more cosmopolitan, shopping expectations than families of earlier generations."[31] As such, the enclosed shopping center model does not suit the demands of the non-traditional and contemporary family group. This new "non-traditional" family group seeks a level of authenticity to their shopping experiences.

As relayed in previous chapters, the enclosed shopping mall had become increasingly homogenous in its construction and features after the property crisis in the early 1990s. Today's consumer is searching for more authentic community aspects. Devlin cites a study on shopping mall design by the University of Pennsylvania and the Verde Group in December of 2008. "Of every complaint by shoppers about malls, three of those targeted the repetition of stores and the 'mundaneness' of malls," says Devlin.[32] "Customers are now seeking authenticity and a deeper sense of connection to their community, culture, climate and daily lives," notes the ULI. Consumers are seeking a more authentic "outdoor" and "Main Street" experience as opposed to the synthetic environment and Main Street signifiers of the enclosed shopping mall. "There is also an emerging preference for outdoor, streetfront shopping experiences," explains the ULI. "Unfortunately, few of today's malls provide such environments."[33]

In the 1970s malls stratified to form several distinct classifications, such as the "fashion mall," the "mid-market mall" and the "outlet mall" to stay viable. Currently, retail competition has reached such a competitive fervor that the enclosed shopping mall is finding it difficult compete. At the high end of the spectrum, boutique retailers positioned as "lifestyle" centers are taking business intended for the high end "fashion malls." At the lower end of the spectrum are the Big Box retailers and Internet shopping, which offer the consumer savings at a level not offered by the "mid-market" enclosed shopping center. "Hundreds of malls have foundered because they provide neither the experience and the shopping environment that appeal to a customer's aspirations and lifestyle," says the ULI, "nor the value and selection association with off-price shopping."[34]

Big Box retailers have significantly affected the viability of traditional department stores, the physical and metaphorical "anchor" of a shopping mall. "Walmart has dramatically impacted all aspects of shopping," says Devlin, "through consolidations and mergers, department store chains have shrunk to 7 from the more than 20 that existed in the 1970s."[35] The ULI agrees, stating: "The disappearance of many department store anchors (because of bankruptcies and consolidations), and the reluctance or inability of surviving chains to expand (because of saturated markets or fragile balance sheets) has limited new construction opportunities for traditional mall, whose formula historically depended on department stores to draw customers."[36]

"Through the growth of the Big Box stores and discount retailers, the concept of the department store has lost its focus," says Devlin.[37] An example

A lifestyle center; Clifton Park Commons in Clifton Park, New York.

of the cannibalization of regional department stores by Big Boxes is the case of the Philadelphia based Boscov's department store chain. Solomon Boscov founded Boscov's department store in 1911 in Philadelphia. The chain, which started out as a small family owned general store, eventually grew to an operation of over 39 stores in the Northeast with some mid-range shopping malls based around Boscov's as an anchor.[38] In 2008 Boscov's filed for Chapter 11 bankruptcy, citing the global financial crisis and the resulting credit crisis as a basis for the claim. Boscov's, with its offering of mid-range goods and flat-packed furniture, have been eclipsed by larger national chains such as Walmart and Target. Burt P. Flickinger III, managing director of Strategic Resource Group, explains: "Regional department store chains are more vulnerable to tightening credit and cuts in allowances from suppliers than national chains."[39] Boscov's emerged from bankruptcy in 2009 a much leaner company, closing 10 of its 39 stores and liquidating large stocks of merchandise. According to Britt Beemer, chairman of America's Research Group in Charleston, South Carolina, retailers such as Boscov's will continue to be at risk, for although their stores are "in excellent locations," they are "still in malls, where customers have cut back on purchases."[40] In a 2008 article in the *Washington Examiner*, Scott Krugman, spokesman for the National Retail Federation, stated: "Malls are starting to rethink the concept of the traditional anchor. Malls are going to have to start considering different options. If we're not seeing it now, we're going to see it soon."[41]

The increase of super-regional malls due to consolidation of regional malls shows that the enclosed shopping mall model still has viability in the super-regional format. As evidenced by the number of struggling regional shopping malls, however, the regional version may face extinction in coming years. The factors in the decline of the regional shopping mall can be described as economic and social. The decrease of household incomes and de-stabilization of property prices due to the global financial crisis has led to the closure of shopping malls and the bankruptcy and subsequent consolidation of some REITs. The increased urbanization of suburban areas has seen the decline of some established regional shopping malls due to a change in demographics and an increase in inaccessibility as a result of traffic congestion.

Regional shopping malls have also been greatly affected by a change in family demographics and shopping preferences. "Non-traditional" family groups now seek authentic, outdoor experiences from their shopping environment, a format that is not provided by the generic enclosed mall format. Increased retail competition is cited as a large factor in the decline of the regional mall. At the higher end of the spectrum, lifestyle centers offer the consumer a more "authentic" experience while Big Box and Internet retailers offer the consumer unrivaled cost benefit at the lower end of the spectrum. Big Box stores have eclipsed the mid-market regional malls in many areas across the country.

Internet Retailing

The popularity of "e-tailing," or electronic retailing via the Internet, has grown in recent years as more people have come to trust online shopping. "There is no doubt that online retail spending is growing," says Devlin. "In total online sales for 2007, the largest spending areas were computer hardware and software, apparel, accessories, footwear and jewelry and home products."[42] Internet retailing has grown steadily over the last few years and will continue to grow, notes Forrester Research. A 2010 survey by the group has revealed that online retail sales were up 11 percent, compared to 2.5 percent for all retail sales.[43] E-retailing has notably affected areas such as music and book sales, as evidenced by the recent bankruptcy of the international book retailer Borders.

"While many readers changed purchasing habits to online book retailers during the past decade, Borders pushed ahead with its superstore model, which involved large rents and labor costs, and it outsourced its eCommerce site to Amazon until 2007," notes retail analyst James Thompson.[44] As such, large empty retail spaces have been left in shopping malls around the country that formerly encompassed a Borders store. While Internet retailing is growing in certain areas, studies show that it will not altogether surpass traditional "bricks and mortar" shops. "We buy only 6.3 percent of our apparel, accessories, footwear and jewelry online, and only 1.1 percent of our groceries and pet food online," says Devlin. "In other words, I think we generally make purchases that fit the qualities of the medium."[45] Researchers note that people prefer to "touch and feel" things like clothing, shoes and food, which is why these products categories still remain viable in bricks and mortar stores.[46] "Human behavior relies on the senses, and consumers are used to the see-feel-smell factor in making decisions based on their own psychological reactions to the inherent feelings generated by these experiences," says Markham.[47] Underhill echoes this sentiment: "Even if web site shopping doubles the catalog's success rate, 80 percent of shopping will continue to be done in the real world."[48] The British Council of Shopping Centers explains that the future of shopping is "multi-channel," and while "e-tailing will never replace the shopping experience," it will be seen as a "complementary tool to support the retail activity" of most consumers.[49]

Big Boxes

Big Boxes, also known as "power centers," are not a new concept. Big Boxes started out in the late 1950s and early 1960s as "community centers." The original community center was a strip mall style center anchored by junior department stores or variety stores, with a supermarket and smaller retailers incorporated into the "strip." The community center specialized in the 1970s to encompass warehouse stores and off-price women's specialty stores and thus the Big Box retailer was born. "The '70s marked the emergence of a single category," says Devlin, "'the category killers,' discount mass merchandiser like Kmart and Target, and warehouse stores such as Costco, Sam's Club and BJ's Wholesale Club."[50] The ULI, writing in 1984, predicted an uncertain future for the community center: "It is too large to thrive off its immediate neighborhood trade area and too small to make a strong impact on the whole community unless it is located in a smaller city with a population ranging from 50,000 to 100,000."[51] From the 1990s onward, with the adaptation of the nineteen standard property types, the Big Box began to edge to the forefront of retailing. Walmart, the "category killer" to end all "category killers," is now the largest retailer in the United States and arguably, the world. "More than half of all Americans live within five miles of a Walmart store," says Fishman, author of *The Wal-Mart Effect*, "less than a ten-minute drive away. Ninety percent of Americans live within fifteen miles of a Walmart."[52] Fishman explains that the rise of Walmart in the 1990s has irrevocably changed the retail climate. "The Walmart Effect"—a phrase coined by Fishman, describes the far-reaching effect that the chain has had on retail across the board. He says it has caused "the suburbanization of shopping [with] the downward pressure on wages of all kinds of stores trying to compete."[53]

Hybrids

Hybrid malls mix traditional malls with Big Boxes and lifestyle centers, creating a hybrid between a "strip-mall" and an enclosed mall. According to the Pyramid Companies' Marketing Director Andra Case: "In order to keep many of the regional malls viable, Pyramid have attempted to move the Big Box to the mall, as many of our malls have attached a Target creating a hybrid between the two."[54] Case noted that although Target is more of a "one stop shop," she does not believe that the nature of a Target takes anything away from the communal aspects of the shopping mall experience. In these malls, Target has its own entrance and functions in the way traditional department stores such as a Macy's once did. Target, however, is a discount version of the traditional mid-market magnet stores, with shopping trolleys and shop fittings that evoke a supermarket rather than a department store.

"Hybrid malls — those that mix indoor and outdoor spaces or traditional retailing with lifestyle or entertainment — have become an increasingly popular new type of development," explains the ULI.[55] Although Pyramid believes this is the solution, it could ultimately lead to the death of the interior mall space. Visitors may frequent only the attached Big Boxes, which provide the bulk and range of goods found at multiple mall stores, and fail to flow into the mall space. Architect Richard Reep supports this theory and believes that the hybrid as a solution to save the shopping mall has failed. He says that instead of using the enclosed mall space as it was intended, as communal space as well as a flow through to the magnet stores, "shoppers parked at the main mall, shopped and then parked in front of the various strips, shopping their way out of the parking lot." Reep goes on to explain: "This [hybrid] model could not rescue malls, so developers started reinventing them as lifestyle centers."[56]

Lifestyle Centers

Introduced in the early 2000s, the "lifestyle center" is a twist on Gruen's retail vision. It is essentially the enclosed mall with the roof removed. The difference, explains *The Economist Online*, is that "the plants are real and rather than vaguely evoking a town center, it is actually done up to look like one ... it performs all the functions of a mall without looking at all like one."[57] The ULI explains that the return to a Main Street style of street-oriented retailing shows a shift to a new perspective in shopping center design. "Street-oriented developments are gaining ground, and enclosed malls are being reinvented by adding open pedestrian components and incorporating other uses on former surface parking lots."[58] Many lifestyle centers incorporate urban grid patterns; creating small laneways with cobble-stone streets dotted with outdoor street lamps, in an attempt to recreate the feel of the Main Street of pre-suburban America that the mall destroyed. These "prelapsarian downtowns where there is no crime or homelessness are only possible because Americans have largely forgotten what downtowns used to be like."[59]

Many ailing malls are ripping off their roofs in an attempt to re-invigorate their dying enclosed core with an open-air re-creation of Main Street. Real estate investors, citing the increasing presence of Big Box centers in the design of these centers, doubt the long-term viability of this type of development. Originally the concept of the lifestyle center was to incorporate high-end specialty retail in an up-market location, similar to the ethos of the "fashion mall." "Lifestyle tenants tend to be those specialty retailers whose product line is focused on a particular ethos or activity," says the ULI. "Nevertheless, the need to expand the notion of convenience and to serve the value conscious consumer has led to the inclusion of Big Box stores in such centers."[60] Miller, an investor with Transwestern, explains: "One sign that developers aren't confident in the model is that more are trying to leave room for 'Big Box' stores."[61] Albright describes a typical lifestyle center model that includes the Big Boxes. "In one corner of the same development, typically there's a Main Street for smaller mall stores, boutiques and Starbucks. Some have offices or condos upstairs. The street is lined with what's called 'teaser parking' so motorists drive a lap before realizing the empty spaces are in a vast lot outback. But dominating center stage is a lineup of Big Boxes."[62] Devlin describes this type of "super-regional open-air shopping center" as a new direction in shopping.

Overall, the following models show a dominance of the Big Box store and presents the case that the Big Box is replacing the regional shopping mall. A decline of the regional mall will lead to a loss of public space in many regional areas across the United States. Big Box stores, while offering opportunities for bargain and bulk shopping, do not provide the consumer with public space. Zepp contrasts the two: "The appeal [of the Big Box store] is a lesser amount of money spent in a limited amount of time with a Zen-like concentration on the business at hand. There is no fun here and no specially programmed Muzak. All space is used for merchandise, with the exception of the necessary room for offices."[63] The appeal of super-regional malls remains strong, as this model offers more entertainment options than the traditional regional mall and draws from a larger catchment area (over 100 miles). Although many super-regional malls remain viable, the 100-mile catchment radius makes it largely inaccessible as a public space to many suburbanites. "In suburbia and small towns, malls often are the only major public spaces and the safest venues for teenagers to shop, hang out and seek part-time work," explain Hudson and O'Connell.[64] The loss of regional malls can be potentially devastating for groups in regional areas that depend on their existence.

The following chapter will focus on the Big Box shopping environment. An overview of this model, as exemplified by retailers Walmart and Target, provides further evidence for its prevalence and the benefits and drawbacks of this shopping environment.

11. The Rise of the Big Box

As noted in the previous chapter, one of the largest factors in the decline of the regional shopping mall has been the rise of Big Box retailers; retail centers that have re-invigorated the strip mall style of "one stop shopping" for time poor and pocket conscious consumers. These Big Boxes are becoming ever more prevalent in suburbia, replacing many viable regional malls or turning them into dead spaces. This shift in retail is founded on many changing factors, including consumer perception and economic rationalism. In essence, the rise of a retailer like Walmart is a natural progression in a free-market capitalist economy such as the United States. However, the implications of a "warehouse" style retail space is the eradication of any space that is not utilized for consumption, thus further diminishing the public space available to suburban Americans. The following will delve into the characteristics of prominent Big Box retailers, Walmart and Target, with a focus on the embedded ideologies inherent in these brands that set them apart from the enclosed shopping mall and how this model is affecting public space across the country. The Big Box retail model, perfected by Sam Walton with his Walmart stores, has many of the same ideological foundations as the shopping mall, as both are squarely rooted in the small-town American vision. As this chapter elucidates, the rise of the Big Box may prove to be even more successful than the shopping mall in inspiring the consumer and in re-constructing the American landscape.

Walmart

Walmart's warehouse shopping model has become the norm in suburbs across America and has ultimately led to a decline in the regional shopping mall. "Developers have been moving away from the enclosed-mall format in favor of Big Box centers anchored by free-standing giants such as Walmart,"[1] say Hudson and O'Connell. In a new age of austerity Big Box retailers offer consumers bulk savings and a sense of satisfaction in their thrifty retail choices. "[Big Box stores] don't just sell products; they sell trophies, when you come home with a huge supply of toilet paper, and the man enters the house with them, he is truly the conquering hero."[2] Walmart is now the world's largest retailer with more than 4,300 stores in the United States and over 8,000 worldwide, with global sales topping $400 billion in 2009. A phrase has been coined; "The Walmart Effect," which describes the company's supremacy and its ability to make every area of the United States into an even more homogenous entity than the shopping mall. "The Walmart Effect happens when Walmart or any Big Box retailer comes into town, reshapes shopping habits, and drains the viability of traditional local shopping areas," says Fishman, author of *The Wal-Mart Effect*.[3] According to a study by Zook and Graham, geographers at the University of Kentucky: "Fully 60 percent of the entire U.S. population lives within 5 miles of a Walmart location and 96 percent are within 20 miles."[4]

When a Walmart opens in any town or region in the country, it has an immediate effect on existing retail. "In the year following entry, mass stores [selling mass-produced goods] suffer a median sales decline of 40 percent," says Parachuri, et al.[5] With its aggressive growth pattern, Walmart has effectively reduced competition across the United States. In a period of 40 years, it has managed to replace many local retailers as well as generating a tide of outsourcing which has in turn crushed many local producers. "Walmart's far flung network of retail outlets ensures that Walmart interacts with and has an impact on virtually every locality within the United States. In effect it is engendering a nation of Walmart based consumption," explains Zook and Graham.[6]

Walmart began humbly in the small town of Bentonville, Arkansas. Its founder, Sam Walton, came from a farming family with roots in the American heartland. Throughout his childhood Walton's family moved multiple times to small farming communities in Oklahoma and Missouri. Walton therefore grew up with a strong sense of what a Main Street community was like. When he started a franchise of the chain Ben Franklin in Arkansas in 1950, Walton imbued this concept of small town community retail into everything he did. Positioning the store in the center of the community, Walton made it accessible to all. He stocked the shelves with a variety of items and stayed open later than other retailers to suit the convenience of the customer. Significantly, in his Ben Franklin franchise, Walton experimented with sourcing directly from suppliers and doing away with excessive staff, unnecessary packaging and decoration in the store to serve the customer's desire for lower prices. This concept took off and Walton's Ben Franklin store in Newport began to outsell the local JCPenney department store.

Top: Walmart Supercenter in Colonie, New York. *Bottom:* Warehouse-style shopping at the Walmart Supercenter in Colonie.

The landlord of Walton's store, who also had vested interest in the department store, decided not to renew his lease for fear of the store overtaking his own. Unfazed, Walton moved to Bentonville and opened another Ben Franklin franchise, this time re-branding it Walton's 5 and 10. Although Walton didn't break away from the Franklin's franchise until 1962, when he opened his self-

A Target store at the Hampshire Mall in Hadley, Massachusetts.

funded Walmart, Walton's 5 and 10 was the starting point for the Walmart vision. With his own store, Walton set about embedding the cultural values of small town America into his retail vision. Burt and Sparks explore this ideology in their article "Walmart's World": "Walmart portrays its culture as 'small town America' ... it's symbolic and community acts reinforce this perception and the ways in which Walmart connects itself symbolically to the dominant ideologies of American life (frugality, family, religion, neighborhood, community and patriotism)."[7]

Unlike the shopping mall, the Main Street U.S.A ideology is not represented in physical elements of public space, such as an atrium space with benches and fountains, or in the use of visual signifiers of Main Street such as colonial moldings or Southwestern stucco and tile styling, in a Walmart. It generates a sense of the small-town American values of frugality, family, religion, neighborhood, community and patriotism through an overarching rhetoric that filters through all areas of the business. Sam Walton's philosophy of retail was that "people make the difference" to a business.[8] The vision that underpins Walton's retail structure is the idea that everyone is important. Thus Walton, in his employee structure, names everyone as an "associate" regardless of his or her duties in the organization. The slogan on the back of an employee smock says "Our people make the difference," which again reiterates the importance of "regular" people in the corporate structure. "This statement of pride in work being conducted by associates provides a symbolic pat on the back, and perhaps a subtle vote of encouragement and appreciation for a difficult job done well," writes Dunnett and Arnold.[9]

In his autobiography, Walton repeats the term "small-town ethics" in practically every chapter. He notes that the associates in his stores function more like a "family" than a team of nameless sales staff. "We break down the barriers, which helps us communicate better with one another. And we make our people feel part of a family in which no one is too important or too puffed up to lead a cheer or be the butt of a joke."[10] This small-town "folksy" attitude permeates all levels of Walmart's company policy. The Walmart company handbook, given to all new employees, reiterates these values and attempts to acculturate them at all levels. "Walmart's human resource strategies have grown from this vision and now facilitate a fully institutionalized company culture that has value for labor discipline," says Rosen.[11]

Despite Walton's disquisition on the importance of staff in his autobiography, Walmart's track record of staff policy in terms of benefits, working conditions and salaries betrays this. Walmart is now the number one private employer in the United States; however, a job at Walmart does not offer the same securities previously available from dominant industrial leaders in America.[12] "Walmart's formula for financial success includes: low-wage labor, limited health benefits, and leveraging of government subsidies," explains Angotti, Paul, Gray and Williams in a 2009 report on Walmart's economic footprint.[13] The social organization, American Rights at Work, explains that this has come through a gradual legislative process that saw a shift from a protected workforce to a free market approach which encroached on the reforms set in place from the '50s through to the early '70s. "Collective bargaining agreements, which once covered a third of all workers, secured regular wage increases, health and pension benefits, and job security for employees at many of the nation's leading companies…. Yet the lifetime career model didn't last. The rightward shift in politics from the Reagan Administration on up to the George W. Bush Administration led to policies that encouraged global free trade at the expense of protections for employees."[14]

A shift to a service based economy in recent years has seen the rise in the power of retailers; however, the retailers do not feel obliged to provide job securities for jobs that had previously been seen as temporary. In Ohio, explains Angotti, et al.: "Walmart has more associates and associate dependents on Medicaid than any other employer, costing taxpayers $44.8 million in 2009."[15] IBISWorld, an independent market research group, quantifies the average wage of a Walmart sale associate to be $8.81 per hour. "This translates to annual pay of $15,576, based upon Walmart's full-time status of 34 hours per week. This is significantly below the 2010 federal poverty level of $22,050 for a family of four," notes *Wal-Mart Watch*.[16] Walmart is no more culpable in this than other retailers and national figures show that Walmart does not pay lower wages than other retailers.

As previously discussed, the shopping mall also promotes this ideology, as most of its jobs are positioned as temporary employment for teenagers and the elderly at the lower end of the job market. However, the implication of the low salary level at America's number one employer could potentially change the entire retail environment. This trend represents a decrease in purchasing power of many Americans, thus in turn decreasing the demand for the higher-end retail available at shopping malls, therefore giving the American public less retail choice in the long run. Scheduling is another issue that is at odds with Walton's "family-values" vision. Random and hectic schedules as a result of a Walmart's extensive opening hours and a continual policy of understaffing stores can lead to staff unrest. Notes Rosen, "Schedule changes can also be used as a way to encourage employees to quit if they are 'uncooperative.'"[17] Survey data collected in 2006 shows that Walmart has an extremely high turnover rate, about 70 percent a year. According to Rosen, this can be attributed to "low wages and poor treatment."[18] This statistic points to the fact that staff, while outwardly portraying a friendly attitude to the customer, have underlying resentment towards the organizational structure of the operation.

"Making the customer number one" is another core value of the company philosophy, one that is held in high regard in the Walmart vision. This is evident in the "Walmart Cheer," which is memorized by management at all Walmart outlets across the globe. On Saturday mornings, employees are obligated to have a weekly meeting where a cheer is invoked, the last line being "Who's number One? THE CUSTOMER."[19] The ideology of the "Customer is number one" is reiterated within the retail environment in many different guises. On first arrival, the customer is met by a "greeter," a staff member specifically employed to greet everyone as they enter the store. Walmart's policy to "meet and greet 'em'" extends beyond the greeter, as it is expected that every staff member "remember the 10 foot rule," to greet anyone who comes within ten feet of their person by smiling and speaking to them.[20] Walton based his retail philosophy on the idea that everyone wants a good deal. The use of large graphics with bright happy faces on them above a sign that says "slashing prices all the time" is a way to show this dedication to the customers' needs. "For many years, we lived entirely off the principles that customers in the country and in small towns are just like their relatives who left the farm and moved to the city: they want a good deal as much as anybody," says Walton.[21]

The policy of extended store hours (many Walmarts are open 24 hours a day) and variety of products also signals a "customer first" attitude. "The sheer variety of goods available in the typical Walmart facilitates one-stop shopping and thus time savings that are central to the store's appeal and success," say Warf and Chapman.[22] The generic store structure, rows and rows of goods laid out in a large warehouse lit by fluorescent tube lighting, is repeated in a near identical format in stores throughout the country. This generic format makes it even more efficient for the customer to find their bargain-priced goods and leave, thus epitomizing the "customer first" attitude.[23] "And really," said Walton, "if you think about it from your point of view as a customer, you want everything: a wide assortment of good quality merchandise; the lowest possible prices; guaranteed satisfaction with what you buy, friendly, knowledgeable service; convenient hours, free parking; a pleasant shopping experience."[24]

The signifiers that Walmart uses to show a "customer first" attitude are often paradoxical. The entry-way "greeter," for example, has a secondary role as a security guard. Unlike the overtly positioned security guards in official uniforms at the shopping mall, the use of a greeter is a subversive means to control who and what comes in and out of the space. The persona of the "friendly home town" greeter is corrupted by the "abrupt security official who stops every shopper who has made a purchase at another store to tag their package upon entrance to Walmart, thus figuratively 'accusing' each one as a potential thief," says Dunnett and Arnold.[25]

Although Walmart touts itself as offering the customer a variety of goods unsurpassed in other stores, it's sheer scale and aggressive buying policies make it possible for the store to inform what the customer wants and not the opposite. For example, Walmart promotes itself as a "family" retailer and as such refuses to sell any CDs with a parental warning sticker. As the number one music distributor in the United States, this policy significantly limits the consumer's choice. This policy also extends to video games, DVDs and literature sold in the store. Walmart regularly declines to sell anything that it sees as being unfit for "families."[26]

Another paradoxical rhetoric that is promoted at Walmart is an overtly patriotic atmosphere that attempts to motivate the patriotic sentiments of the consumer and mask the fact that the majority of products sold in the store are produced overseas. Huge American flags and graphics portraying stars and stripes adorn the interiors and exteriors of the stores. "While Walmart was engaging in a 'Buy American' campaign in the 1990s, it simultaneously became China's sixth largest trading partner," notes Warf and Chapman.[27] In his biography, Walton rationalized this as such: "In some cases — too many in my opinion — importing is really our only alternative because a lot of American-made goods simply aren't competitive, either in price, or quality, or both."[28]

However powerful Sam Walton's "folksy" rhetoric of small town values, reiterated on the staff member's vests, symbolic community gestures, constructed attitudes and signage in the store, the reality of a highly rationalized retail chain is that it more closely resembles a finely tuned machine than a living breathing "family." The physical space of a Walmart is an example of this, as it creates an environment that is unconducive to genuine community interaction. In essence the Walmart outlet is just a terminus point for an extended logistics network and as such Walmart structures adopt a utilitarian design format. Walmart, as opposed to the traditional Main Street, is "a retail location distant from the downtown area ... a large "cinderblock box" dropped on a parcel of land and surrounded by acres of asphalt."[29] The overarching design behind Walmart is one of "discount space, a place where the experiential mode of shopping is replaced with 'Always Low Prices — Always.'"[30] "Walmart Stores have a distinctive design that contrasts sharply with the typical pastiches of rural building styles," writes Barcus.[31]

Walmart does not offer the built-in allocation of a space for consumers to linger or relax as enclosed shopping malls once did. "Discount space is mass-produced merchandise, arranged on standardized shelving, in a large warehouse environment where all attention is shifted toward savings," says The BoxTank group.[32] The BoxTank goes on to explain: "This infinitely reproduced interior is modulated by the shell of the Big Box, the discrete unit of discount space, which renders the box lifeless. Both inside and outside, quality is replaced with quantity and experience is replaced with economy."[33] The design of a Walmart extends beyond the interiors, explains LeCavalier of *Design Observer*: "The Walmart environment includes not only the commercial enclosures themselves but also the environs they produce: the parking lots, street lights, traffic lanes, median strips, freeway exits, drainage systems, retaining walls, grass berms, gutters, sidewalks, curbs, fire lanes, etc., that characterize the suburban commercial landscape — and in fact have come to dominate it."[34] Thus the landscapes of suburban spaces have taken on an even more utilitarian format, and the shopping center stripped of all interior decoration, is no longer a place where one can escape the bland expanses of concrete and tarmac for a fantasy world. "The separation of retail environments and community heritage environments suggests a clearly defined distinction between the roles of Big Box retailers and community heritage environments," writes Barcus.[35] In a Walmart vs. the Mall survey on *debate.org*, a debater notes, "Malls are much more eye-pleasing than Walmart. The roomyness [*sic*] of the hall ways, the 2 levels (or more), and general decoration are much better than a common Walmart. The one I go to has a nice little forest in the center, and little ponds in places.... Walmart has to be plain because its made for everybody, and can't seem to slide towards any specific trend. Boring and generic."[36] In this sense, Walmart's generic warehouse-type construction model, the "Big Box," is a bland alternative to the suburban shopping mall.

"Since people feel forced to go to Walmart as a social center, time might be wisely spent advocating for government funding for parks, community centers, and libraries, new stores on traditional main streets — to create a center for one-stop shopping and entertainment on the scale of Walmart so that people feel they have a choice," says Smith.[37] Examples of how the public has attempted to utilize Walmart as more than a warehouse are indicative of the lack of public space and desire for human interaction in these environments. The same groups previously discussed as having a strong need for the public space of the shopping mall, teenagers and the elderly, have attempted to re-create community in Walmarts across the country. "High school and college students often use Walmart's size and late hours to play games such as scavenger hunts, aisle foot ball and A–Z 'Alphabet Shopping.' The Walmart in Madison, Wisconsin, offers bingo for older folks at the McDonald's inside," continues Warf and Chapman.[38] As the interior offers little in the way of public space, parking lots have been used as social spaces in many areas across the country. "We knew that the Walmart parking lot has been replacing traditional venues for public space for years," says The BoxTank,[39] including 9-11 memorial gatherings, army recruiting and as an overnight camping spot for people in RV homes. The BoxTank focuses on the concept of the parking lot as public space, noting, "this is merely a representation of a larger phenomenon found in the American landscape that favors Fordist models of specialization: strict diagrams that favor efficiency and uniformity while generating landscapes that don't allow for the flexibility demanded of local conditions."[40]

A popular Web site, *People of Walmart* invites Americans to send in candid shots of people shopping in Walmart in outlandish clothes or cars in the parking lot adorned with stuffed animals and other over-the-top decorative elements. This online community is another attempt by the public to imbue Walmart with the interesting and sociable quality it lacks by making a game out of shopping there. The creators of the site explain, "This site is simply a satirical social commentary of the extraordinary sights found at America's favorite stores. Walmart is Americana baby, Enjoy!"[41] These examples show that, confined to the homogenous aisles of a warehouse, the young and old in America have tried in vain to make this cold, inhuman space a bit more like "home."

"Walmart has always tried to build up its image as a community member," says Arnold, Bu, Gerhard, Pioch and Sun. "In a reflection of its small-town origins, it wishes to be perceived as a responsible member of the town or city in which it resides."[42] Similar to the Disney vision, over time Sam Walton's framework of ideal community values embodied in the Midwestern

Main Street became skewed, morphing into a corporate vision more squarely rooted in free-market capitalism than in a utopian vision of community well-being. "Walmart is not just a reflection of American society and values," says Fishman, "It is a mirror of us as individuals. In a democracy, our individual ambivalence about such a concentration of economic power, even when that power is ostensibly on our side, is a signal."[43]

Walmart is far from an ideal community retailer, as it has significantly altered the American landscape and erased many community aspects from its surface. However, Walmart has not done this unsupported. Millions of Americans have helped to drive this trend. "Most people know on some level that Walmart is hurting them, or at least that theirs is a dependent relationship," explains Smith, "but we shop at Walmart anyway. It carries styles of clothes and media the customers there want to buy, it offers low prices a large percentage of U.S. consumers can afford, and it also fits into a larger narrative that many ascribe to their own lives, a narrative about being simple, hardworking and friends."[44] In this sense, the American public is as culpable in the decline of community as the corporation itself. In a hunger for bargain goods, the general public has systematically destroyed viable manufacturing in the United States, allowing a retailer with a drive towards efficiency and control rather than human interest to become the number one employer of Americans. "Walmart of course, can't be charged single-handedly with driving manufacturing jobs overseas," says Fishman. "That is, in fact, the American dilemma: We find the abandonment of U.S. factories from Georgia to Michigan unnerving; we find cheaper stuff on store shelves addictive. And we don't connect the two."[45]

In the quest for a bargain, American consumers are willing to give up any sense of public space. "Why would you want to spend a whole day at the mall when you can spend thirty minutes getting everything in one place?" says a debater on Walmart vs. the Mall.[46] "Walmart's generic buildings and the environments that result have saturated the United States," says LeCavalier of *Design Observer*.[47] Our communities have been greatly affected by this retail behemoth but often there is little reflection or revision of this model. "Both as individuals and as a society, we have an obligation to answer the unanswered questions about Walmart," says Fishman. "Otherwise we have surrendered control — of our communities, or our economy, of some measure of our destiny — to Bentonville."[48]

Target

Target is the second largest discount retailer, behind Walmart, in the United States. Their "designer-discount" approach gives them a point of difference from Walmart and has helped them dominate in the area traditionally covered by department stores. Target started as a discount offshoot of the department store Dayton's in the 1960s. Dayton's department store, founded by George Draper Dayton in 1902 as a dry-goods store in Minneapolis, became one of the dominant department stores in the Midwest. The store prided itself as being a quality mid-market retailer with a commitment to the community. In 1918 the company created an endowment fund to "aid in the promoting of the welfare of mankind anywhere in the world." "Success is making ourselves useful in the world," George Draper Dayton wrote in 1918, "helping in lifting in the level of humanity so conducting ourselves that when we go the world will be somewhat better of our having lived the brief span of our lives."[49] In 1946, the company established a policy of giving 5 percent of pretax profits back to the community, thus solidifying their position as a community benefactor.

Significantly, Dayton's was an anchor tenant in the 1956 development of the first enclosed shopping mall, Southdale, in Edina, MN. With the success of their suburban outlets, Dayton's segmented their brand into different areas as a means to expand their market. The company created five autonomous divisions: Dayton's department stores, Target discount retailing, B. Dalton Booksellers, Dayton Jewelers and the Dayton Development Company. Target discount retailer was created to service the mass market. "At the time, the move is considered risky by some industry experts as it moves away from the company's dominant position as a department store retailer," explains *Target.com*, "By demonstrating visionary leadership, the company took the first step towards transforming the organization from a family-run department store chain into one of the nation's greatest discount-store chains."[50]

Dayton's created Target to bridge the gap between the high-quality service and offerings of a traditional department store with the poor-quality offerings, budget reputation and service of a discount store. "Target differentiates itself from the other retail stores by combining many of the best department store features — fashion quality and service — with the low prices of a discounter," explains *Target.com*.[51] The first Target store opened with great fanfare in May of 1962 in Roseville, MN, and subsequently four more Midwestern stores were added later that year. The Target retailing concept took off, and by the late 1960s Target began expanding on a national level.

In the late 1960s Dayton's merged with the Hudson Corporation to create a single entity, Dayton-Hudson Corporation. Hudson's Department store, founded in Detroit in the early 1900s, was one of the largest department stores in the Midwest. Of note is the fact that Hudson's was the second anchor store in the 1956 Southdale Mall development.[52] As a single entity, the corporation became a powerhouse in retailing, eventually purchasing the California based retailer Mervyns in the late 1970s and iconic Chicago-based retailer Marshall Field's in the early 1990s. In 1975, Target surpassed all other divisions of the corporation in profit revenue and became a focus for the corporation. By the late 1970s, Target reached $1 billion in annual sales with 74 Targets in 11 states.[53]

It continued to expand rapidly throughout the 1980s, and in the mid–1990s, the Super Target was introduced in an effort to directly compete with Walmart. Target became such a major focus of the Dayton and Hudson brand, that in the year 2000 the company decided to change the corporation's name to the Target Corporation. They retained an aspect of the department store trade, however, they re-branded all remaining Daytons and Hudsons "Marshall Field's." In 2005, the Target Corporation sold their Marshall Field's and Mervyns holdings to the May company (which later became Federated Department Stores) and thus put all the focus on its discount brand Target.[54]

Currently Target is the second largest discount retailer and the fourth largest overall retailer in the United States. It has 1556 stores in 47 states and has recently expanded its offerings to Canada.[55] Target has kept an edge over Walmart with a continued focus on high quality and designer goods at discount prices. To facilitate this, Target formed alliances with popular fashion designers and architects to create designer goods at budget prices. Designer alliances are key to Target's success and differentiate it from Walmart. "Shoppers go to Target for a selection that includes detergent and batteries, in the tradition of all discount stores," writes Constance Hays of the *New York Times*, "but also for designs from Philippe Starck, Stephen Sprouse, Sonia Kashuk and Todd Oldham that can be found only at Target…. Executives say good design should be democratized."[56] Although the stores compete for business, they define their target audience in different terms. "People who are oriented toward quality and design do more of their shopping at Target," says former Target CEO Bob Ulrich. "People who are focused on price tend to go to Walmart."[57] This approach to retail has also helped Target slip into the areas left by failed department stores in hybrid shopping malls much more seamlessly than Walmart stores. Unlike Walmart's embedded "small town" family values approach, Target relies on its glamorous advertising and "designers for Target" appeal to attract the aspiration buyer — patrons who had formerly frequented mid-market and up-market department stores.

In 2001, Target spent over $924 million on advertising their designer offerings, something that the brand sees as essential in keeping the customer engaged.[58] Walmart, on the other hand, does not see marketing as essential as the ability to keep the prices as low as possible and therefore does not allocate as extensive a budget to yearly advertising. Although distinguished by the "designer elements" of their products, both Target and Walmart can be described as the same "beast." They both stand for a similar ethos of discount shopping at a cost to true community well being. "Remember, if you take away Method cleaners, Issac Mizrihi-designed items, and glowing endorsements on David Letterman's show from Sarah Jessica Parker, then Target is the same beast [as Walmart]," writes Smith. "[It] is just smaller and wrapped in red instead of blue."[59]

Big Boxes as Public Space

Overall, Walmart and Target can be seen as the United States' "power houses" in the contemporary retail environment. Both companies approach discount retailing with a warehouse-type set up and extensive distribution networks that make them very difficult to compete with. Whereas Walmart is squarely focused on the lowest possible price, Target's focus is on "designer discount," a factor that has enabled Target to distinguish itself in the discount retail market. Both retailers attempt to build up their image of a community-minded institution through institutional image, advertising campaigns, offerings to charity and internally funded foundations. The Big Box stores, however, do not function as a meeting place or town center in the way a traditional enclosed shopping center once did. Although the stores offer some form of seating (a small amount of indoor or outdoor park benches) and in some stores, a small food area, a community space akin to a mall atrium or food court is lacking in the store design layouts of both Target and Walmart. The visual signifiers of water, light, and nature present in the enclosed shopping mall, which evoke a similar symbolism as churches or other houses of worship (as discussed in Chapter 4), are therefore absent in the warehouse model.

The Big Box store aims to be an "all-encompassing, one-stop shopping trip" experience for the consumer who values convenience and low price.[60] "Walmart's creation of an independently sited substitute market at a driving distance from other merchants attempts to displace shopping from downtowns and shopping malls by providing a corporate island of only those choices purveyed by Walmart," notes VanderVelde.[61] Although Target has some stores that are attached to hybrid shopping malls, they effectively displace the competition by offering a large variety of products at discount price points, eliminating the need to flow into other outlets. In the Target stores attached to shopping malls there is often a physical barrier between the Target and the mall space where shopping carts are no longer allowed in the mall space. This barrier prompts the patron to first return to their car with their Target purchases before commencing their mall experience, thus breaking the leisurely flow into the mall. Similarly, the shopping carts in Walmart function in pushing the consumer to purchase all their needs quickly and efficiently. Once the consumer has filled their cart full of goods, the store offers no space to "park" your cart to allow the mind and body a rest during the shopping experience. An atrium space or indoor pedestrian city, as Gruen's original mall designs constructed, is redundant as the Big Box retailer is not interested in the "Main Street" or pseudo-spiritual experience presented in the enclosed shopping mall. The Big Box retailer is more squarely focused on purveying the convenient distribution of discount goods than in the creation of a leisurely shopping environment.

"The infinity of products Walmart sells reveals the store as a center both of Fordist consumption and simultaneously of postmodern consumption, as it targets multiple niche markets, filling the need of every conceivable sociodemographic group," explains Warf and Chapman.[62] Current sales figures of Big Box retailers relay the American consumer is highly receptive to this type of retail. A report on U.S. 2010 holiday spending reveals higher sales at discount retailers Target and Kohl's than traditional department stores located in malls, such as Sears.[63] During times of economic stress, explains the *New York Times*, consumers are more cautious with their spending; preferring discount stores when the cost of food and gas rises.[64] These statements relay a sustained dominance of the Big Box model over the enclosed regional shopping mall.

The decline of the shopping mall comes at a cost of suburban public space. The next section looks at several case studies of regional shopping malls. Case studies offer an understanding of the decline of these centers and the effects of their decline on the local community.

12. Regional Mall Case Studies

"Few cities, towns, or suburbs have escaped the debilitating effects of underused or vacant shopping centers," says Smiley and Robbins.[1] For insight into this observation, the author studied retail development in New York State during November 2010. According to U.S. census figures, November and December represent the highest periods of retail traffic and sales in the United States.[2] New York State exhibits the third highest gross domestic product (GDP) and state population in the United States.[3] New York State cannot be said to represent the whole of the United States, but as the home of the first suburb in Levittown and Gruens' first urban shopping mall in Rochester, it offers relevant insight to the current state of the regional shopping mall. Mall sites were sourced through the author's personal contacts, word of mouth and through mall documentation sites *Deadmalls.com* and *Labelscar.com*. In comparison to data collected from other states, both *Deadmalls.com* and *Labelscar.com* show a high percentage of "greyfields" or "dead malls" in New York State. In the period of observation, 20 regional malls were studied. As discussed in previous chapters, regional malls can be defined as those with two to three department stores that draw customers from a 20 to 30 mile radius. The shopping malls in the case studies are all located in suburban areas of New York State and offer a cross-section of demographic areas, spanning from southern New York to western New York. The research utilized a covert observation technique with collection of information through photo documentation. Interviews with the Simon Group and the Pyramid Companies were also carried out. With the aim of providing a current snapshot of the regional shopping mall, the following case studies provide insight into area demographics, mall history, current viability, and community response to regional shopping malls in New York State.

Nanuet Mall (visited November 8, 2010)

LOCATION: Southern New York State

HISTORY

Nanuet Mall opened in 1969 and was the first enclosed shopping center in Rockland County, New York. Sears and Bamberger's were the original anchors of this traditional two department store mall. In 1986, Macy's took over Bamberger's and the mall was further expanded in the early 1990s to include another wing. In the 1990s expansion, the department store Abraham and Straus was added. Abraham and Straus was later replaced by the department store Sterns and finally Boscov's, which closed in 2008.[4] The mall is owned by the Simon Property group, which acquired it in 1989.

AREA DEMOGRAPHICS

Rockland County is a well-to-do area 30 miles outside of New York City. According to the latest figures from the United States Department of Labor, Rockland County has the lowest level of unemployment in Southern New York State and at 6 percent is lower than the national average, which as of June 20, 2011, is listed at 9 percent. Rockland has a population of 311,687, of which 73 percent are white, 27 percent are under 18 and only 13.7 percent are over 65. The median housing value is $381,000 with a median household income of $78,218 (in 2009).[5] With an 8.7 percent growth over the period from 2000 to 2010, Rockland represents a stable economic climate.

CURRENT VIABILITY

Nanuet Mall was still open (as of July 2011) and had 120 retail spaces; 42 spaces were occupied with Macy's and Sears as the remaining anchors. The wing that once housed Boscov's department store was completely empty. Nine of the 42 retail outlets in the mall were national chain stores; all other occupants were local retailers or local service providers. Les Morris of Simon Property Group announced in May 2011 that the mall was to be demolished and replaced by a Big Box "lifestyle center" hybrid. "We expect to make our formal announcement in the next month or so. We do plan on tearing down the mall and putting up an open air regional center anchored by a Sears, Macy's, a theater and a grocery store," explained Morris.[6]

REASONS FOR DECLINE

The decline of Nanuet Mall has been attributed to a change in shopping habits and an oversaturation of shopping centers in the area that offer Big

Box and cut price offerings. The Nanuet Mall is competing with the Spring Valley Marketplace "power center" just two miles away. Spring Valley Marketplace is an open-air community center that houses a Costco, Target and TJ Maxx. The super-regional Palisades Mall, completed in 1998 by the Pyramid Companies, is another big competitor for the Nanuet Mall. Palisades is a fully enclosed mall approximately four miles from the Nanuet Mall. According to the International Council of Shopping Centers (ICSC), the Palisades mall is a "1.85 million-square-foot so-called 'power mall,' features an unusual combination of traditional tenants, power anchors, category killers, food and entertainment."[7] The Palisades is essentially a hybrid that combines traditional retailers such as Macy's and JCPenney with discount retailers such as Home Depot, Target and BJ's Wholesale Club. "We should be able to accommodate 99.9% of the shoppers' needs," explains Mark Congel, a senior partner in The Pyramid Companies development group, "A traditional mall probably satisfies maybe 50 percent of their needs. Here we have it all — it's one-stop shopping in its truest sense."[8] Palisades also exhibits characteristics of an "entertainment mall," as it houses a regulation-sized skating rink, one of the largest food courts in the northeast (2,000 seats), a Ferris wheel, carousel, stadium seating in center court, and an Imax theater. As a super-regional mall, the Palisades draws from a much larger radius than the regional Nanuet Mall. It accommodates approximately 20 million shoppers per year from New York City, Southern New York, Pennsylvania and New Jersey. Pyramid spent approximately $16 million on road improvements and parking to accommodate this number of shoppers.[9] The road improvements and transport access to the mall is another advantage over the Nanuet Mall. The 2008 bankruptcy of retailer Boscov's (explained in Chapter 10) can also be cited as a reason for a decrease in viability for the Nanuet Mall. The closing of Boscov's resulted in a loss of tenants in the wing of the shopping center that housed the department store.

COMMUNITY RESPONSE

The Nanuet Mall has serviced the community of Rockland for over forty years and as such the space has become an important cultural site for many in the community. "Like the Tappan Zee Bridge and the Palisades Interstate Parkway, the Nanuet Mall symbolized the area's changing landscape," explains Alexander J. Gromack, supervisor of the Town of Clarkstown (which includes Nanuet).[10] The Facebook page "I Don't Care, The Nanuet Mall Will Always Be Part Of My Childhood" documents responses to the potential demolition of the mall and is a group with over 369 members.[11] "I have great memories of hanging there in the mid–70's. Going to the movies and for pizza. In 1979–

80 I worked at Music Den ... that was pretty cool because my friends were pumping gas & flipping burgers. Beer & onion rings at the Hungry Lion.... Sad to see her die off," says Gary Endlich.[12] "I remember the opening of the Nanuet Mall. We would all go almost every Saturday. Go to [Friendly's restaurant] for lunch. Walk around for hours. Sad to see it is closing," says Mariann Cedo Simpson.[13] "I remember when it was first built, and the best hangout ever! Scoping the boys, giggling when they'd walk by, and talking about it at school (Pomona Jr. High) the next day ('69–'72), then coming back in '07–'08 and finding it so lonely and changed inside and out! So sad.... 'They paved paradise and put up a parking lot!,'" says Karen F. Guth Holland.[14] Hundreds of comments on the site show nostalgia for the space and relay its relevance to many in the area.

On the shopping mall documentation site *Labelscar.com*, the sentiment for the loss of the space is palpable. "I have lived in Rockland my whole life. I am 41 years old and I have seen a tremendous amount of change here. The Nanuet Mall was and still is a beautiful mall," says Ava. "It used to have a Friendly's downstairs and on Friday nights I would go there with my family and 'wait' on line to get a table!... The mall used to be packed because of great stores and restaurants. Now the Palisades dump [*sic*] is packed because people have no where else to go."[15]

Nanuet Mall signage.

Nanuet Mall atrium space.

Comments on the *Labelscar* site show an overtly negative response to the Palisades Mall, citing the size, impersonal nature and mass clientele as drawbacks to the space. A sense of ownership is evident in many of the comments which refer the space as "my mall." A comment by Peggy Sullivan exhibits a strong feeling for the Nanuet mall and a direct negativity to the Palisades:

Top: Empty park benches and shop fronts at the Nanuet Mall. *Bottom:* Water-damaged ceiling of the Nanuet Mall.

Nanuet Mall food court.

"Hate to see Nanuet Mall go — needs improvement but not to the point of elimination. Believe it or not, many people do not like and will not go to the Palisades Mall. It is a monster place with no warmth — Nanuet Mall always had this for me. It is my mall," writes Sullivan.[16] The Nanuet Mall is also described in terms of its overt "beauty" in comparison to the Palisades, which exhibits a more "industrial" look with exposed air-conditioning vents and bare concrete floors, a style that is meant to appeal to today's teenagers.[17] Writes Max: "The Nanuet Mall is such a beautiful mall, which is a sharp contrast to the Palisades Center (which is the ugliest mall I have ever seen, given the fact that the HVAC units are exposed everywhere.)"[18] A perception of safety is also conveyed in the smaller Nanuet Mall. "As a teenager living in Nanuet, I can tell you that the only reason that anyone my age goes to that mall is because parents think it is "safer" (which I know is true) than the Palisades," writes Eric. "As everyone knows, the Palisades has much more desirable stores, although it is a bad atmosphere. I am sad to see the Nanuet Mall go, since it has been a part of my life since I moved here in 1997, as a 3 year old."[19]

Responses from the community about turning the mall into a "lifestyle" center are mixed. Many consumers are unclear as to what a "lifestyle center" actually encompasses. On *Labelscar*: "Instead of speaking more on low points, why not solutions, because really, what is a 'lifestyle center'?" writes Jasn.[20]

"What the bleep [*sic*] is a 'lifestyle center'"? says Lindsay Nichols.[21] "lifestyle center???" writes Afua Adjei-Brenyah, "that just sounds suspicious."[22] Consumers have criticized the concept due to the cold climate of Rockland and suggest that this would be a deterrent for spending any significant amount time in the public spaces in a lifestyle center. "An open air center — a good suggestion — still won't be able to compete against the Palisades Center and other regional malls," writes Jeff, "Also not the best idea for a northern climate location where 'foot traffic' will rather be somewhere warmer for a large part of the year."[23] The addition of more retail to an overly saturated area is another point of criticism of the "lifestyle center" concept. "Even when the Lifestyle center finally opens there might not be a market for it. At some point Macy's could decide to close that location, being so close to its Palisades store. As for Sears — there [*sic*] financial problems could seal their fate, or they could also build a new store in West Nyack as well. No matter how you look at it, it doesn't look good for Nanuet mall's future," writes Sean.[24]

Latham Circle Mall (visited November 10, 2010)

LOCATION: Capital Region of New York State

HISTORY

Latham Circle Mall started out as "Latham Corners Shopping Mall," an open-air community center, in 1957. It was re-developed as a mid-market enclosed "fashion mall" in 1977, attracting high profile retailers The Boston Store and JCPenney and Woolworth as major anchors. Significantly, Latham Circle was the first enclosed mall in the Capital Region. In the 1980s the mall shifted to more of a discount approach by adding the major tenant Caldor. The Boston Store closed in the late 1980s when a fire ravaged the department store and was replaced by the Burlington Coat Factory. In the 1990s both Caldor and Woolworth went bankrupt and subsequently both stores were closed. The wing housing Caldor was demolished and the property was sold to Lowe's, which opened a stand-alone store next to the Latham Circle Mall. Woolworth was replaced by the department store Stein Mart, which remained in the mall until it went out of business in 2001.[25] Developer Eugene Weiss purchased the "Latham Corners Shopping Mall" from Latham Circle Realty Corporation in 1973 and remained the primary owner until recently when the property was foreclosed on by the financing firm that loaned the mall owner $21 million in December 2006. Realty Financial Partners in Wellesley, Massachusetts, has since hired KeyPoint Partners to manage the center during foreclosure procedures.[26]

Area retail experts are currently speculating that the shopping mall will be demolished to make way for an open-air community center with anchor Whole Foods Market or the Big Box retailer Dick's Sporting Goods.[27] These reports are unconfirmed by Realty Financial Partners and seem unlikely considering the proximity to a large Dick's Sporting Goods store in the Latham Farm Power Center and the newly constructed up-market grocery store Fresh Market, both less than one mile from the Latham Circle mall site.

Area Demographics

Latham Circle mall is situated in the suburb of Latham in Albany County. Located in the Capital Region of New York State, Latham benefits from an economy boosted by the presence of state government offices. Albany County has a population of 304,204, with a 78 percent majority of white residents. In 2009, the median household income of the area was $54,395 with 11 percent of the population below the poverty level. Recent statistics (June 2011) show a 6.8 percent unemployment rate, which is lower than the national average of 9 percent.[28] Albany County has a population growth of 3.3 percent over the period of 2000–2010, which is slightly higher than the state average of 2.1 percent.

Current Viability

The Latham Circle Mall was still open (as of July 2011) and housed two anchors, JCPenney and the Burlington Coat Factory. The 675,000-square-foot shopping center had approximately 250,000 square feet of retail space. Along with JCPenney and Burlington Coat Factory, Regal Cinemas and a handful of local retailers occupied the mall. As there were no tenants in the food court, local retailers offered coffee in carafes to make up for the fact that no food or drink was available in the mall. The last renovation of the space was completed in 1988. Although it was still open, the mall was undergoing foreclosure negotiations, so its future was uncertain.

Reasons for Decline

The Latham Circle Mall was successful in the 1970s and 1980s. Recalls Weiss, "I threw in a fortune to rebuild it, rent went up to $12 to $15 per square foot. It was a power house. It was a very successful mall."[29] The decline of the center can be attributed to many factors. The closing of Caldor and The Boston Store were significant in that they caused the loss of smaller tenants. Subsequently the demolition of the Caldor building decreased the surface area of the mall. The Big Box retailer Lowe's was built as a stand-alone retailer and did not attempt to "blend" by opening an access point in the mall. Over-saturation of retail in the area is another reason for the decline. Less than one mile away from Latham Circle is the Latham Farms Big Box "power center," which houses a Home Depot, Walmart, Dick's Sporting Goods, Hannaford supermarket and Staples. It also houses a thriving collection of stand-alone chain restaurants, including Applebee's and Dakota Steakhouse.

Seven miles from Latham Circle is the Crossgates and Colonie Center Mall. Crossgates is a super-regional shopping mall with a leasable area of 1,700,000 square feet. Crossgates was built in 1984 by the Pyramid Companies and was expanded in the early 1990s to double its size. The mall has 250

Latham Circle Mall signage.

Top: Main entrance to the Latham Circle Mall. *Bottom:* Latham Circle Mall food court.

Vacant shops at the Latham Circle Mall.

A vacant hallway at the Latham Circle Mall.

stores with the major anchors of Macy's, JCPenney, Burlington Coat Factory, H&M, Best Buy and Dick's Sporting Goods. The mall also houses a large Regal Cinema and seven full service restaurants. The Pyramid owned Cross-gates Commons' Big Box center, which houses one of the nation's largest Wal-marts, borders Crossgates. The Simon owned Colonie Center, a regional "fashion mall" with two department stores, is an up-market mall with a large cinema and several popular restaurants. Colonie Center generates business from a compact, up-market approach by blending quality retail with enter-tainment. Latham Circle failed to adapt to changing market conditions in a timely manner and thus lost market share, while at the same time suffered from an influx of discount Big Box retailers in the area. With the loss of tenant income, the mall fell into disrepair. According to *Deadmalls.com*, due to vio-lations of the fire safety code, food outlets in the mall have been restricted.[30] The lack of a food court and restaurants can also be cited as a reason for the decline of retail viability.

COMMUNITY RESPONSE

Community response to the decline of Latham Circle mall is mixed. Some say it is a long neglected eyesore and others lament the decline of a space that has serviced the Latham community for nearly sixty years. Some patrons fear that the mall will close and are upset about this prospect. When visiting the space on the 11th of November 2010, the author was casually approached by an elderly gentleman named Stavros, who discussed his attachment to the mall. Stavros introduced himself as "the mayor" of the mall and displayed a sense of ownership and pride in the space. "I have been walking around this mall for forty years," explained Stavros. "I worked as a tailor for the Macy's in Colonie, but this is my local mall so I preferred to spend time here."[31] Stavros was very disappointed in the current owner, Eugene Weiss, for letting the mall deteriorate. He doubted that the mall could be renovated to any standard but couldn't fathom not having the space to visit everyday should it be demolished. When asked if he would frequent the Latham Farms Big Box center, Crossgates or Colonie, Stavros said he found all of the sites "too large and impersonal" and that Latham Farms would be "too cold" to walk outside. Other patrons offer similar responses to the decline of the Latham Circle Mall. "I would be disappointed if the mall closed," writes Patrick. "It was part of my childhood, and would hate to see it go. I honestly don't think anyone will sink the money into it to update it, especially with Crossgates and Colonie Mall nearby."[32] On *Labelscar*, Scott writes: "I used to come here as a kid and loved it. The mall used to be packed with stores and there was a lot to do there."[33] The president of the Colonie Chamber of Commerce, Tom Nolte, is upset about the "dead mall" status of Latham Circle Mall. "It was very disappointing [to see Latham Circle Mall on the Dead mall.com Web site]." Nolte understands, however, that in its current state Latham Circle will not last much longer. He cites the prime location as a reason for the mall to invest in renovations. "This mall is a big part of our Chamber and we know it's a great, great location."[34]

Shoppingtown Mall, Dewitt (visited November 15, 2010)

LOCATION: Central New York State

HISTORY

Shoppingtown Mall is one of the first shopping centers in suburban Syracuse. It was developed as an open-air community center in 1954 in the suburb of Dewitt and originally housed W.T. Grant's, Woolworth, E.W. Edwards, Dey's, and the Addis Co. as anchor stores.[35] Shoppingtown was converted into an enclosed mall in 1975 with the anchors JCPenney, Chapell's and Dey's. The mall was renovated and expanded in the early 1990s to include a new wing with the retailer Sears. In 1993, Kaufmans purchased Dey's and Addis

Co. and Chapell's was bought out by The Bon-Ton in 1995. Shoppingtown Mall is currently owned by the Santa Monica based Macerich Company. Macerich acquired the mall in 2005 when it purchased major retail holdings of Wilmorite Properties.[36] Wilmorite, a Syracuse based development company founded in 1950, managed several failed regional malls in the area, including the Penn-Can Mall, Irondequoit Mall and the Fayetteville Mall. Shoppingtown has been on the decline since the early 2000s when it lost the department store Bon-Ton, Media Play and subsequently many other smaller retailers.

According to Tim Frateschi, an attorney representing Shoppingtown's owner, Macerich Co., Macerich owns 71 shopping centers across the country and Shoppingtown is the least profitable shopping mall in their portfolio. In 2007, Macerich announced plans to demolish a wing of the mall and significantly renovate the remaining space. The plans were waylaid due to a poor economic climate. Macerich pursued a legal battle with the Town of Dewitt in 2008, claiming the city overvalued the shopping center for tax assessment purposes. The city valued the property at $54 million while the Macerich group claimed that the property was only worth $25 to $30 million. In 2010, the property was re-assessed at $25 million, cutting the company's annual tax payment from $1.8 million to $1 million. This agreement could potentially provide the impetus for the planned renovation. Karen Kitney, chairwoman of the Onondaga County industrial development agency, is unsure whether the property will in fact be renovated. "The proposed agreement did not firmly commit Macerich to renovating the mall or to preserving the 950 jobs there," says Kitney.[37] According to Macerich, however, they are fully committed to renovating the property, noting that the industrial development group would have the right to withdraw the tax agreement if the company did not "substantially complete" the renovations within three years.

AREA DEMOGRAPHICS

Shoppingtown mall is situated in the town of Dewitt, which is located in Onondaga County. Onondaga County has a population of 467,026, with an 81 percent majority of white residents. The median household income in the area is $49,886, with a poverty level of 13.7 percent.[38] From 2000 to 2010, the area has experienced a growth rate of 1.9 percent, slightly lower than the state average of 2.1 percent. The unemployment rate, as of May 2011, is 7.7 percent, 1.5 percent lower than the national average.[39]

CURRENT VIABILITY

At the time of observation, Shoppingtown Mall was still open and housed the department stores Macy's and Sears as well as the anchor Dick's Sporting

Goods. While the mall exhibited a level of occupancy that could be considered healthy, a third of retail space was empty and the shopping center has not been renovated since the 1990s expansion. In the wing anchored by Sears, many low-rent local retailers populate this area, including several local sports studios, a skateboard park, a driving school, and a railroad museum. In 2007 Macerich proposed plans to demolish this wing; these plans have yet to be enacted.

REASONS FOR DECLINE

Shoppingtown Mall has suffered heavily from the poor economic climate in the Syracuse area, from competing Big Box retailers and the close proximity of the super-regional Carousel Center. The close proximity to many open-air plazas with Big Box stores — Kmart, Barnes and Nobles, Old Navy and Marshalls — is a cause for the decline of the Shoppingtown Mall. Old Navy was once a major retailer in the Shoppingtown Mall, however, it closed in 2005 and moved to its own premises in a Big Box "power center" down the road. The Carousel Center is a super-regional mall on the outskirts of the city of Syracuse approximately seven miles from Shoppingtown. Carousel is a seven story, 1.5 million square foot shopping center, built in 1990 by the Pyramid Companies. The retail space encompasses seven anchor stores, a seventeen screen Regal Cinemas and space for over 150 retail outlets and several full service restaurants. Along with the abundance of retail in the area, the poor economy, which has seen the unemployment rate of Syracuse spike to 9 percent in January 2011, is a major cause of the decline of retail in the area. In this poor economic climate, discount and Big Box retailers are more viable than the mid-range fashion mall offerings of Shoppingtown. The poor economic climate was cited by the Macerich group in the case against the Town of Dewitt in re-assessing the value of the property.

COMMUNITY RESPONSE

The community response to the decline of the mall is varied; while some patrons feel a nostalgia for the space as it was, others champion the new "community" feel of the mall due to the influx of low-rent tenants. Patrons, however, reveal that the decline of the mall is very symbolic of the economic climate in the area and doubt its ability to remain a viable entity much longer into the future. Similar to the case studies of other declining regional malls, patrons' comments reveal a sense of ownership and nostalgia for the space. "I grew up in the area and Shoppingtown was the best mallrat hangout for anyone who didn't live directly in downtown Syracuse," writes Erik.[40] One patron explains that Shoppingtown, once a beacon of local department stores, is a symbol of the loss of Syracuse-based retailing. "This mall speaks volumes about the rise and decline of local Syracuse retailing," writes Jim. "For those of us who grew up in that great old city, it is sad to see all of the generic stores which one can find anywhere in America, standing in the place of wonderful Syracuse stores which, one by one, were bought out by the inane 'bon tons' of this world." Jim goes on to explain: "These local stores followed population shifts and trends and slowly their downtown flagships closed and then their suburban satellites were absorbed by generic stores and the great old names disappeared forever. This pattern was repeated in every city across America. How sad."[41]

The decline of viable retail in Shoppingtown has led to the creation of more "community" space in the mall as the low rents have spurred many community and social groups to enter the space. A center for teenagers, many sports studios and a library offer the general public the community aspects that Gruen had initially intended when creating the enclosed shopping mall model. Although this use of space seems alien to a population of people who are used to the mall as a purely commercial space, patrons relay that this is a positive use of the space and it should not be re-proposed. "Shoppingtown is a really cool mall, and the Sears wing is possibly the best part. It would be

An interesting disguise for a leaking fountain at the Shoppingtown Mall.

Top: A family bathroom in a vacant shop at the Shoppingtown Mall. *Bottom:* Center for teens at the Shoppingtown Mall.

Top: A skateboard park in the shell of a disused department store at the Shoppingtown Mall. *Bottom:* Vacant shop front at the Shoppingtown Mall.

Top: A golf range in the Shoppingtown Mall. *Bottom:* Public library in the Shoppingtown Mall.

a shame for them to de-mall it, especially in a city that could use indoor gathering spaces," writes Caldor.[42]

Although open-air Big Box retail in the area seems to be the preferred shopping destination, some patrons have noted that they do not wish this mall to be converted into open-air shopping. "Shoppingtown does NOT I repeat NOT need to be a strip mall!!! Way to much snow for a strip mall!! People want to be INSIDE," says Ruth.[43] This is echoed by Timothy, who writes, "I hope they revitalize the Sears wing and do not close it off/tear it down, making Sears an Open Store ... all the mall needs is a Solid Anchor Store in the old Media Play space and the area would revitalize."[44]

The Summit Mall, Wheatfield (visited November 18, 2010)

LOCATION: Western New York State

HISTORY

The Summit Mall opened in 1972 with the major anchor of Sears and local department stores: AM&A's (now The Bon-Ton), Hens and Kelly and Jenss. It is located in the town of Wheatfield, approximately twelve miles from Niagara Falls. Once a thriving regional mall, the shopping mall has struggled to attract tenants since the late 1990s. Forest Enterprises, the original owners of the mall, foreclosed on the property in 1998. It was sold to Oberlin Plaza One by the holding company in 2002. Oberlin attempted to revitalize the mall through a renovation and a new roof. Under Oberlin's management, the shopping mall retained the anchors Bon-Ton and Sears as well as adding the store Steve and Barry's (in 2005) and Toys R Us. Oberlin had previously proposed an "Oz" theme park to correlate with the "rainbow" theme that persists around Niagara Falls as well as a year-round Christmas theme for the shopping mall, however, none of these concepts were ever carried to fruition.[45] Although it experienced a brief period of revival, the mall failed to attract steady business and Oberlin filed for bankruptcy in 2009. "Once in our possession, we were determined to make the mall successful for the tenants and the community," says Oberlin Plaza One's James Anthony. "We made extraordinary efforts but it was difficult to find and maintain enough tenants to be viable." In 2010, when the author visited the mall, the Bon-Ton, Sears and a dollar store were open; however, the interior area of the mall was closed.[46]

AREA DEMOGRAPHICS

The Summit Mall is located in the small town of Wheatfield in Niagara County, approximately 12 miles from Niagara Falls. The population of Niagara

County is 216,469 with a negative population growth of -1.5 percent over the period of 2000–2010. The population of Niagara County is predominately white; 88.5 percent, with a median household income of $42,580 (in 2009).[47] The unemployment level for Niagara County is 7.5 percent (as of May 2011).[48] With a negative population growth and high rate of unemployment, the area exhibits symptoms of economic depression.

CURRENT VIABILITY

Summit Mall has been closed since 2009 when Oberlin declared bankruptcy. Sears, The Bon-Ton and a dollar store still functioned in the space; however, the rest of the space remained empty and was starting to become derelict. According to the *Niagara Falls Reporter*, in 2009, State Senator George Maziarz announced that the New York Power Authority would purchase the mall and relocate its offices there; as of July 2011, this plan has not come to action.[49]

REASONS FOR DECLINE

The Summit Mall fell into decline for many reasons, although primarily it is the result of the poor economic state of the area. The proximity of dis-

Entrance to the Summit Mall.

Interior of the Macy's store at the Summit Mall with "disguised" Mall entrance.

count retailers, Walmart Supercenter and Prime Outlet Mall, is also cause for the decline. "What killed the Summit Park Mall is debatable," writes the *Niagara Falls Reporter*. "Some say it was the arrival of Walmart. Others point to the rise of the Prime Outlets mall."[50] John Grdovich, on *Deadmalls.com*, cites the demise of the mall as gradual, although he believes the decline was spurred on by the "Love Canal" toxic waste scandal of the late 70s. "The Summit Park Mall is just a stone's throw away from the infamous Love Canal neighborhood. As everyone old enough may recall, the neighborhood was evacuated in '78 and '79. Over 800 families were moved from the area, and the Summit Park Mall, built to service the area, suffered. The Summit Park Mall is probably built on top of a toxic dump, like the Love Canal neighborhood was," says Grdovich.[51]

COMMUNITY RESPONSE

Patrons lament the decline of the Summit Mall, however, despite its closure and the fact that the mall has struggled for over two decades, many believe that it can still be resurrected. "The mall still has a fighting chance, but action must come quickly and decisively," writes The Niagara Reporter in 2009.[52] Deborah Perry, writing in 2005 on *Deadmalls.com*, optimistically states, "It has been tough, but I only see a rainbow ahead."[53]

Lockport Mall, Lockport (visited November 18, 2010)

LOCATION: Western New York State

HISTORY

The Lockport Mall was completed in 1971 and was built as a mid-range fashion mall with two anchors and a cinema. The original anchors of the mall were AM&A's department store and Montgomery Ward. AM&A's was later bought out by the Bon-Ton in 1995. Montgomery Ward went into bankruptcy in 1997 and subsequently the store was closed and converted to a Rosa's Home Goods for three years. A new wing was added to the mall in the 1990s and originally housed the discount store Hills, which was later replaced by Ames discount department store. Ames, which went bankrupt in 2002, was removed from the mall in 2001 and the wing remained empty until present. In 2006, the interior of the mall was closed and only the Bon-Ton continued to function.[54] General Growth Properties, which went bankrupt in 2008, has owned the shopping mall for the past 25 years. The Lockport Mall was sold to Walmart in 2010 and demolition of the site began in April 2011 to make way for a Walmart supercenter.[55] General Growth Properties still retains ownership of the Bon-Ton property and the proposed Walmart supercenter will allow space for a stand-alone Bon-Ton store.

AREA DEMOGRAPHICS

The Lockport Mall is located in the town of Lockport, approximately 30 miles from Buffalo, NY, and 26 miles from Niagara Falls. It is located in Niagara County. The population of Niagara County is 216,469 with a negative population growth of -1.5 percent over the period of 2000–2010. The population of Niagara County is predominately white; 88.5 percent, with a median household income of $42,580 (in 2009).[56] The unemployment level for Niagara County is 7.5 percent (as of May 2011).[57] With a negative population growth and high rate of unemployment, the area exhibits symptoms of economic depression.

CURRENT VIABILITY

At the time of observation, The Bon-Ton store was still open but the shopping mall was closed. The mall has been closed since 2006. As of April 2011, the mall was in the process of being demolished. Walmart, which purchased the site from GGP for $3.95 million in December 2010, has plans to erect a 185,000-square-foot supercenter on the property.[58] The supercenter is scheduled to be completed by 2012 and will replace a smaller store a quarter-mile south of the vacant mall.

COMMUNITY RESPONSE

While some people in the community welcome the arrival of a super Walmart, others lament the loss of the Lockport Mall. The Walmart is perceived as bringing fresh life to the area in terms of employment opportunities; however, mall patrons have criticized its presence as an unsuitable replacement.

Potholes and cracked tarmac in the parking lot of the Lockport Mall.

Top: A vacant Ames store at the Lockport Mall. *Bottom:* Main entrance to the Lockport Mall.

Chris Lazarou, manager of the existing Lockport Walmart, explains that there will be "at least double" the amount of jobs offered at the current Walmart, which employs 200 people.[59] Councilwoman Cheryl Antkowiak feels that the Walmart is a very positive addition to Lockport. "This is a wonderful day for the Town of Lockport, and good days are coming for the town and city of Lockport," said Antkowiak at a ceremony marking the mall's demolition on

the April 14, 2011.[60] "It is about damn time," writes a community member
(D34dm4n) on The Buffalo Range local community site. "According to the
Buffalo News, they have scheduled to have the Lockport Mall demolished the
week of April 18th.... Hopefully this means that the construction for the Walmart can begin very soon. This project has been in the works for years and I
am happy that it finally seems to be getting going."[61]

Many patrons, however, regret the loss of the mall and feel that Walmart
will not replace the sense of public space that existed at Lockport Mall. "I
grew up at this mall. It was local, it was convenient, it had everything a mall
should have, and it was perfectly sized for the population of my fair city,"
writes Erica Hayes, "which is why it came as such a shock to me when I came
home from college to discover the mall over 75 percent empty. The rumors
were that leases weren't being renewed because the owners wanted to demolish
the mall and build a Walmart in its place, save for the Bon-Ton which does
good business and would remain as a stand-alone store.... It turns out that
much of the community is very against this Walmart. So much so that I came
home from college in 2003, and the mall (with only the Bon-Ton left) is still
standing in 2008." Hayes goes on to lament the decline of the mall, explaining
that it had immense personal relevance to her. "I went back on May 27, 2006,
to buy a book from Waldenbooks on its final day of operation," explains
Hayes. "I've been a bookworm all my life, and I can't tell you how many hundreds of dollars my mother spent at that store over the years to keep me hap-
pily immersed in reading. I admit, I cried when I walked out. It was almost
symbolic that the store that meant the most to me was the last to go."[62] A
similar feeling of nostalgia and sense of ownership of the space is echoed by
Jewel Kazacami: "This mall is a mall I grew up with. I remember in the 3rd
grade when I had my ears pierced at Claire's.... This mall is to be demolished
soon, for a super Walmart. It has been closed for about (12?) years now. It
has been and will be missed," writes Kazacami.[63] Kazacami feels that the Walmart is not a suitable replacement for the loss of the mall. "Walmart pretty
much ruins everything. We have a Walmart already — we're building a supercenter — then abandoning the old one.... Walmart is pretty much horrible,"
says Kazacami.[64] Some members of the community feel that a supercenter is
unnecessary for the area and will not provide the community with any further
value than the old Walmart that it is replacing. "Well I guess Lockport is
completely giving up on its downtown and its potential to ever have real retail
again by bringing in the ultimate category killer," writes a community member
(sabredan17) on The Buffalo Range.[65] "They [Walmart] aren't really cheaper
on many things. And as we are only a family of three, we don't need to buy
in bulk. I have a 5 lbs. jar of dill pickles I bought there 5 years ago — still
unopened," writes another community member on The Buffalo Range.[66]

The Medley Center (visited November 17, 2010)

LOCATION: Western New York State

HISTORY

    The Medley Center is located in the Rochester suburb of Irondequoit, 2 miles from downtown Rochester. Originally named "The Irondequoit Mall," it was developed by Wilmorite Properties in 1990 as a mid-market fashion mall with anchors Kaufmann's, JCPenney and Sears. Initially a successful mall, it was expanded in 1993 to include a new wing for the McCurdy's department store. McCurdy's was later bought out by Bon-Ton (in 1995) and Kaufmann's became Macy's when the company consolidated in 2006.[67] The mall began to decline in the mid–90s, due to increased retail competition and a perception of crime in the area. JCPenney left the mall in 2003 and many other smaller retailers left the mall, making it 80 percent vacant.

    Irondequoit Mall was sold to Bersin Properties in 2005 and subsequently renamed "Medley Center." Under Bersin, the mall received a temporary boost by attracting the retailer Steve and Barry's; however, the outlet closed two years later due to bankruptcy. A stand-alone Target was completed in the

Entrance to the Medley Center.

Top: Medley Center signage. *Bottom:* Atrium of the Medley Center.

Food court of the Medley Center.

Children's play area at the Medley Center.

expansive parking lot of the center in 2006, and a large playground was added in the interior of the mall space. Bersin staged a large Halloween event in the near empty mall in 2006 to generate interest in the space but all of these ventures failed to re-stimulate the retail space of the Medley Center.[68] Despite securing $200,000 in federal funds for infrastructure, which Bersin used to update access roads, parking and lighting, as well as claiming $442,966 in tax credits in 2007, the mall continued to do poorly. In March of 2007, the Bon-Ton closed, taking with it other smaller retailers. With the interior of the mall largely vacant, Pyramid Companies purchased Bersin Properties in April of 2007 and the next year announced plans for a mixed-use development.

The Pyramid Companies plan encompasses the creation of 94,000 square feet of office space, a 421-room, 30-story hotel as the centerpiece of the development, along with 330 residential units, and 1.2 million square feet of retail and restaurant space.[69] Under the plan, Medley Center is to be renamed Lake Ridge Centre. The plan, proposed in December of 2008, is currently being held up due to red tape surrounding the re-zoning required to re-purpose this space as a mixed-use development. Currently, the interior space of the mall is closed and Macy's and Sears department stores, along with the stand-alone Target in the parking lot, are the only surviving operators.

Area Demographics

The Medley Center is located in the Rochester suburb of Irondequoit, approximately 2 miles from downtown Rochester. The population of Rochester is 208,123, with 48.3 percent white residents and 38.5 percent black residents. Rochester has a negative population growth of -5.3 percent over the period of 2000–2010 and a current unemployment rate of 7.1 percent.[70] With a median household income of $27,123 and 25.9 percent of the population living below the poverty level, this area exhibits symptoms of economic depression.[71]

Reasons for Decline

The decline of the Medley Center is attributed to many factors; however, the poor economic state of the area is a major contributor. As noted previously, the perception that the mall is in a high crime area is also a factor. *Labelscar* theorizes that the decline of the Medley Center is a direct result of the decline of the Midtown Plaza shopping mall in Downtown Rochester. "Shoppers who used to go downtown began to shift their preferences toward suburban malls, and Irondequoit Mall was the closest mall to most of the city of Rochester," writes Prange Way. "Many residents of the city of Rochester, especially the area closest to Irondequoit Mall, are low income and minority. In typical 'white flight' fashion, the more affluent suburban shoppers Irondequoit Mall so desperately wished to court began to avoid the mall, citing a perception of crime that ironically wasn't really there."[72]

In addition to the perception of crime in the area, the Medley Center suffers from high competition from other suburban malls in the area. In 1995 Wilmorite consolidated the Greece Towne Mall and Long Ridge Mall into a single site called "The Mall at Greece Ridge." Positioned further from downtown Rochester, in the eastern suburb of Greece, this mid-market fashion mall later added space for 10 Big Box stores.[73] The Eastview Mall, built in 1971 by Wilmorite, is located in Victor, 18 miles from downtown Rochester. Eastview was expanded in the mid–90s to become a Super-regional mall, with 180 retail spaces in the 1,300,000-square-foot space. Eastview houses five anchor stores and many up-market boutiques and attracts customers from a large radius.[74] "Ironically, both of these projects were Wilmorite's, the same company that built Irondequoit Mall only 5 years earlier. The competition from these two expansions, combined with a perception of crime and dab of racism, would soon slide Irondequoit Mall into obsolescence," notes Prange Way.[75]

A further factor cited in the decline of the mall is the alienation of patrons due to a change in policy regarding the use of the food court area in 2005. "Controversial changes surrounding the food court and mall traffic in general have caused some minor resentment among the mall's remaining loyal visitors," writes Phillip Dampier in 2005.

> Since the mall opened, the food court, especially during the day, has been a gathering place for retired locals who literally spend hours sitting and visiting with their friends. Chess and card games were a common [sight] to help pass the time. Frequently the only people in the food court, they were surprised to learn that a policy change now prohibited chess and card games during regular mall hours. The policy change, attributed to Bersin, came as a result of his efforts to make the mall's appearance more conducive to a "family friendly shopping experience."[76]

This change, cites Prange Way, was a major deterrent to the senior patrons that considered this their primary third-space. "The new rules created deep-seated resentment from a large customer base, and was probably not the greatest decision."[77]

COMMUNITY RESPONSE

The community response to the decline of the Medley Center differs from others in this section due to the fact that, since it's opening, it has enjoyed only a short period of viability. Although some community members feel sad that the structure is defunct, they cite the "overmalling" as endemic in the area. "Rochester is definitely overmalled. It is sad to see Irondequoit failed ... and it's surprising that Wilmorite couldn't better market it," writes mallguy on *Labelscar.com*.[78] This sentiment is echoed by Rich: "This is a mall that never should have been built — too close to downtown which had its own mall. Wilmorite should have known better ... given that this was their home turf."[79] Michele writes: "This mall was great when it opened. Interesting stores, great looking, etc. It's too bad it's like this now."[80] Other community members discuss the fall of Medley Center is a symbol of an area that has suffered with low population growth, high unemployment and property taxes for too long. "I've lived in the Roch [*sic*] area most of my 48 years and in Irondequoit about 5 years so I can say with some authority that the Medley Centre is a pretty wretched place," writes IronWest. "It was mega-cool when it first opened.... The place should have taken off bigtime and it was pretty great at first."[81] IronWest goes on to explain that as the economy declined, the area perception of the mall followed.

> I personally wouldn't park my car and walk into the Medley on a dark night alone if you paid me. It's just not wise. Probably nothing bad would happen but I know it does, local word of mouth, bragging, etc.... They even pulled the annual carnival that takes place in the parking lot there every summer because of wilding teenagers,

just pulled the whole thing down in the middle of its run, left and said they weren't coming back, we're off their schedule from now on. Those are the reasons these places get shut down. Too many bored people with no money just hanging around with nothing to do but complain and make trouble. I got laid off a year and a half ago and still haven't found work in good ol' Rochester. They raised my property taxes in IronWest, too ... people like me are taking up the slack and getting nothing in return for it but empty malls, no town center, no sidewalk clearing ... the area is pretty enough but it's just not worth the money to live here anymore. Of course, I also can't afford to move now so I just keep plugging along.... Hopefully someday I will be able to move away and stop wasting my money here.

The community is skeptical that the planned Lake Ridge Center will in fact come to fruition. "Okay, folks it could never cut it as a mall, and now we are going to put a 30 story HOTEL in there? For visitors to Rochester to actually stay in? I say that because no one who is actually FROM Rochester would stay for even one night in a hotel at that location!" writes Meami Craig on *herRochester.com*.[82] Others doubt the viability of the center should the plan be realized. "When you here [*sic*] and read how NYS population keeps on shrinking, a fare [*sic*] percentage of that comes from Buffalo, Syracuse and Rochester do to poor employment prospects among other issues," writes Sean on *Labelscar.com*, "in that light how is a new mall type development going to be successful there?"[83]

Analysis and Conclusions

Case studies of declining regional shopping malls in New York State exhibit similar characteristics. All of the malls in the sample suffer from close competition by other retailers, specifically Big Box centers and super-regional malls. Three malls in the sample, Nanuet, Latham Circle and Shoppingtown, were the first shopping malls in the area and have suffered from a change in the nature of the suburbs that they are situated in. This is also the case in the Medley Center, which has declined due to a perception of crime in the area. At the far western end of New York State, both the Summit and Lockport mall have declined due to the poor economic climate in the area. High unemployment coupled with negative growth has greatly affected these shopping malls. The Medley Center, near the downtown area of Rochester, also suffers from the poor economic climate. With the exception of the Medley Center and the Summit Mall, all of the malls in the sample have proposed re-development into new shopping areas with elements of Big Box type facilities. The Lockport mall is currently in the stages of demolition in order to make way for the town approved Walmart Supercenter. Both Latham Circle mall and Shoppingtown have proposed plans for open-air "power centers" while Nanuet mall owners, the Simon Group, have announced plans to create an open-air lifestyle center with attached Big Box retailers.

While community response to the decline of individual shopping malls is diverse, an underlying similarity is a powerful nostalgia for the mall spaces and a feeling of sadness for the death or decline of the mall. In the case of Lockport Mall, the community feeling towards the repurposing of the space as a Walmart Supercenter tended to be negative. Nanuet Mall patrons were equally scathing about the decline of the mall due to competition from the Palisades Mall, which was described as a poor community gathering space. Patrons exhibited optimistic feelings that the mall might revive itself in comments about Latham Circle, Shoppingtown and Summit Mall. Plans for open-air "lifestyle" developments were largely spoken of in negative terms and deemed not suitable for the harsh winter conditions of New York State.

INTERVIEWS WITH MALL DEVELOPERS

In interviews with representatives from the Pyramid Companies and Simon Group, both companies displayed an overtly positive position on the enclosed regional shopping mall. An interview with Les Morris, director of public relations for Simon Property Group, was carried out via e-mail on February 15, 2011. Though the company has not developed any new regional malls since 2006, Morris feels that the regional mall is the superior development model for suburban retail. "There has yet to be a retail format developed for the delivery of goods and services that is better than the regional enclosed mall," says Morris. The Simon Group foresees a long and lucrative future for the regional enclosed mall format. "We believe that regional malls have a very bright future," he says. "There hasn't been much new development at all in the past few years which means as retailers expand their existing businesses and broaden their brand, they will be looking at current space and this portends well for regional malls."

While Morris believes that Big Boxes centers are very viable, he does not foresee them replacing the regional mall. Morris also notes that Simon malls have not adopted the "hybrid" model of incorporating Big Box retail into traditional shopping malls. Simon has a number of lifestyle malls in its portfolio; however, the company does not cite this as the dominant trend in shopping center development. "They have a place in today's retail environment but from a sales standpoint, they aren't the 'powerhouses' that their proponents initially envisioned them to be," says Morris. They do have characteristics which make them more attractive than enclosed malls. "They allow for freedom of design and some of our lifestyle centers incorporate wooden pedestrian bridges, outside fireplaces and fire pits, sculpture, parks, etc. This type of freedom isn't available in a regional enclosed mall," explains Morris. When asked how Simon, the largest mall owner in the country, revitalizes failing or declining malls, Morris states that they try to engage an exciting anchor store or clusters of popular restaurants. "We feel that our development, management, and leasing teams are the best in the business," he says.

An interview with Andra Case, marketing director of Pyramid Companies, was carried out on November 15, 2010, at Pyramid Headquarters in downtown Syracuse, New York. Pyramid has not developed any new malls since 1996. The last fully enclosed mall built by Pyramid was the Palisades Mall in 1996. Regardless, Case was very positive about the regional mall, describing the mall in terms of its community value and stating that the mall is an important public space. Case refers to regional shopping malls as "community hubs" and notes that Pyramid welcomes local events, fundraisers and stalls in its malls. When asked about the mall in association with the church, Case noted that she believes that the mall has replaced church to some degree, despite the fact that the Syracuse area has a very strong Catholic base. Case goes on to explain that people like to make the mall a weekly experience and agrees that in this sense, the mall has surpassed the church as a community venue for people who do not attend church weekly. In this sense, Case explains that the Big Box model cannot replace the regional shopping mall. She admits that to remain viable, Pyramid companies have utilized the hybrid development model of attaching Big Box stores to the enclosed mall. "Pyramid is the market leader in the area," says Case. "We have moved the 'Big Box' to the mall." Case does not believe that the discount nature of a Big Box takes anything away from the traditional mid-market attitude of the shopping mall. In correlation with Simon's responses, Case showed indifference to the lifestyle center model. She noted that Pyramid does not have any lifestyle malls in their portfolio, as they feel that the centers "don't work in our market (upstate New York and Massachusetts) because of the harsh winter climate."

In conclusion, despite the figures presented in Chapter 10 and case studies showing the decline of the regional shopping mall, development companies Simon Group and Pyramid Companies believe that the regional mall is still a very viable development model that has longevity. Both companies doubt the longevity and profitability of the lifestyle center model. While the Simon Group does not support the concept that Big Boxes will takeover the role of the regional shopping mall in the community, Pyramid has created more hybrid malls to compete with stand-alone power centers such as Walmart Supercenter. The next chapter presents case studies of super-regional, hybrid and lifestyle centers as a means for comparison to the traditional enclosed regional mall format.

13. Case Studies: Super-Regional Malls, Lifestyle Centers, and Hybrids

The author studied three super-regional malls, two hybrid malls and a lifestyle center in the vicinity of the regional malls observed as a means to form a comparison between the models. Using the same research methods as the observation of regional malls, the following observations explore the histories of the center, their current viability and the community response to the shopping environment.

A super-regional mall has a mix of retail and entertainment. It normally has five anchor stores or more, covers a large surface area and draws from a radius of over 100 miles. A lifestyle center can be defined as an uncovered specialty retail center that mimics design features of a historic Main Street. A hybrid center is a regional shopping mall that has added Big Box retailers in place of traditional anchor stores. All of the malls studied show a combination of all features.

"Compared with other mall formats, the super-regionals are prospering," explains Sokol. "That's partly because of their size — they're so powerful in their trading areas that they're sometimes referred to as 'fortress' malls. But it's also because the behemoths are adapting to changing market conditions. They're adding new, open-air lifestyle areas and re-tenanting to bring in the Big Box discounters that consumers now favor."[1]

The following case studies review these models as a means to explore their current viability in the marketplace. An understanding of these models will give solid grounding for analyzing the future of retailing in the United States.

SUPER-REGIONAL MALLS

The Palisades Center Mall (visited November 8, 2010)

LOCATION: Southern New York State

HISTORY

Developed by the Pyramid Companies, the Palisades Mall was completed in 1998. Located in the southern New York area of West Nyack, the Palisades offers over 1.85 million square feet of retail space and draws customers from the surrounding states of New Jersey, Pennsylvania, and Connecticut as well as from Canada.[2] This mall combines elements of Big Box retailing with traditional department stores and houses the major tenants of Macy's and JCPenney with discount retailers such as Home Depot, Target and BJ's Wholesale Club. Palisades also exhibits characteristics of an "entertainment" mall, as it houses a regulation-sized skating rink, one of the largest food courts in the Northeast (2,000 seats), a Ferris wheel, carousel, stadium seating in center court, and an Imax theater. The mall was built on top of two adjoining landfill sites and cost approximately $390 million to develop. Approximately $16 million was spent on road improvement and parking to accommodate a large number of shoppers.[3] Andra Case, marketing director of Pyramid Companies, explains that The Palisades has been a successful mall since opening and is one of the highest grossing malls in their portfolio. According to Case, Pyramid specifically pitches this mall at teenagers, employing a surface treatment which utilizes polished concrete floors, exposed HVAC systems and brightly colored neon accents for a "young and trendy feel."[4]

AREA DEMOGRAPHICS

The Palisades Center Mall is situated in Rockland County, a well-to-do area 30 miles outside of New York City. According to the latest figures from the U.S. Department of Labor, Rockland County has the lowest level of unemployment in Southern New York State and at 6 percent is lower than the national average, which as of June 20, 2011, is listed at 9 percent.[5] Rockland has a population of 311,687, of which 73 percent are white, 27 percent are under 18 and 13.7 percent are over 65. The median housing value is $381,000 with a median household income of $78,218 (in 2009).[6] With an 8.7 percent growth over the period from 2000 to 2010, Rockland represents a stable economic climate.

CURRENT VIABILITY

At the time of observation, the Palisades was highly populated, with a low level of vacant retail space. According to Spodek of *The Real Deal,* the

Palisades Center, in 2002, averaged $596 per square foot in sales volume.[7] While significantly lower than the highest grossing mall in New York State, the Simon-owned Roosevelt Field Mall on Long Island, which grossed $900 per square foot, it represented a healthy figure for the population density of the West Nyack area and surrounds. The mall managed to keep its center viable by adopting a "ThEATery" concept that clusters a solid base of sit-down restaurants and fast food around a large cinema complex. Milford Pre-witt explains that Palisades generated a large share of profits from the restaurant trade. "Of the $700 million in total retail sales the center is expected to gen-erate this year [2000], more than $130 million will be made from the third-floor restaurant row, which the center dubs the "ThEATery." Another $10 million is generated from the fast-food foodcourt below," says Milford.[8]

COMMUNITY RESPONSE

The mall has been a controversial development since its initial proposal. Pyramid Companies received approval for the mall after many years of com-munity disproval, lawsuits and petitions. "This project was fiercely opposed the whole time we were building it," says Thomas J. Valenti, the managing partner in charge of the Palisades Center at the time of opening.[9] As such, the mall has dodged rumors of criminal activity and building instability from its opening day. "First, there were whisperings that a serial rapist was attacking shoppers," says Debra West of the *New York Times*. "Then a story went around that the developers were on the verge of bankruptcy. Some heard that the underground parking lot was sinking and the four-story megamall would soon collapse under its own girth. Right after a bustling holiday season, the rumor mill had it, the three-million-square-foot, $390 million mall would close."[10] According to Pyramid, these rumors are unfounded; however, they continue to propagate even after twelve years of successful retailing at the center. In 2009, Independent filmmaker Bullfrog Films and Stone Lantern Films released the documentary film *Megamall*. *Megamall* charts the 20-year community battle over the Palisades Mall construction and discusses the impact it has had in destroying small businesses in the area. In the film, dis-gruntled community members explain that the Palisades Mall has effectively killed the "small town" ambience that once existed in West Nyack.[11]

Patrons writing on *Yelp.com*, however, have mixed reviews of this mall. Those who have given the mall 5 out of 5 stars explain that they like the mall because it is "big" and therefore houses everything they need in one central location. Many who give the mall a 5 star rating travel to the mall from a dis-tance, coming from New Jersey or New York City. "I'm one of those Jersey people that only comes to this mall on Sundays when everything in Bergen

Top: Façade of the Palisades Mall. *Bottom:* Towering entrance arcade to the Palisades Mall.

The populated parking lot of the Palisades Mall.

County is closed. I'm not much of a mall person to begin with, but I like this place because it's SO big that, even when it's super crowded, it doesn't seem so bad," writes patron Christina P.[12] A noted negative response is evident in local area resident reviews of this mall, with many giving the mall a three star or less rating. "Perhaps I'm biased because I live in Nyack? However, I grew up near Paramus, NJ, the ultimate of Malls-per-square-mile, and so I feel like I'm pretty familiar with mall culture, etc. Palisades just seems to attract the total dregs of society," writes Jennifer D.[13] "I guess when you have nowhere else to go, and the mom & pop stores close down, because they can't afford to stay open ... then you don't really have a choice, do you? Because after all, this ugly mess has wiped out the competition and where else are you going to see a movie or buy those clothes/scented candles/toilet paper/cds/etc.?" writes Eva K, a former area resident who once worked at the mall.[14]

Walden Galleria (visited November 18, 2010)

LOCATION: Western New York

HISTORY

Owned by the Pyramid Companies, Walden Galleria was completed in 1989. This super-regional mall services the Buffalo-Niagara area and originally included a traditional mix of department stores. Walden Galleria comprises more than 1,600,000 square feet of retail space, with 250 stores on two levels.[15] In the 1990s, the regional anchors — Bonwit Tellers, Sibleys, LL Bergers and The Sample — were either closed or consolidated, leaving room for Big Box retailers to enter the mix. The current anchors of the center include Best Buy, Dick's Sporting Goods, DSW Shoe Warehouse, JCPenney, Macy's, Lord and Taylor, Old Navy and Sears. The mall was renovated and expanded in 2006 and is now the "crown jewel" in Pyramid's offerings.[16] At a cost approximately $60 million, the 2006 renovation encompassed the creation of a new 50,000 square foot Best Buy outlet, the demolition of the old Bon-Ton department store to make way for the addition of a new 12-screen cinema and an extensive renovation of the interior and exterior of the mall. The 2006 renovation saw the center adopt a lifestyle center approach in one section of the mall, with the entrance to the "ThEATery" area evoking a Main Street setting. This area, which features a large Cheesecake Factory and PF Changs restaurant, has outward facing shop fronts, street lights and shop access via valet parking services in front of the restaurants.[17] In comparison to the Palisades and Carousel Malls, the Walden Galleria does not rely as heavily on an entertainment approach catering specifically to teens. It lacks theme park-like attractions (such as a carousel, rollercoaster and skating rink) and markets itself as a more "classy, upscale and Berkshire" style center, says Case.[18]

Walden Galleria atrium.

Top: Upscale finishes in the Walden Galleria. *Bottom:* Street front view of the lifestyle section of Walden Galleria.

AREA DEMOGRAPHICS

The Walden Galleria is located in Erie County, NY. Erie County has a population of 919,040, with a majority (80 percent) of white residents. The median household income of the area is $46,739 with 13.9 percent of the population living below the poverty level. With an unemployment rate 7.75 percent (as of June 2011) and a negative growth of -3.3 percent (over the period of 2000–2010), the area exhibits signs of economic stress.[19]

CURRENT VIABILITY

The Walden Gallery was the largest mall in Western New York at the time of the study and attracted approximately 20 million shoppers annually. High foot traffic and low amount of vacant retail space demonstrated that the mall was very viable. Andra Case, marketing director of Pyramid Companies, described it as the second highest grossing mall in their portfolio. Case cites a 30 percent patronage of Canadian shoppers as well as the recent renovation as a reason for the mall's consistent performance.[20]

COMMUNITY RESPONSE

As evidenced by comments on the review site *Yelp.com*, community response to the Galleria Mall is largely positive; however, many positive responses are from Canadian residents who travel to the mall for a more diverse blend of shops. "So many great stores that aren't in Canada!" comments Ashley S. of Ontario.[21] "Walden Galleria is a fantastic mall," writes Naureen H. "Its [*sic*] got most of all the stores you would want for men, women, kids and even pets!"[22] Some local residents commented negatively, citing the traffic and presence of Canadian shoppers. "Be prepared to have patience on the weekends. Due to the U.S.'s poor economy and lowered dollar, there is a glut of Canadian shoppers," writes Erica M. of Buffalo. "It's really fantastic for Erie county's taxes, but stressful for someone like me that likes to get in, get what I want and get out."[23] This sentiment is echoed by Cookie x. of Buffalo, who writes: "Over the past year or so it has grown and now has become too crowded. On an average weekend expect to be annoyed by slow walkers and people standing in the middle of the walkway."[24]

Carousel Center Mall (visited November 15, 2010)

LOCATION: Central New York State

HISTORY

Developed by the Pyramid Companies, the Carousel Center Mall was completed in 1990. Named after a historic 1909 carousel acquired by the Pyramid Companies in 1985, it was built on a former landfill bordering Lake Onondaga. The historic carousel placed in the food court is the centerpiece of the 1.5 million-square-foot mall.[25] Initially planning it as a mixed-use community, the Pyramid Companies had proposed building 2000 new residences, a hotel and a marina on the site. Due to this expansive development plan, the city government offered Pyramid a 25-year payment in lieu of taxes (PILOT) agreement that freed it from ordinary property tax.[26] Although approved for tax credits, the Carousel Mall did not add mixed-use facilities in its original development plan, citing that they would be added later; however, to date residential units are still absent. From its inception, Carousel housed a variety of stores that catered to a large audience such as the discount retailer Hills and up-market department store Bonwit Teller.

Currently the Carousel Center houses eight anchor stores, with a mix of Big Box and traditional tenants. Macy's, Bon-Ton, H&M, and JCPenney constitute the traditional tenants, whereas a Best Buy, Borders and Sport Authority offer Big Box style retailing. Carousel has a large 12-screen cinema and five restaurants, with an expansive food court housing 18 outlets.[27] In 2000, Pyramid announced plans to further expand the center to create a mega mall akin to the Mall of America. The plan, dubbed "Destiny U.S.A," called for the

Exterior of the Carousel Center with new outlet center addition.

Top: Historic carousel at the Carousel Center Mall. *Bottom:* Atrium of Carousel Center Mall.

Multiple floors of retail space at the Carousel Center Mall.

construction of an "indoor city" that would mimic the feel of a European town square. In order to create a center of this magnitude, Pyramid proposed expanding the mall by several million square feet. The Destiny U.S.A project enabled Pyramid to secure another PILOT plan, as it promised to "renew" the city of Syracuse by making it a national tourist destination.[28] Pyramid was also able to secure $228 million in "green bonds" from the U.S. government by promoting a completely energy efficient construction plan for Destiny. The plan included supporting the use of renewable energy through a reliance on non-fossil fuels. To achieve this, "a 45-megawatt electricity generating plant running on "biofuel" made from soybean oil and recycled cooking grease" was proposed along with "290,000 square feet of solar panels on the mall's roofs and other surfaces."[29]

Opened with great fanfare and promise in 2007, the Destiny project stalled in 2009 when the Citigroup stopped its funding. Citing a lack of secured tenants and concerns over cost overruns and construction delays, the bank stopped advancing funds to Pyramid on their $155 million construction loan.[30] Only a quarter of the proposed development has been finished and at the time of observation, the new structure remained empty. Due to pressure from the city government to pay back PILOT credits, in 2010 Pyramid proposed a downscaling of the initial development plan, instead creating an up-market outlet village in the new expansion. With the Destiny project stalled, the "green" mall initiative to use 100 percent renewable energy fell by the wayside. The inclusion of three windmills on the roof of the mall and a collection of large banners on the exterior and interior announcing the mall's commitment to the environment are the only signs of the green mall initiative. Currently, Pyramid has secured 14 tenants (a mix of retailers and restaurants) for the outlet village but will require more to fill the space. The company is currently in talks to secure a movie theater/bowling alley concept play area called "Revolutions" to fill the space.[31] If the plan comes to fruition, Carousel will become the ultimate hybrid center combining cut-price and up-scale retailing with a large entertainment element.

AREA DEMOGRAPHICS

The Carousel Mall is located in Syracuse, NY. The City of Syracuse has a population of 140,658 with a negative population growth of -4.0 percent over the period of 2000–2010. The median household income is $25,000 with 27.3 percent of the population living below the poverty level. The unemployment rate of Syracuse city is 7.7 percent. The statistics relay symptoms of a depressed economic climate in this area.[32]

Top: Destiny USA grand plan at the Carousel Center Mall. *Bottom:* Plan showing the most current footprint of the Carousel Center Mall.

CURRENT VIABILITY

The Carousel Mall is the second largest mall in Central New York, attracting approximately 17 million visitors annually.[33] At the time of observation, the new addition to the mall was closed to the public. Also noted was a series of large, empty parking lots near the new addition (which were meant to be part of the planned Destiny center); they were blocked for entry on the day of observation. Otherwise, the mall appeared to be vibrant with few empty retail spaces. Despite the recent financial woes, Andra Case explained the mall was very viable and that the planned outlet center was seen as a positive step in securing the future of this center.

COMMUNITY RESPONSE

Due to the controversy surrounding the construction of Destiny U.S.A, many people have a poor opinion of the Carousel Mall. At the time of observation, the author asked Syracuse area residents their thoughts on the Carousel Mall. Of the ten residents interviewed, all felt that the construction of Destiny U.S.A was flawed and doomed to be redundant. A strong negativity towards the tax credits given to the mall developers was mentioned as well as a feeling of hostility towards the president and owner of Pyramid Companies, Bob Congel. A collection of comments from the review site *Yelp.com* mirrors this negativity. "For a mall that promotes green energy they do nothing to accommodate those of us who chose walking or bicycling over driving a car," writes Daryl A. of Syracuse, "no crosswalks, no bicycle racks, no nothing. I would love to see bicycle racks installed in a sheltered area with camera monitoring so you don't have to feel like your bike is going to be stolen."[34] "Lime Green paint? Can't even keep a Borders open? This place is going downhill fast. Destiny for Despair!" says Mark M. of Niagara Falls.[35] This sentiment is echoed by Kyle E. of East Syracuse: "I think the project is ridiculous and should have never been started."[36]

While many of the comments regarding the Carousel Mall on the review site *Yelp.com* are negative, there are some positive replies from patrons. "I'm not gonna lie, I love Carousel Mall," writes Samantha H. of Syracuse. "I'll probably always be a mall girl seeing as I was born and raised in Syracuse suburbia, and this one has a lot of places to shop and eat."[37] For patrons from out of town who may not be aware of the controversy involved with the mall, a more overtly positive response was noted. "I love the new eco-friendly focus, it's nice to see them encouraging people to go green. And the carousel in the food court is always worth a ride," says Rachel C. of Stonybrook, NY.[38] "Very nice mall on the inside," writes Jasmine A. of Dallas, Texas; however, Jasmine is confused as to why the outside is so shabby.[39]

LIFESTYLE CENTER

Clifton Park Center (visited November 10, 2010)

LOCATION: Capital District of New York State

HISTORY

The Clifton Country Mall was developed in the mid–1970s as a mid-market fashion mall and was originally anchored by a JCPenney and Steinbach. The mall was re-developed in 1984 to include a significant addition to house a branch of the discount store Caldor. The mall struggled after losing Steinbach and Caldor, due to bankruptcy of the chains, in the late 1990s. By the year 2000, the mall was barely tenanted, retaining the JCPenney and Marshalls as anchors with the Caldor wing remaining empty. In 2001, the mall managed to attract the department store Boscov's to fill the empty space left by Caldor and attracted some mid-range national chain stores as a result. The mall continued to struggle, however, due to heavy competition in the area.[40] Acquired by 2006 by DCG Development, Clifton Country Mall was re-named Clifton Park Center. In 2007, plans were enacted to demolish a portion of the enclosed mall and re-develop the mall as a lifestyle center. A portion (the 1984 enclosed addition) was retained so the mall is essentially a hybrid of an enclosed mall and a lifestyle center. "We wanted the customer and the tenant to have an opportunity to have access externally to our local shops, as well as have the inside mall to be protected from weather," says Susan Keegan, Clifton Country Mall general manager.[41] The mall now includes a mix of local and chain restaurants as well as local and national retail outlets. The façade of the mall has been renovated to look like an outdoor town center and includes heated sidewalks, park benches, spaces for outdoor dining and storefront parking. Future plans include the addition of a new 10-screen cinema and 104-room hotel. Currently, the old cinema is in the process of demolition.

AREA DEMOGRAPHICS

Clifton Park Center is located in Saratoga County, New York; it is within commuting distance to Albany. Saratoga County has a population of 219,607, mostly (94 percent) white residents. The median household income is $66,634 with 6.3 percent of the population living below the poverty level.[42] The area has a population growth of 2.1 percent over the period of 2000–2010 and an unemployment rate of 6.2 percent (as of May 2011).[43]

CURRENT VIABILITY

At the time of observation, the mall had several un-tenanted spaces in both the "lifestyle" and indoor sections. Entry to the enclosed section was not obvious, as it appears that the stores are all accessible from the front (so no need to go inside). Despite having three large empty retail spaces in the "lifestyle" section, it appeared vibrant. The enclosed mall, however, had several closed shop-fronts. Aeropostale, American Eagle, a piano retailer, and a movie theater (which was closed during the period of observation) appeared to be functioning in the mall space; however, many retail spaces in the enclosed section had signs announcing "space available."

During the period of observation, the anchor store Boscov's was still functioning to the rear of the building. None of the lifestyle section stores faced inward except Marshalls, which appeared to be a detriment to the stores on the interior. The other anchor, JCPenney was a separate shop which functioned like a Big Box. The enclosed section originally joining JCPenney to the mall had been demolished. According to the *Times Union*, JCPenney would

Mall entry signage on the Clifton Park Center lifestyle center.

Top: Interior of the enclosed mall section of the Clifton Park Center. *Bottom:* Food court in the enclosed mall section of the Clifton Park Center.

Top: Elderly man reading a novel in the enclosed mall section of the Clifton Park Center. *Bottom:* External façade of the Clifton Park Center.

undergo significant renovation in 2011 and would include a branch of the Sephora cosmetics chain in their store. An Olive Garden restaurant and Jos. A. Bank men's clothing store was also slated to enter the mall in 2011.[44] While the mall appeared to have a substantial amount of empty retail space at the time of observation, the ability to attract new retail and restaurant space relays the future potential of this space.

COMMUNITY RESPONSE

Community response to the space is mixed with many patrons finding the Main Street appeal "forced" and others finding the new layout more convenient. On the site *Labelscar*, Droman writes: "I still don't get the appeal of a faux-main street lifestyle retail strip. Especially because it looks like it's unsafe for shoppers to walk around and a mess to drive and park in. Plus it's an ugly hybrid of a downtown street and a strip plaza."[45] This sentiment is echoed by Xismzero, who writes: "The lifestyle adaption looks like it doesn't adapt.... Also, it looks very uninspired and rather cookie cutter but that's no surprise with mall renovations today."[46] Patron Steve Swain comments on the "faux" Main Street appeal as being very unauthentic. "The outdoor portion of this mall looks horrible; like cardboard cutouts covered in construction paper," says Steve.[47]

When interviewing the manager of the Mocha Lisa café in the new "lifestyle section" of the center, however, a positive response to the new layout was implied. "People don't want to be enclosed in the mall anymore; they want to drive right up to the shops," explains the Mocha Lisa manager. The coffee shop appeared to be doing very well; during the period of observation, several groups of young people were spending time in the shop chatting and enjoying the atmosphere. Posters on the wall noted that the coffee shop won the best local business award in the Capital District that year. "Perfect atmosphere for coffee with friends, they have free wi-fi. their chairs are comfortable. They have a meeting room if you needed for parties or meetings. They have something for everyone even if you don't drink coffee!" writes Kristina T.[48] "I am a regular at Mocha's and there's a reason for that. I love coming here ... getting cheap refills on my coffee ... getting lots of work done in a comfortable and warm atmosphere. The staff is always kind and friendly — especially the younger ones. The seating is comfortable ... the wifi is always free and working.... It's a wonderful place for couples to relax or for friends to catch up," writes a patron (spl23311) on *citysearch.com*.[49] Reviews of the café are very positive and show that the café is an embodiment of what a "lifestyle" center aims to be — a friendly, local Main Street–like environment.

HYBRIDS

The Shops at Ithaca Mall (formerly The Pyramid Mall) (visited November 15, 2010)

LOCATION: Fingerlakes Region of New York State

HISTORY

The Pyramid Mall was developed by the Pyramid Companies and opened in 1976. Developed as a regional mid-market fashion mall, it housed a JW Rhodes, JCPenney, Montgomery Ward and Hills as its original anchors. In 2000, the Pyramid Mall was renovated to include several Big Box stores. JCPenney left in 2001 and in the wing that housed JCPenney, Pyramid Companies added the Big Box retailers Dick's Sporting Goods, Borders Books and Music, and Best Buy. In 2002, Old Navy was added to the space left by the defunct Montgomery Ward and a new addition of a Target, attached to the mall by a small corridor, was also added at this time.[50] All of the Big Box retailers are accessible from the exterior and interior. Traditional department stores, Sears and The Bon-Ton, as well as several other smaller retailers, remain in the enclosed section, making it a hybrid of an enclosed mall and a Big Box

Vacant retail space at The Shops at Ithaca Mall.

center. The Pyramid Companies sold this hybrid mall in 2007 to the Triax group, which changed its name to The Shops at Ithaca Mall. The Triax group added a new 14 screen Regal Cinema complex in 2007. In the new theater area, Triax hopes to create a "lifestyle center" like setting. "Today as the retail market and shopping center industry changes, very few new malls are being built," says Gena Speno, general manager of The Shops at Ithaca Mall. "What you are seeing is old malls, and things that are called 'lifestyle centers' where you have retail on the first floor, you have nice sidewalks and trees and benches. They have businesses located above them, doctor's offices, and residential. That's where a lot of things are going."[51]

Triax announced plans to create a mixed-use development complex on the site with an additional 82,000 square meters of retail space, 12 senior housing units, wetlands and a bird sanctuary in 2009.[52] The group received approval for the construction of a stand alone BJ's Wholesale Club and began construction of the store in April 2011.[53] A new BJ's will add to the Big Box appeal of The Shops at Ithaca Mall.

AREA DEMOGRAPHICS

The Shops at Ithaca Mall is located in the college town of Ithaca, NY, in Tompkins County. Tompkins County has a population of 101,564 with a majority (82.6 percent) of white residents. The median household income is $45,535 with 18.8 percent of the population living below the poverty level.[54] Tompkins County has a positive growth rate of 5.2 percent over the period of 2000–2010. With an unemployment rate of 5.4 percent, this area is one of the healthiest economically in the state.[55]

CURRENT VIABILITY

At the time of observation, the Big Box section of the mall appeared very viable; however, there were a few large empty retail spaces and many empty kiosks in the older enclosed mall space. The Sears wing had a particularly noticeable amount of empty shops. In February of 2011, the Borders store closed due to bankruptcy, leaving a large empty retail space. As evidenced by the new BJ's store, the mall had a viable future as a Big Box center. Overall, it was a highly functional mall, which benefited from the healthy economic climate of the area and the proximity to two large universities.

COMMUNITY RESPONSE

Community response to this mall is largely positive; however, some patrons feel the Big Box approach takes away from the function of the enclosed mall. "The mall looks painfully ugly, and there are way too many Big Box stores," says Johanh Norason. "What I suggest is an auxiliary Big Box center to take away all the Big Boxes except Old Navy and Target. Old Navy needs to move to a less-conspicuous location. Then, bring in the stores!"[56] Patrons admit, however, that the addition of Big Box stores has effectively saved many regional malls from decline. "Another observation I've noticed is all of those Pyramid malls [Hampshire Mall, Aviation Mall, Pyramid Mall] you mentioned were all saved by Target," writes Xismzero.[57]

The Fingerlakes Mall (15/11/2010)

LOCATION: Fingerlakes Region of New York State

HISTORY

The Pyramid Companies completed the Fingerlakes Mall in 1979. Originally housing a Chappell's, JCPenney, Sears and Kmart, it represented a mix of mid-range and discount retailers. From its inception, the mall offered an interesting mix of retailing and entertainment, with a roller-skating rink and 4-screen cinema, making it an early hybrid of sorts. The mall fell into financial strife due to the loss of the anchors Kmart and Chappell's in the 1990s and subsequently 60 percent of the tenants left the mall. Pyramid sold the struggling mall to the Jager management group in 1999. Jager then sold it to Gregory Greenfield and Associates (GG&A) five months later.[58] GGA was able to attract the Big Box specialty retailer Bass Pro Shops to the mall in 2003. The mall was significantly renovated during this period, to allow for the Bass Pro Shops to add its own entry and extensive entry display.[59] With the addition of the popular Bass Pro Shops, the Fingerlakes Mall was able to attract thirty new retailers and eateries. In 2005 the mall was at 80 percent occupancy. The Bass Pro Shops, a major specialty retailer, draws customers from 100 miles and beyond. "Bass Pro was pretty much the single tenant we had targeted as being the one that could turn the property around," explained Greenfield in 2005.[60] In 2006, the Cameron Group completed construction of a Big Box power center directly opposite the Fingerlakes Mall. The power center includes the retailers Home Depot, Dick's Sporting Goods, Circuit City and Kohl's.

AREA DEMOGRAPHICS

The Fingerlakes Mall is located in Cayuga County in Central New York. Cayuga County has a population of 80,026 with a majority of white (92.5 percent) residents. The county has a median household income of $47,926 with 13.5 percent of the population living below the poverty level.[61] The area has experienced a negative growth of -2.4 percent over 2000–2010 and has an unemployment rate of 7.3 percent.[62] Based on these figures, it can be assumed that the area exhibits signs of economic stress.

CURRENT VIABILITY

The Fingerlakes Mall was sold to a private development group in 2008 and has since gone downhill. At the time of observation, the mall had many empty stores. It was down to 30 stores as opposed to the 70 that were open in 2005. Empty shops had been masked with printed canvas featuring faux shop fronts. Bass Pro Shops was still functional and appeared to be the most frequented store in the mall, as most of the cars in the parking lot were grouped there. At the time of observation, Sears and JCPenney still functioned in the mall; however, the décor in these sections appear dated and the wings housing them were filled with local retail and temporary "pop-up" shops. Reasons for the decline are cited as the increase of rents due to the popularity of the Bass Pro Shops and competition from the Fingerlakes Crossing Big Box center across the road.

COMMUNITY RESPONSE

The community response to this mall is mixed due to its revival and subsequent quick decline. Community members on the FingerLakes Forums

Exterior of the Fingerlakes Mall.

Top: Food court at the Fingerlakes Mall. ***Bottom:*** Bass Pro Shops at the Fingerlakes Mall.

express sadness that the mall has fallen into further decline under the new ownership. "The mall has never had less business, or more empty stores at any time in its history," writes Timbo50. "It's a sad state of affairs. Several existing clients are barely holding on and probably won't renew their leases. If Bass Pro, Penny's or Sears ever leave they may as well bulldoze it." Timbo goes on to explain that Kohl's (in the Fingerlakes Crossings) has taken over as a major retailer in the area.[63] "I recently spoke with a store manager at the mall. She stated that rents are going up," writes runner 97, "I am uncertain as to why this would happen given the fact that more stores are leaving and none are coming in. What is the mall manager thinking? Does he not realize that there are 28 vacancies now? I emailed the mall and I was told it is our fault that we don't support the mall. I really think it's a double edged sword. Bring more stores in and we will shop there, but they need the foot traffic. It is like what came first the chicken or the egg?"[64] Blogger Josephus is more optimistic, stating that the mall is not a lost case: "It seems like the mall was a ghost town until the Bass Pro Shop came in. Now it seems to be pretty busy! Maybe not at the big stores like Penny's, but the smaller ones. I was at the Verizon store there just two weeks ago, and the place was a bustle of activity."[65]

An empty shop at the Fingerlakes Mall.

Dated fountain display at the Fingerlakes Mall.

ANALYSIS AND CONCLUSIONS

Overall, the case studies point to the dominance and sustainability of super-regional malls, hybrid malls with a significant amount of Big Box tenants and stand-alone Big Box power centers in the area studied. Despite the financial difficulties with the Destiny U.S.A. project, all of the super-regional malls in the area (owned exclusively by Pyramid Companies). have a relatively high occupancy and foot traffic as opposed to the regional malls studied. As well has dominating the areas with their physical space and number of anchor stores, the super-regional malls exhibit a hybrid approach to retailing with a mix of Big Box, lifestyle and traditional department stores. This supports Sokol's statement that super-regionals remain viable due to their multi-faceted approach to retail. "The behemoths are adapting to changing market conditions. They're adding new, open-air lifestyle areas and re-tenanting to bring in the Big Box discounters that consumers now favor," says Sokol.[66] Community response to the super-regional malls relays a tendency for the malls to be impersonal, as local community members exhibited a marked hostility to patrons from other states or countries. In this case, patrons felt that a mall that draws from such a large radius detracts from a true feeling of local community.

The lifestyle model is not an overly popular model in the area studied. Several super-regional malls have added elements of a lifestyle center to their original design; however, they did not totally convert to this outdoor model, as the malls are still essentially enclosed. Andra Case, marketing direction of Pyramid Companies, explains that they do not apply this model due to pro-hibitive weather conditions in the area. The Simon Group (Morris interview) doubts the long-term viability of this model. The lifestyle center that was observed, Clifton Park Center, was itself a hybrid of a lifestyle center and a traditional enclosed mall. Perhaps due to the weather conditions in the area, developers felt it necessary to retain some of the enclosed mall; however, this section is struggling to retain shops. The majority of the shop fronts exist in the outdoor lifestyle section; therefore, this mall can be classified as more of a lifestyle center than a traditional enclosed regional mall. The community response to this center was mixed with many patrons enjoying the new "com-munity" feel, especially in the Mocha Lisa coffee shop wing. Some patrons, however, felt the community concept was forced and unnatural. The layout of the center was also forbidding for actual pedestrian traffic and the pastel "faux Main Street" style shop fronts were unconvincing in this area of the state.

In the area of observation, the viability of regional malls as hybrids is uncertain. Of the two in the sample, The Shops at Ithaca Mall appeared to be stable, whereas the Fingerlakes Mall is displaying signs of decline. Both malls are former Pyramid properties that had attempted to revitalize their dwindling centers by adding on Big Box stores. While The Shops at Ithaca Mall added a large Big Box section with several retailers, the Fingerlakes Mall only added one large Big Box specialty retailer. This was a disadvantage to the smaller retailers in the Fingerlakes Mall who now suffer from the compe-tition of a large Big Box power center across the road. Perhaps the key to a successful hybrid is creating a dominant collection of Big Box retailers to stave off potential competition from the stand-alone Big Box power centers. The downfall of the hybrid model, however, is that the attached Big Boxes often deter the focus from the enclosed mall area. Patrons can go in and out of the Big Boxes without entering the interior mall space. This can have a negative effect on the viability of the interior shops, as seen in both hybrid malls in the study.

From a mall development perspective, the Big Box stores also pose chal-lenges not previously seen with traditional department stores. "Managing Big Box tenants is much more intensive," says the Urban Land Institute, "A pri-mary difference with Big Box retailers is the notification process they demand ... most Big Box tenants require multiple notices, some extending as far as 180 days before turnover. Additional required notices might involve the availability of utilities, pad preparation, or other construction-related issues. The leases of many Big Box retailers require a penalty — as much as six figures — for failure to receive any one of these notifications from the landlord, a lesson some developers have learned the hard way."[67] Therefore, smaller regional malls may not have the ability or capacity to weather these demands. Both hybrid malls in the observation had similar responses from patrons about the viability of the enclosed mall space. Many doubted that it would remain viable and some patrons suggested that the Big Boxes move to a stand-alone section so as not to deter from the original enclosed format of the mall. Patrons, however, admit that the Big Box stores have effectively aided in saving an ailing mall, although in the end they lead to dominance by the Big Box retailer. In both malls in the observation, the Big Box remained successful with the enclosed mall suffering.

The next chapter presents case studies of urban shopping malls and assesses their current viability. Through a discussion of the "new urbanism" happening in cities across the U.S., correlations are drawn to the future of retail in these areas. This chapter also looks at the rise of Big Box power centers in urban areas and possible implications of their inclusion in this environment.

14. New Urbanism and the Death of the Urban Mall

"Walkable urban development is already a growing part of the American built environment," says Leinburger. "It will even become part of the next American Dream over the next generation.... The only question is whether the market will just take its course over many decades or whether walkable urbanism will be part of new American domestic policy to speed up the process."[1] As stated in Chapter 3, the downtown areas of American cities have been in relative decline since the suburban movement of the 1950s. Mall developers James Rouse and Victor Gruen proposed the construction of shopping malls in downtown areas to revitalize their dwindling economies. Revisiting many urban shopping malls in 2010 is a sobering experience. In the cities of Buffalo, Rochester and Syracuse, inner city malls exhibit high vacancy and in some cases, demolition. Retail in these areas is limited to local shops and lack sufficient grocery stores. Surrounding these spaces are large empty office buildings, derelict homes and empty city streets — signs of economic depression. The urban areas, however, exhibit some glimmers of re-development in new up-market housing developments in old department stores and former industrial spaces as well as small pockets of boutique retail and restaurant spaces. Walmart has revealed plans to develop smaller outlets in central urban areas, and has already carried out this plan in larger urban areas such as downtown Chicago.

This development will be discussed in comparison to the inner-city malls, which had once offered the promise of renewed urban growth. Case studies of four urban shopping malls provide insight into this model and also provide a means of comparison with regional shopping malls. The observations provide a snapshot of the current state of retail in downtown areas in New York State. Coupled with recent theories of "new-urbanism" in America, the following case studies give insight into the concept of "walkable urbanism" as the "new American Dream."

Galleries of Syracuse (visited November 15, 2010)

LOCATION: Central New York

HISTORY

The Galleries of Syracuse are located on Salina Street in Downtown Syracuse. At the turn of the century, Salina Street was the retail heart of the city, housing department stores Addis, Chappell's and Dey's as well as the city theater. In the 1940s, at the height of downtown activity, the street featured a thriving retail environment with retail giants Sibley's, Chappell's, Flah's, E.D. Edwards, F.W. Woolworth, Grant's, Lincoln Stores, The Mohican, David's, Kmart, Walgreens, McCrory's, Dey Brothers, Addis Company, Wells and Coverly, Whitney, Witherill's, Wilson's Jewelry, Goldberg's Furniture and Raymour's Furniture (which became Raymour and Flanigan). "In the 1910s, Salina Street brimmed with activity. Shops lined the street and people easily outnumbered cars," explains the Web site *Yestercuse*, a retrospective on the city of Syracuse.[2] As the suburban movement took hold in the 1950s, retail gradually left Salina Street. Sibley's closed in 1986 and Dey's in 1992, followed by smaller retailers who found the suburban shopping malls much more appealing and accessible to their consumer base.

In an effort to revitalize downtown Syracuse, the Galleries of Syracuse was built by demolishing the former Flah's department store next to the Dey's store. Dey's and Flah's had been connected to the Sibley's building by a covered walkway over Salina Street since 1976. Therefore, when the mall was developed, it had an access point to the walkway to allow the pedestrian covered access to the other side of the road. The Galleries, constructed in 1987, are fronted by a large glass atrium space and offers covered spaces for commuters to walk between city streets without having to face traffic or the harsh weather. Similar to their suburban cousins, the Galleries functioned as an enclosed retail space, complete with fountains and palms, interior street lamps and park benches.

Urban development of this style was built in many inner cities during this period. On a larger scale, the St. Louis Center in downtown St. Louis, MO, also completed in the 1980s, is of a similar design and connects the old Famous and Barr department store [now Macy's] with Associated Dry Goods, and Stix, Baer and Fuller. St. Louis Center was demolished in 2010 after years of decline and re-purposed as a parking garage.[3] The Galleries of Syracuse did not succumb to the same fate as St. Louis Center. The Galleries is still functioning largely as office spaces; however, as a retail venture, the space was not successful.

Atrium space of the Galleries of Syracuse.

Top: Second level of the Galleries of Syracuse. ***Bottom:*** Entrance hallway in the Galleries of Syracuse.

Office spaces in the Galleries of Syracuse.

According to *Yestercuse*, "Syracuse's population dropped by 12,000 in the 1990s thanks to flight from the rust belt. Another reason for the drop was Syracuse's employment picture. From 1990 to 1993, the city lost 12,000 jobs."[4] With employment options drained from the city, the Galleries, which has stayed viable mainly through its food court, which offered downtown employees lunch options, continued to lose tenants. "The Galleries, despite its high cost, brought no more businesses than the buildings they replaced. In fact, for many of its early years, the Galleries had serious problems filling its commercial space," explains *Yestercuse*.[5] Retail spaces were soon converted into office spaces with the Onondaga Library moving the city library into the space once populated by anchor Kaufmann's. In 2004, the Galleries defaulted on a loan repayment of $800,000 and were loaned the money by the Syracuse Industrial Development Agency, which appointed Flaun Management to run the space. According to *Yestercuse*, Flaun closed the second floor food court in February of 2004 to create more office space. "Behind the Galleries on Warren Street, the Dorset Apartments were demolished to create yet another parking lot," to offer adequate parking allowance for the new offices.[6] At the time of observation, The Galleries of Syracuse houses a library and several law offices, Christo's café, Olympic News store and a menswear store. There were noticeable empty spaces, but as a whole the space appeared to be functioning. While no longer a retail space, The Galleries of Syracuse relays the potential adaptability of inner city malls into offices and community minded space.

Area Demographics

The City of Syracuse has a population of 140,658 with a negative growth of -4.0 percent over the period of 2000–2010. The median household income is $25,000 with 27.3 percent of the population living below the poverty level. The unemployment rate of Syracuse city is 7.7 percent. The statistics reveal symptoms of a depressed economic climate in this area.[7]

Retail Potential of Downtown Syracuse

At the time of observation, the old Dey's department store was in the process of being re-purposed as a boutique apartment building called Dey's Plaza. The developers, Rich DeVito and Bob Doucette, had also sought planning approval for Dey's Fresh Market to be placed in the retail space in the ground floor of the apartment building. "The Dey's Fresh Market is envisioned as an indoor place where customers would buy food or other items from individual vendors, not from a cashier," says Cazentre of *The Post-Standard*, "the idea is to connect consumers with the food producers and sellers."[8] Dey's Market was proposed to open in June of 2010 in correlation with the final phase of renovation. As of June 2011, the 45 apartments on the upper floors of the project have since been rented; however, Dey's Fresh Market is not open nor has the ground floor of the building been renovated to support the opening of the market. The project could potentially bring a much needed boost and generate a renewed vibrancy to retail in the area. Retail development, however, is essential in keeping the initial interest in the area. "A neighborhood is created when the vitality of a street is brought out. Having residential units is helpful, but doesn't mean you'll have vitality on the street. So retail development is as crucial if not more crucial than the apartments," said DeVito.[9]

Armory Square, a retail and restaurant hub in downtown Syracuse, is another example of positive retail potential in the area. Built in the early 1880s, the square was designated a National Historic District in 1984. "At the turn of the century, the area was densely built up and bustling with activity," explains the Armory Square official Web site, "There were more than twenty hotels in the neighborhood, servicing the railroads. The Jefferson Street Armory, built around this time, is actually three buildings and was once used to quarter the cavalry and the infantry."[10] In keeping with the rest of downtown Syracuse, the area declined in the late 1940s and early 1950s as more and more people moved to suburban housing. According to the Armory Square Web site, between 1940 and 1960, many buildings were vacated or demolished. In the mid–1990s efforts were made to revitalize the district, when several buildings were converted into retail and restaurant space and new buildings were developed that retained the historic characteristics of the area. Today the area is populated with several popular up-scale restaurants and cafes, a branch of the clothing outlet Urban Outfitters and several coffee shops. It is a popular destination for college students and office workers alike. At the time of observation, the area exhibited high lunch hour foot traffic, but had a handful of empty retail and restaurant spaces.

While the Armory Square and Dey's developments display positive signs of urban renewal and a trend towards walkable urbanism, *Yestercuse* argues that this will not save the city of Syracuse. "Downtown's role as the business center of Syracuse is over," says *Yestercuse*. "Of the renovation activity downtown, the vast majority is conversion of unrented and unwanted commercial space into residential space. However, the methods chosen may backfire. Rather than build affordable housing, the city and property owners have focused on luxury 'market rate' apartment conversions with rents anywhere from $800 to well over $1000 for one bedroom units." *Yestercuse* goes on to explain that the luxury market is unfit for the economic climate in the area.

"The emphasis on high-end apartments may not benefit downtown merchants as much as civic leaders assume. Downtown residents generally work outside of downtown, so their lunch business and after-work shopping will be in their workplace neighborhoods rather than downtown. Another factor is that each formerly commercial space that once held many employees may now house only one or two residents, providing a much smaller pool of potential customers for downtown businesses. The small number of downtown residents cannot support a downtown supermarket."[11] Should the Syracuse economy face further decline, as many residents predict, the luxury apartments would most likely be the first to be vacated.

Main Place Mall (visited November 18, 2010)

LOCATION: Western New York State

HISTORY

The Main Place mall is in downtown Buffalo on Main Street. It was built in 1968 as part of an urban renewal effort. According to *Deadmalls.com*, "The mall was located on the site of the former Adam, Meldrum, and Anderson store (AM&A's)."[12] AM&A's moved across the street in 1961. The mall was once anchored by Kobacker's, which later changed to Sattler's. It is linked to the Main Place office building by a covered pedestrian walkway. Currently a large food court stands in the area that once housed the anchor store. The food court is populated on weekdays during office hours; however, as a retail space the mall is barely functioning. Payless Shoes, an Optical Store and a dollar store are the few tenants left. It is the only mall in downtown Buffalo and is owned by the Liberty Property group. Liberty owns the Main Place office building across the street and the historic Liberty building.[13]

At the turn of the century Buffalo was an expanding industrial city with several steel mills and granaries. It was the terminus point of the Erie Canal, the main transportation system for goods across New York State. Buffalo benefited from close proximity to Niagara Falls and through harnessing the hydroelectric power of the falls, it was one of the first cities in the country to have widespread electricity. Buffalo was host of the 1901 Pan American Expo in which the city was deemed the "City of Light" due to its close links with the hydroelectric plant at Niagara Falls. During this period, Main Street Buffalo was a thriving retail center with the department stores Hens & Kelly, L.L Berger, AM&A's, Hengerer's and Sattler's. The downtown area began its decline in the late 1940s with the mass movement to suburbia. Buffalo also

Empty shops in the Main Place Mall.

suffered from the opening of the St. Lawrence Seaway in 1957, which allowed barges to bypass Buffalo through a series of canals and locks on the St. Lawrence River.[14]

The city has been in relative decline since the 1950s, though several measures were taken in the late 1960s and 70s to revive the city core. A light rail system was created in 1978 to help stimulate the city core. The Buffalo Metro Rail was meant to encompass a series of lines that would connect the city to surrounding suburbs, but only one line of the proposed plan was ever realized. This was due to the prohibitive cost of the railway and the dwindling population growth of the area. With the construction of the Buffalo Metro Rail, Main Street was converted to a pedestrian mall and remains so today. The metro system and pedestrian street, along with the covered overhead walkway, complemented the Main Place Mall and created a pedestrian-friendly retail space. The Metro has one 6.2 mile line which links the Buffalo University campus to the Erie Canal Harbor.

Like the Main Place Mall, the Metro failed to resuscitate the ailing downtown of Buffalo. Due to the declining population in the area, and as a direct result a declining tax base, the rail system is barely functional. In 1990, the system was shut for two days due to funding issues and in 1995 it lost significant financial assistance from the state, which caused the company to

Atrium of the Main Place Mall.

Vacant retail space in the Main Place Mall.

increase fares.[15] With a loss of passengers and funding, some of the stops on the line closed. Buffalo Metro Rail continues to struggle today as evidenced by reports that Main Street is due to return to an auto-accessible street.[16]

At the time of observation, the Main Place Mall food court was populated, however, many stores were empty. Shops open in the mall included a Payless Shoes, a gift store and a menswear store. The area surrounding the Main Place Mall appeared depressed, with many vacant storefronts and buildings. On the day of observation, people were loitering listlessly near the entry to the shopping mall. An interview with a former mall patron revealed that area residents are afraid to shop after hours at the mall due to a perception of crime. The patron said the jewelry shop that had been in the mall for 30 years recently closed. Before the closing, the proprietor put the jewelry in a Kmart or Walmart bag to disguise the contents for fear of theft.

AREA DEMOGRAPHICS

The city of Buffalo has a population of 276,059 with a negative population growth of -5.7 percent over the period of 2000 to 2010. Buffalo has a median household income of $24,536 with 26.6 percent of the population living below the poverty level.[17] As of May 2011, the unemployment rate in

Buffalo was 7.5 percent.[18] The statistics relay symptoms of a depressed economic climate.

RETAIL POTENTIAL

Elmwood Avenue District in downtown Buffalo exhibits signs of urban vitality. The area has been nominated for PPS (Project for Public Spaces) award for its attempts to revitalize the area. According to Christian Calleri on the PPS Web site, "Elmwood Avenue is a beautiful, fun and laid back street and neighborhood that is punctuated by a few parks, many funky shops, delicious food, cafes, great architecture and vibrant street life."[19] The street atmosphere is an example of the benefit of an authentic neighborhood approach to retail.

In 2007, the Erie Canal Harbor Development Corporation (ECHDC) proposed plans for a redevelopment of the harbor area of Buffalo. The $6 million plan called for the re-creation of a fake canal system next to the genuine terminus of the Erie Canal and the construction of a Big Box center on the site with Bass Pro Shops as the main anchor. The plan included the construction of a 300-car parking garage, an Erie Canal museum, an aquarium and several spaces for smaller retailers. The Bass Pro Shop's 2010 decision to pull out of the development along with community criticism of the plan caused the ECHDC to revise their plans to a "lighter, cheaper, quicker" layout that works to highlight the area's unique historic sensibilities.[20] The current development being undertaken is the reconstruction of four cobblestone streets, installation of granite curbs, exposed aggregate concrete sidewalks, new street lighting, landscaping, and traffic signal work. All efforts have been made to mesh the new development with the current grid layout of the city. "By taking full advantage of our proximity to water, historic Erie Canal and cobblestone streets we work project by project to build a waterfront that is not only attractive to visitors and economic development, but one that is uniquely Western New York," says Congressman Brian Higgins.[21]

The new development plans highlight the need for retail to draw people to the site; however, for the moment the focus is on bringing restaurants to stimulate the area. "What we'd like to do is something quick (for now)," explains Thomas Dee, president of the ECHDC. "The biggest thing we get down there is that people need food. So we think restaurants are the first things. We don't even have permanent rest rooms down there either. So we need to do that as well."[22] The plan also calls for the creation of a "marketplace" in the style of an old grain elevator, which combines market stall operators with traditional retailers. "It would be a combined wholesale and retail marketplace centered around food, with production such as bakeries in the back and booths or counters in front for patrons to buy individual meals," explains Sommer and Epstein of the *Buffalo News*.[23]

Despite the economic situation facing Buffalo, both Elmwood Avenue and the Harbor Development relay that a return to authentic and area-specific spaces offer potential for growth. It also shows a move away from the construction of homogenous retail structures and chain stores that do not highlight the unique characteristics of the area. The inclusion of a marketplace in the harbor development mirrors the plans of "Dey's Market" in Syracuse and shows the need for downtown supermarkets with a focus on fresh food and locally produced products to attract and sustain consumers. Both approaches are an effort to create genuine neighborhoods, rather than tourist specific sites. This marks a point of difference to Rouse's "Festival Marketplaces," which largely served as tourist destinations rather than local community hubs.

Midtown Plaza (visited November 17, 2010)

LOCATION: Western New York State

HISTORY

Midtown Plaza was designed by Victor Gruen in the early 1960s as a means to re-vitalize the urban core of Rochester. Midtown was the first urban enclosed shopping mall in the United States. The mixed-use development, which included a dual-level shopping mall, a hotel, a thirty-story office building and an expansive underground parking system, was initially successful in breathing life back into the downtown area of Rochester. Positioned opposite to the Sibley's department stores, a pedestrian "skyway" was added in the 1960s to connect the two structures. In the 1980s, with the further development of suburban shopping malls, Midtown Plaza began to decline. Sibley's was bought out by the May Company in 1986 and closed the downtown store in 1989. From the 1980s onward, Midtown Plaza began to lose tenants. The Midtown hotel closed in 1981 and in 1994, McCurdy's, Midtown's original anchor tenant, sold the majority of its holdings to the May Company. The May Company closed the Midtown McCurdy's and Forman's stores three months after the acquisition.

Without anchor stores, Midtown struggled to retain retail tenants and in 1997, the mall was sold to California based Arnold Enterprises for $27.3 million. Arnold was unable to revive the center, declaring bankruptcy in 2000. Blackacre Bridge Capital assumed the Plaza for $14.9 million in 2001 and attempted to lease the empty retail spaces. In the same year, Blackacre Capital Management and Pembroke Companies merged to form Midtown Rochester

Properties and detailed significant plans for redevelopment for Midtown. By 2003, 90 percent of the retail space in Midtown was vacant.[24]

Unable to justify the property tax on the site, in 2006 Midtown's property manager, Lawrence Cohen, offered the city of Rochester the opportunity to purchase the site. According to *rochesterdowntown.com*, in 2006, "Rochester's City Council votes to purchase option on Midtown Plaza for $250,000 and empowers Bergmann Associates to carry out a $55,000 analysis of the property. The option allows the City to hold a sale price of $6M until February 2007."[25] After the city assumed control of Midtown, Mayor Duffy facilitated the signing of a contract with the vice president of Italy's Parma province in 2006 to create an "Italian-theme park and retail development" in the Midtown plaza. The contract was non-binding and did not come to fruition due to budget constraints.

In 2007, the city relinquished plans for the final purchase of Midtown Plaza; subsequently state Governor Eliot Spitzer took on plans for its development. The Spitzer administration effectively condemned the structure and announced the demolition of the plaza for the construction of a mixed-use development. The highlight of the proposed development was the creation of a new corporate headquarters for the PAETEC Company. The Rochester City Council signed a memorandum of understanding in October of 2007,

Midtown Plaza Office tower from street level.

Top: Demolition of the atrium space of Midtown Plaza. ***Bottom:*** Cross-section view of the Midtown Plaza demolition.

Midtown Plaza signage.

which stated that the city would acquire the site from the current owner under the condition that the state will cover the cost of demolition needed to make the site ready for the PAETEC building. Under the development plan, most of the original Midtown Plaza structure, save the thirty story office tower, would be demolished.[26]

Originally, the PAETEC company proposed the construction of 50,000 square feet of office space with a tower of more than 10 stories. Since the 2008 proposal, however, PAETEC has significantly scaled down the development, citing the economic downturn and the unstable commercial real estate market. "PAETEC is now considering a smaller structure that would partly use the existing Seneca Building," said spokesman Christopher Muller in 2010.[27] Demolition of the Midtown Plaza began in 2010 and was scheduled to be complete by the end of 2011. The final structure was proposed to open in June 2012. PAETEC is contractually obligated to occupy the proposed building for 20 years. The remainder of the 50,000 square foot Midtown site has had various plans proposed. A casino, a school, college or other educational campus exceeding 50,000 square feet, surface parking or a medical clinic for non-resident patients have all been proposed as potential tenants.

During the period of observation, the mall was in the first phase of demolition. All access points to the structure were closed and the skybridge was in the process of being dismantled. The former central atrium space, the first proposed demolition site, was exposed. Area residents evoked a feeling of nostalgia for the Midtown mall, especially for the displays set up during the Christmas period. All residents interviewed, however, noted that they welcomed the PAETEC building and were optimistic about the structure renewing the area.

Area Demographics

The population of Rochester is 208,123, with 48.3 percent white residents and 38.5 percent black residents. Rochester has a negative population growth of -5.3 percent over the period of 2000–2010 and a current unemployment rate of 7.1 percent.[28] With a median household income of $27,123 and 25.9 percent of the population living below the poverty level, this area exhibits symptoms of economic depression.[29]

Retail Potential

The ULI completed a survey of downtown Rochester in 2005 with a view to suggesting development options for urban renewal. In the report, the ULI cited the East End and High Falls areas as offering the most potential in terms of vibrancy and retail activity. "Primarily attracting younger patrons, these districts feature restaurants, nightclubs, and bars," says the ULI. "The East End is convenient to the Eastman School of Music while High Falls is convenient to Eastman Kodak headquarters and the Frontier Field baseball stadium."[30] Using the East End and High Falls as exemplars, the Urban Land Institute suggests that the city of Rochester build on the concept of "neighborhoods" and proposes a three-step plan for redevelopment. "The first [step] is to re-create downtown [Rochester] as a neighborhood," says the ULI. "The second strategy is to re-create downtown as a center of commerce [and] the third strategy is to promote downtown as a center of arts and culture."[31] In order to do this, the ULI suggests that Rochester revitalize the collection of historical buildings that exist downtown and demolish post-war office buildings that do not add to that character. "Continued construction of downtown housing units will be the primary driver of retail sales growth during the next several years," says the ULI.[32]

Repurposing the historic infrastructure to persuade "creative entrepreneurs" to settle in the city will bring back foot traffic and revitalize the city core. The ULI also suggests the construction of a specialized grocery store and a part-time farmer's market to promote growth in downtown Rochester and create a neighborhood feel. Overall, the goal is to bring foot traffic back to the city core through the creation of a unique historically relevant space.

A return of foot traffic will ultimately promote and stimulate retail in the area. "Bringing pedestrians back to downtown will help sustain new retail in the urban core and eliminate the perception of danger," says the ULI.[33]

Aspects of the ULI's proposal have been taken into action by the city of Rochester, as evidenced by the demolition of Midtown. With an emphasis on authentic, neighborhood environments that showcase the unique characteristics of the area, the ULI recommendations for Rochester follow similar lines of development happening in other economically stressed urban areas of Western New York.

Rainbow Center Mall (visited November 18, 2010)

LOCATION: Western New York State

HISTORY

The Cordish Company, as part of an urban renewal effort, built the Rainbow Center Mall in 1982. Connected to the Cesar Pelli designed Wintergarden with a glass walkway, the complex was meant to stimulate tourism in the area. With 280,000 square feet of retail space, a large atrium filled with live tropical plants and a glass elevator, the Rainbow Center Mall seemed to be a vibrant new addition to the faltering economy of Niagara Falls at the time. It was originally anchored by Beir's Department store; however, Beir's closed in 1990 and was replaced by the Burlington Coat Factory. With the arrival of the Burlington Coat Factory, the Rainbow Center Mall experienced success for a few years by repositioning itself as an outlet center. It slid into decline in the late 1990s when Prime Outlets purchased Niagara Factory Outlets and converted it into the upscale Fashion Outlets at the edge of town. The Burlington Coat Factory left the mall in 1999 and with them went a majority of tenants. The mall ceased to function as a retail space in 2000, but housed an off track betting site in the interior until 2005 and an Indian restaurant accessible from the exterior until 2009. In 18 years of existence, the Rainbow Center Mall was only operational for 10.[34]

Niagara Falls has been a popular tourist destination and center of hydroelectric power since the turn of the century. It was a burgeoning industrial center in the 1950s and 1960s. Falls Street, where the Rainbow Center is placed, was once a bustling tourist Mecca, with a collection of restaurants and shops. It was partially redeveloped in 1977 to encompass the Wintergarden structure, a large enclosed greenhouse in the middle of the city. "Built in 1977, the old Wintergarden served as a popular arboretum that residents and

Rainbow Center Mall front profile.

Signage at the Rainbow Center.

out-of-towners visited, hosted parties and even served as a backdrop for marriage ceremonies. Its glass frame is among the most recognizable in the city's skyline," said a *Niagara Gazette* article.[35] Niagara Falls fell into decline after the Love Canal toxic waste contamination crisis of the 1970s. In 1978, *The New York Times* carried a story documenting links between birth defects,

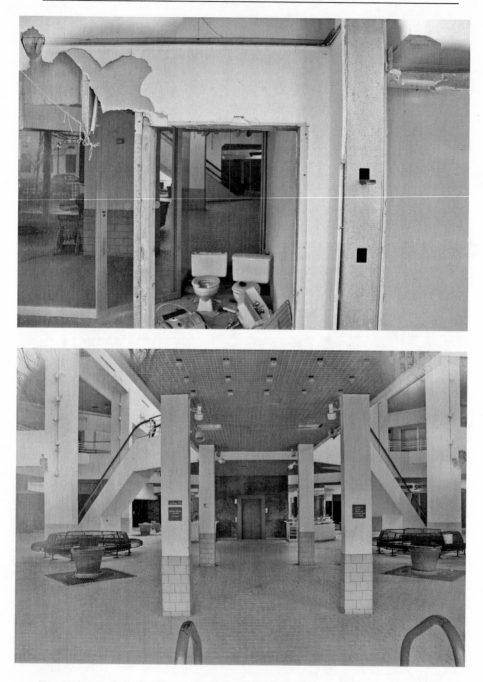

Top: Interior of the Rainbow Center Mall. *Bottom:* Entry hallway of the Rainbow Center Mall.

Food stall in the Rainbow Center Mall.

infections, miscarriages, cancer, and asthma of the residents of the Love Canal neighborhood with the toxic waste buried in the area. Love Canal, located in a white-collar section of Niagara Falls, was declared a federal emergency in August of 1978 and many residents were relocated. A second stage of relocation occurred in 1980 when further contamination was discovered in the area.[36] The nationally significant Love Canal incident has had serious aftereffects on the economic climate of the area and can be noted as a reason for economic decline in the area.

In 2001, Niagara Falls received a boost to its faltering economy when the State of New York came to an agreement with the Seneca Tribe to allow for the construction of several casinos in Western New York. The Seneca Tribe constructed a casino and hotel at the terminus of Old Falls Street, with 147,000 square feet of gaming space, six restaurants, three cafes and retail outlets. The Seneca Niagara Casino, completed in 2003, has become a big draw for the area. According to *rochesterdowntown.com*, "The Seneca Niagara Casino enjoyed an estimated six million visitors in 2004 and enrollment in its Seneca Player's Club reportedly totaled 575,000 members. For its part, the City of Niagara Falls's share of the casino revenues is to total approximately $12.5 million, or approximately $2 million more than in 2003. City monies have been earmarked or already spent on the Niagara Falls Airport; the Heart

Seneca Casino in Niagara Falls.

Center at the Memorial Medical Center; the Tourism and Convention Corporation; and the City School District."[37]

On the back of the success of the Seneca Niagara Casino, a conference center was built across the road from the Rainbow Mall in 2004. The adjoining Wintergarden was eventually demolished in 2008 after a failed attempt to repurpose it as a family fun center. By demolishing the Wintergarden, the Old Falls Street is now a through road to the Seneca Niagara Casino. Old Falls Street has been tastefully re-purposed in a way that replicates the historic feel of Old Falls Street. "Falls Street was once the economic center of the downtown tourist area and this Project component is intended to help recapture some of this former setting," explains the U.S.A Niagara Development Corporation.[38]

At the time of observation, Rainbow Center Mall was closed but still intact. The attached parking garage was still functional. Since 2000, the mall has remained closed despite several efforts to revitalize it. In October of 2010, the owner of the Rainbow Center, David Cornish, donated the site to the Niagara Community College. Following this announcement, plans were unveiled to re-develop the mall as the home of Niagara Community College's culinary school. The project calls for the construction of a street level, student-run restaurant, pastry store, wine shop and Barnes and Noble Bookstore.

Niagara Community College will only take up a third of the old Rainbow Center Mall site. The rest of the site will be cleared to prepare for potential future development.[39]

AREA DEMOGRAPHICS

The population of Niagara Falls is 52,326, with a negative population growth of -5.9 percent from the period of 2000 to 2010. The area has a majority, 76.2 percent, of white residents with a median household income of $26,800.[40] With 19.5 percent of the population living below the poverty level and a 7.5 percent unemployment rate, the area shows signs of economic depression.[41]

RETAIL POTENTIAL

With the new casino, conference center and proposed Niagara Community College development, the downtown of Niagara Falls seems to project a healthy future. Despite the depressed economic state, the proposed development will aid in bringing tourism back to the area, which will in turn stimulate retail growth. The 2009 change in passport regulations, which now requires U.S. citizens to have passports to enter Canada, will perhaps curb the number of U.S. citizens choosing to access the more economically stable Canadian side of Niagara Falls. *The New York Times* cites an initial negative reaction to the new regulation, stating that it would significantly detract from tourism in the area. "The new rules could discourage millions of visitors from coming to one of the nation's most majestic and romantic tourist attractions and result in billions of dollars a year in lost revenue," writes David Staba for *The New York Times* in 2007.[42] Current statistics from the Seneca Casino, however, and the new development in the area show the opposite.

The development in and around Old Falls Street shows the city's efforts in returning the area to its original street structure. The area has been re-developed in a historically sensitive character, with cobblestone paving, wrought iron street lamps and street furniture with a vintage feel. In keeping with the proposed fresh food market concepts in Syracuse, Rochester and Buffalo, in May of 2011 an Idaho based Brix and Company has suggested the opening of a seasonal holiday market on Old Falls Street. "Niagara Holiday Market will be a European-style, outdoor/indoor holiday themed market featuring world-class offerings of regional, national and international goods, foods and entertainment," explains Mark Rivers, president and CEO of Brix.[43] While the Old Falls Street development has an overt tourism focus, it shows the tendency to return to a more authentic neighborhood approach to urban renewal.

Case Study: Walmart in the City

In 2006, Walmart announced that it would open 50 stores in economically depressed urban areas throughout the U.S. "Walmart will donate $1.5 million in cash and free advertising in those 10 communities and could look to eventually expand the program," said a company spokesperson in 2006.[44] The announcement, largely a PR stunt at the time to take the focus away from negative press, marks a new page in urban renewal. Whereas the enclosed shopping mall was promoted as the "savior" of downtown in the '70s, '80s and '90s, the Big Box is now being positioned as such. The downsizing of its large warehouse-style suburban outlets to suit the urban environment facilitates Walmart's urban plan.

A typical suburban Walmart is 195,000 square feet, but to fit into an inner-city location, Walmart needed to re-scale its stores to roughly 20,000 feet. Walmart has several "Neighborhood Markets" that offer fresh food, pharmacy, beauty, stationery and pet supplies at a size of 42,000 square feet. The "Neighborhood Market" format has fit in some urban spaces; however, Walmart has also developed a re-branded 15,000 square feet up-market grocery store called "Marketside" to suit the trend for neighborhood style fresh food markets (as discussed in the urban mall case studies).[45] "Marketside" mimics the historic feel of a local grocer with faux historic trims that are meant to meld with inner-city storefronts. To appeal to the large Hispanic populations in many inner-city areas, Walmart has created a "Supermercado de Walmart." Supermercado de Walmart is a Mexican-style supermarket offering a range of Latin American brands and products.[46]

The first urban Walmart opened in Chicago in 2006. Walmart #5,402, built in the depressed West Chicago area of Austin, marked a shift in Walmart's primarily suburban development. Walmart's urban expansion plans have sparked criticism across the board. "Dozen of stores in depressed urban communities?" says Fishman, author of *The Wal-Mart Effect*, "what a great way to exploit the urban poor as both customers and employees and get praise for stores you were going to open anyway."[47] A study of Walmart #5,402 by the Center for Urban Research and Learning at Loyola University, Chicago revealed that the store had significantly affected local business in the area. "The weight of evidence suggests that the Walmart opening on the West Side led to the displacement of a range of businesses. There is no evidence that Walmart sparked any significant net growth in economic activity or employment in the area," states the 2009 study.[48]

Since the initial entry into the Chicago inner-city market in 2006, Walmart has had difficulties getting unions onside to construct further stores. "The UFCW grocery worker's union sees Walmart's grocery-selling supercenter stores as a threat to the superior wage and health benefit packages paid by the city's traditional unionized supermarkets," writes Birchall in the *Financial Times*.[49] In 2010, after constant lobbying, Walmart gained union support and was able to secure the development of a new store on Chicago's South Side.[50] Walmart announced plans to construct 4 stores in inner-city Washington, DC, in November 2010 and is scouting for locations in New York City in the boroughs of Queens and Manhattan.

The first "Marketside" was opened in 2009 in Phoenix, Arizona. After opening four test stores that year in the same city, Walmart halted plans for further development, citing economic concerns.[51] "We're pleased with it, but at this point in time given the current condition in the marketplace ... we are not accelerating that effort until we have better data to make a decision," explained Vice Chairman Castro-Wright at the company's 2009 annual meeting.[52] The first "Supermercado de Walmart" stores opened in Houston and Arizona in 2009 and have been initially successful for the company. "While the recession has hindered Walmart's plans to open more Marketside stores, it said it is very pleased with the Supermercados," write Schwartz and Maestri.[53]

Walmart's urban expansion plans, particularly the Supermercado and Marketside models, support Leinburger's theory of a New American Dream of "walk-able urbanism." It relays that the economic crisis has caused Americans to re-visit the potential of long-neglected urban areas. In this sense, the growth of Walmart in the inner-city to address the issues of "food deserts"— inner-city areas devoid of supermarkets — seems like a welcome addition. Many are skeptical of Walmart's plans, however, believing that its urban expansion will cause the inner-city areas to sink further into depression. "With our city struggling with persistent unemployment and 3 million New Yorkers lacking access to fresh produce in their neighborhoods, the jobs problem and food desert problem are unquestionably real. But asking Walmart to fix those problems is like asking a fox to fix a henhouse," says Matt Ryan, executive director of New York Jobs with Justice and Urban Agenda.[54] Reflecting on Walmart's suburban dominance, placed in an urban setting this super-retailer may override the opportunities for localized marketplaces to create authentic neighborhoods in downtown areas. Walmart's aggressive strategy, purchasing power and retail dominance are cause for concern, as they could limit the growth of small niche retail offerings in downtown areas.

Analysis and Conclusions

The case studies presented show a failure of the enclosed shopping mall model to provide effective urban renewal. All of the studies show a similar pattern of decline. Of the four malls studied, the Main Place Mall and Galleries of Syracuse were open; however, their viability as retail centers were limited. Both the Midtown Plaza and Rainbow Center Mall were in the process of demolition and repurposing. All major renewal projects in the urban areas studied show a focus on creating an authentic neighborhood environment in the downtown area. A renewal of historic buildings and street layouts were proposed in the development of all urban areas studied. The inclusion of a "fresh food" marketplace that offered high-end localized offerings was a strategy that was proposed in all environments as a way to stimulate urban growth.

In Niagara Falls, there was a much higher emphasis on tourism to stimulate the area due to the proximity to a national landmark; however, as a whole the urban areas in the sample displayed a similar preference toward the creation of authentic neighborhood areas that would promote long-term growth rather than short-term tourist spending. Although most projects are in early stages, the urban renewal strategies support Leinburger's theory of walk-able urbanism and a return to a more community-minded approach to urban development. The presence of a Walmart as a major competitor in these areas may undermine the ability to generate an authentic neighborhood approach to urban renewal. Walmart's urban expansion plans, if enacted en masse, could replicate the blight left by the enclosed urban shopping mall. By pushing out smaller retailers the urban shopping mall left the city core devoid of vibrancy; Walmart, known as a "category killer," may function in the same way.

The next section will look at the future of retailing in the United States. A discussion on new and potential models for retail development and community engagement provides a potential picture of the future of public space.

15. The Future of Public Space in America

Based on the case studies and research presented, the regional enclosed shopping mall is on the decline. One implication of this decline is the loss of public space for the elderly and teens, which use the regional mall for their primary community and social interaction. Data collected reveals that regional malls are increasingly being replaced with Big Box power centers, which do not offer the same sense of a "town center" or public space as the enclosed shopping mall. Hybrid malls, super-regional "entertainment" centers and life-style centers are models that have replaced the regional mall in many areas across the country; however, similar to the regional mall, the models are flawed in offering a true local community environment.

The decline of the regional shopping mall offers opportunities for reassessing its use as a public space. As presented in the previous chapter, Leinburger and Glaeser both predict that Americans will return to urban environments and will stimulate a new walkable American Dream that would offer renewed possibility for the revitalization of public squares, parks and shared urban spaces. Rising oil prices and declining economic conditions may prove to aid in the creation of this new American Dream. A history of American auto-dependence and the infrastructure supporting this, however, poses a significant threat to the fruition of this new dream. If the auto-dependent American Dream shifts to a walkable American Dream, what are the implications for retail and its role in providing public space to the community? This chapter looks at proposed solutions to the generation of community space and provides multiple viewpoints on the future of American public space.

In his 1960 book *Shopping Towns USA*, Victor Gruen predicted the future of the enclosed shopping center. Gruen prophesized that atomic power would be used "for peaceful purposes" in the automation of factories, thus facilitating a shorter work week and creating more leisure time for the American public. "The shorter work week and work day will result not only in more leisure time for the individual, but in more shopping time for the family as a unit."[1] Based on this prediction, Gruen asserted a continued importance of the suburban shopping mall with an expansion of its social areas. "The pedestrian area will gain in importance as the main shopping areas, while entrances and shop windows, directed toward parking areas may gradually disappear."[2] Gruen believed that the future design of shopping malls would incorporate "a more enjoyable atmosphere" and "a better construction" that would "achieve greater integration of architecture, landscape and art."[3] In his future vision, the regional shopping mall would be an exemplar of community space, and would serve as a model for saving the downtown areas of cities. "The lessons learned and the experience gained in the planning of regional shopping centers will contribute immeasurably to the successful carrying out of this [revitalizing downtown areas] task."[4]

In 1985, the Urban Land Institute presented its predictions for the future of the enclosed shopping mall in *The Shopping Center Development Handbook*. Relating that the regional shopping mall had become "an integral part of the social structure of most communities," the ULI predicted that it would remain "an important part of the American lifestyle."[5] ULI asserted that the American family structure would change, traditional families with one partner working and the other staying at home would be replaced by both partners working, therefore making families more inclined to eat out and seek entertainment outside the home. "A greater percentage of personal services and entertainment activities, previously provided within the home, will be obtained from outside the home."[6] In their survey of U.S. demographic trends in the 1980s, the ULI predicted that Asian and Hispanic populations would grow to be a significant consumer group with "special social characteristics and needs, which the shopping center industry has not responded to directly."[7] Following these assertions, the ULI stated that despite changing demographic structures, "all of the current or emerging social changes would appear to benefit the long-term viability of shopping centers."

Significantly, in their 1985 predictions, the ULI recognized the power of off-price retailers as potential competitors to the shopping malls. "The off-price and outlet malls now being developed are seen by many as a whole new type of shopping center and by others as a temporary accommodation for tenants that are threatening to conventional retailers now but will likely be welcome in more traditional center," explains the ULI.[8] Finally, the ULI predicted the shopping center will face difficult times due to over-saturation and population stagnation, all of which will lead to the further stratification and hybridization of known shopping center models. "Retailing in general seems to be heading toward some rather dramatic restructuring in terms of traditional manufacturer/wholesaler/retailer/consumer relationships," cites the ULI. "Certainly one manifestation has been the growth in off-price retailing, a new type of discounting, which has in turn led to a new type of shopping center."[9] "Should such a restructuring take place," warns the ULI, "it will have a significant impact on how shopping centers are developed, organized, and managed."[10]

While Gruen's predictions for a "shorter work-week" facilitated by atomic power was not realized, nor was his assertion of the ability of urban shopping malls to save the downtown areas of cities across the country, he was correct in assuming that the urban environments would eventually become a focus for retail and community regeneration. This can be seen in current revitalization efforts taking place in urban areas (as covered in the case studies in Chapter 14) as well as the increased focus of Big Box retailer Walmart to populate these areas. Leinburger and Glaeser's predictions that the new American Dream is an urban, rather than a suburban, dream also support this theory. What Gruen was unable to predict, however, was the rise and eventual dominance of the discount retailer in the suburban environment and with it the degeneration of pedestrian and community spaces. As discussed in previous chapters, the Big Box power center, offering "off-price" retailing, has eclipsed the regional shopping mall as a model for suburban retail construction. This development has led to a decrease in areas for pedestrian traffic and social spaces in the commercial environment. While this represents a regression of the public space in suburban communities, it also offers opportunities for repurposing the use of privatized enclosed retail spaces as a replacement for genuine public spaces. The decline of the regional shopping mall can also be seen as a factor in stimulating a new retail vision, one that more fully incorporates the community into the planning of the center.

"The regional shopping center faces a crisis today; some even speculate that it might die," writes Mattson. "Therefore, it is important to recognize that there are bottom-line economic reasons for developers to listen to those who want to make the mall into something more than a conduit for consumerism."[11] In discussing the future of retail space in America, the ULI notes that existing planned communities will increasingly adapt regional shopping mall and strip malls into "town centers." "Retail in planned communities or in locations that serve new communities will be configured as town centers, expanding the early function of the marketplace as the central part of a community," explains the ULI.[12] Some developers have sought to repurpose the regional mall in a way that offers the community a mixed-use space with a significant amount of opportunities for genuine community interaction. Mattson cites a project in Willingboro, New Jersey, in which a developer turned a ghost mall into a center that mixes smaller retail and light industry with a library and community college.[13] "The Willingboro Town Center development plan employs sustainable building practices in creating a mix of retail and commercial establishments, adult housing and community-oriented institutions," says *Real Estate Weekly*.[14] A further example of renewing a shopping mall by making it a genuine place of civic and public space is Mashpee Commons on Cape Cod. Developer Doug Storrs transformed a derelict strip mall into a mixed-use space that includes stores, offices, residential space, a post office, library, church school and police station. Storrs developed the space in a way that assimilates characteristics of historic New England towns into the center and incorporates the use of a public square.[15] The mixed-use development is not a new concept; it was introduced as early as the 1960s in the development of urban shopping malls such as Midtown Plaza, which incorporated offices with retail and community space.

Mixed-use development today, however, as illustrated by the Willingboro and Mashpee Commons projects, has a much more clearly defined focus on the community as a whole and incorporates the elements of a traditional town center with equal grounding in the commercial elements of the space. Community services, such as libraries and churches, are integrated into the design of the center as standard and not, as often occur in the planning of a shopping mall, as a secondary concession to community groups. The ULI asserts that this model will replace the regional shopping mall with "streetfront retail" and "public space and may also have residential, civic or other commercial uses vertically or horizontally integrated with the retail."[16]

"The mall is an island — a retail venue surrounded by a sea of parking, and set apart from everything except highways — does not meet the expectations of 21st century shoppers," says the ULI. "Today's shoppers demand a more urban experience — specifically, pedestrian friendly street front retail."[17] The urban areas of the country have begun to come back in focus as potential sites for growth. In its *Retail Development Handbook*, the ULI asserts that changing demographic factors will create a focus on generating an urban environment in the suburbs. The ULI predicts that old and young will converge in tastes for mixed-use development, creating a need for urban environments that encompass "shopping, entertainment, and public transportation" in a "high-density setting."[18] Young and old will prefer this urban high-density environment as opposed to the "boredom of single-purpose, low-density development," explains the ULI. Therefore, the ULI suggests that the construction of high-density urban housing — in areas that have been initially built up as suburban, low-density, single purpose housing — should be a focus for developers.[19] "Developers who have recently marketed housing above retail confirm that retail sets the tone of the project and that residents include a mix of retirees, professionals of all ages and young singles," says the ULI.[20]

Writing in 1973, Gruen asserted the relevance of trade in shaping and revitalizing the urban environment. "Thus it appears that trade, in following its own economic interests, has made as so often throughout history, a meaningful contribution to the shaping of the urban environment."[21] As predicted by Leinburger, Glaeser and the ULI, the urban areas across the United States will again become a major focus for retail activity. "The untapped market potential of urban communities is vast," explains the ULI. "The 2008 opening of DC USA, a vertical center in Washington D.C., anchored by a Target, brought major retail to a neighborhood dominated by an immigrant and minority population. Within weeks of opening, it became a destination for the surrounding segment of the city, drawing from higher-income areas, as this type of shopping previously required travel to the outlying suburbs."[22]

As discussed in Chapter 14, Walmart has made a similar push to the urban areas, announcing in April 2007 that it would "build stores in fifty urban areas around the United States that are economically depressed."[23] Although these types of urban developments are often more costly, cites Leinburger, due to "more expensive multiple-story construction, better finishes, and increased marketing risks," they are essential in creating a viable urban environment.[24] While many community members are suspect of large super-retailers entering into urban neighborhoods and potentially destroying any existing local retail, "the level of service needed for a downtown or other walk-able urban place to complete with regional malls, is much higher than any city can afford to provide alone."[25] Therefore, retail giants such as Walmart and Target will be able to provide the sort of capital needed to regenerate urban areas. Increased dominance of these retailers is worrying, however, as it may lead to homogenization of the urban environment, as it has done in suburbia. The ULI, however, insists that the influx of Big Boxes in the urban environment will lead to an overall influx of retail opportunities, thus stimulating the growth of not only the retail but also social and community aspects. "These experiences [developments such as DC USA] will become commonplace," asserts the ULI, "the range of interested stores will expand, and even more varied opportunities for retail development will become available. Coupled with city support for infill and revitalization, most of these projects will likely be involved in some form of increasingly sophisticated public/private partnership."[26]

The continued rise of the Internet as a consumer tool will re-define American retail environments. "The connection between highly branded virtual stores and their actual stores is one indication of the future of retail development," cites the ULI.[27] A prediction that consumers will increasingly choose their products online before shopping, along with the realization that many goods are more suited to purchase in the online environment, will shape the way that retail spaces of the future are organized, says the ULI. Already some large department store chains and large bookstores have succumbed to changing market trends and this will continue to be the case. "The most successful retail centers will capitalize on this [the tactile and experiential] aspect of shopping, continually adapting to the public's tastes in social settings, need for community and search for entertainment." The ULI asserts: "Outdoor public spaces and clusters of restaurants and movie theaters have successfully become established anchors [of malls] in the last ten years."[28] This will continue to be the case, with shopping malls becoming more "outdoor," "entertainment" and "cultural" based centers with an increased community, rather than strictly retail, focus. "[Cultural and community] centers will become the 'third place' in people's lives, and customers will shop when they go out rather then go out to shop."[29] The ULI cites the Village at Shirlington in Arlington, Virginia, which has a playhouse and a library housed in the playhouse, as well as Rancho Cucamonga, California, which incorporates a cultural center with a library and children's theater, as exemplars of this model.

In response to environmental concerns of global warming and depleting fossil fuels, the retail environments of the future, predicts the ULI, will be "greener." "Retail center developers who ignore the trend to build green will soon be behind the times," says the ULI. Developers will be increasingly employing architects to create structures that "use less energy, produce fewer carbon emissions, and make a contribution to the surrounding environment."[30] Thus, the ULI predicts that retailers will opt for smaller stores and "main street-type developments with buildings on blocks rather than strip buildings" to promote a more walkable environment.[31] "Consumers will recognize well-planned retail projects within walking distance of transit as smart, trendy, and worth their patronage," says the ULI, "even if they arrive by car!"[32] This type of development, explains Leinburger, will not only ease the impact on the environment, but will "build wealth for the residents and property owners, revive or continue the economic growth by providing increased densities in existing communities, and take the pressure off land consumption on the fringe of the metropolitan areas."[33]

"The car enables us to go out into the world ourselves. Communication of ideas and emotions thus established has the effect of bringing the country into a closer unity," wrote Bel Geddes in 1940. "In this way an enormous influence is brought to bear on the manners and morals of this nation. Old ideas of education are revised; new antidotes for ennui are discovered. Isolated communities are knit together and congested centers can spread out."[34] Bel Geddes was correct in asserting that the car "enables us to go out into the world ourselves," but in this sense it has also isolated the average American from his fellow man. The car, as predicted by Bel Geddes, has brought many areas that were once difficult to reach within our grasps, however, it has also stratified communities by creating homogenous suburban environments. The automobile played a large role in shaping contemporary American values and lifestyles. America, in its current state, is an auto-reliant society linked by a vast series of highways which provide individuals with the freedom to come and go as they please. The shopping mall was a natural extension of this auto-dependency and suffices to provide an indoor pedestrian paradise with an exterior of bland concrete and tarmac so that the consumer can park his car. As suggested by the dominance of Big Box retailers and the viability of super-regional malls, the automobile is still the most popular means of transportation in the United States. Economic and environmental factors will dictate the future of the automobile as the primary means of transport for Americans, and as suggested in this chapter, it may only be a matter of years before walkable urban environments replace suburban sprawl.

"As a democratic society, we need places where citizens can congregate and associate with one another," writes Mattson. "Public space is a prerequisite for a healthy society. But this sort of argument often sounds abstract in the world of real-estate and development."[35] Often the shopping mall's negative tendencies resonate more strongly than the positive, and in this sense reinvigorating the regional shopping mall with a more community-minded perspective will serve to produce more meaningful public spaces for the next generation of Americans. Writing in 1940, Bel Geddes proclaimed that suburban life would be "full of light, fresh air, open parks," and "easy movement.... The man of 1960 will more naturally place his full part in the community and develop his mind and body."[36]

As a physical environment, both the suburban environment and the shopping mall can be seen as deceptively persuasive and yet sterile in its ability to provide the citizen with a true form of public space. The shopping mall, as a private space, demands a sense of control that is at odds with the constitutional rights guaranteed in true public places. "Developers are starting to learn that people are not just consumers but also citizens," says Mattson. "That is what makes the issue of the civic redesign of shopping centers so pertinent today."[37] Provided that the models discussed in this chapter come to fruition, and are not stalled by the continued preference for personal auto-transport and the proliferation of the Big Box model, the potential for community minded, walkable environments is vast. "The environment in which we live out our lives in is not a cafeteria containing an endless variety of passively arrayed settings and experiences," says Oldenburg, "it is an active, dictorial force that adds experiences or subtracts them according to the way it has been shaped."[38] Should this new walkable American Dream eventuate, future generations of Americans will experience the true community feel of a Main Street and not simply the kitsch recreations in shopping malls and theme parks. Suburban neighborhoods will become dynamic interdependent communities and not sterile homogenous boxes separated by manicured lawns. "If there is one message I wish to leave with those who despair of suburbia's lifeless streets, of the plastic places along our 'strips' or of the congested and inhospitable mess that is 'downtown,' it is: *It doesn't have to be like this!*" writes Oldenburg.[39]

"Malls embody the values and ideals of what we might call 'commercial utopianism,'" says Farrell, "freedom, abundance, leisure happiness, individualism and community."[40] As this book asserts, the shopping mall represents a utopian Main Street vision. As a physical space, it takes cues from historic American Main Streets and mixes them with the spiritual signifiers of light, water, bodies and "centeredness." The mall has been described as an American "temple of consumerism" and in many communities it has become more than simply a consumer space, it has replaced the church as an integral part of the community. The loss of this space may happen gradually, as seen through case studies, or perhaps rapidly should economic forces dramatically change course. However, the research presented in this book relates that this model is on the decline and that retail in suburban areas will take on new forms. The proposed models for revitalizing retail environments, disussed in this chapter, all provide opportunities for increased community interaction and a more relevant and authentic social space to support human development.

Gruen's enclosed shopping mall design, although posing issues of control, environmental and social concern, cannot be dismissed as a completely flawed model. It has provided Americans, young and old, with a relevant form of public space for generations and it has served as a cultural symbol for the power of American capitalism. In this sense, it lives up to Gruen's original conception of "an experimental utopia," for the mall provides the consumer with a fantasy world of excess, a permanently temperate world of bright lights, fountains and palm trees, a world where consumption can give us the "salvation" that we are looking for in our daily lives. Whatever the future may hold for this model, the regional enclosed shopping mall will always remain a symbol of the 1950s American optimism and need for control that permeated the nation. For current and previous generations of Americans, it will live on in their collective memories as a place where a significant amount of formative and elder years were spent walking the halls with friends. The enclosed regional shopping mall will also live on in the films and novels of the last fifty years, which frequently used this "temple of consumerism" as the natural backdrop for discussing the American condition. While not an ideal form of civic space, it is, after all, a genuine American creation, a capitalist "utopia," that embodies American's unique brand of freedom. It is an environment that, however impermanent its physical presence may prove to be, will live on in our collective memories for many years to come.

Notes

Introduction

1. Mark Dery, "Dawn of the Dead Mall." *Change Observer*, December 11, 2009. http://changeobserver.designobserver.com/feature/dawn-of-the-dead-mall/11747/ (accessed 11 November 2010).

2. Dery, "Dawn of the Dead Mall."

3. "Birth, Death and Shopping," *The Economist*, December 19, 2007. http://www.economist.com/node/10278717?story_id=10278717 (accessed December 15, 2010).

4. James J. Farrell, *One Nation Under Goods: Malls and the Seductions of American Shopping* (Washington, DC: Smithsonian Books, 2003), xii.

5. Farrell, xi.

6. Farrell, 264.

7. Jon Phal, *Shopping Malls and Other Sacred Spaces: Putting God in Place* (Grand Rapids, MI: Brazos Press, 2003), 67.

8. Phal, 65.

9. Karen Stabiner, "New Lives for 'Dead' Suburban Malls." *The New York Times*, June 28, 2011. http://newoldage.blogs.nytimes.com/2011/01/21/new-lives-for-dead-suburban-malls/ (accessed January 25, 2011).

10. Charles Redell, "Dead Malls." http://sustainableindustries.com/articles/2009/03/dead-malls?page=3 (accessed November 20, 2010).

11. Farrell, xv.

12. Ray Oldenburg, *The Great Good Place* (New York: Paragon Books, 1989), 13.

13. Christopher B. Leinburger, *The Option of Urbanism* (Washington, DC: Island Press, 2008), 176.

Chapter 1

1. Anita Kramer, *Retail Development* (Washington, DC: ULI — the Urban Land Institute, 2008), 4.

2. Kramer, *Retail Development*, 4.

3. Kramer, 27.

4. Kramer, 28.

5. Kramer, 28.

6. Kramer, 28.

7. Alex Wall, *Victor Gruen: From Urban Shop to New City* (Barcelona: Actar, 2005), 12.

8. In Mark Dery, "Dawn of the Dead Mall," *Change Observer*, December 11, 2009, http://changeobserver.designobserver.com/feature/dawn-of-the-dead-mall/11747/ (accessed 11 November 2010).

9. Wall, *Urban Shop*, 56.

10. Harvey M. Rubenstein, *Pedestrian Malls, Streetscapes and Urban Spaces* (New York: John Wiley and Sons, 1992), 14.

11. Wall, 65.

12. Wall, 65.

13. Wall, 67.

14. Wall, 85.

15. Wall, 92.

16. Victor Gruen and Larry Smith, *Shopping Towns USA* (New York: Reinhold, 1960), 149.

17. Wall, 96.

18. Wall, 97. Quoted from Victor Gruen, "The Planned Shopping Centers of America." *Zodiac* 1, 1957, 159–167, 167.

19. Wall, 99. Quoted from Victor Gruen, "Winter or Summer," *Architectural Forum*, March 1953, 126–132, 127.

20. Wall, 101.

21. Margaret Crawford, "The World in a Shopping Mall," in *Variations of a Theme Park*, ed., Michael Sorkin (New York: Hill and Wang, 1992), 21.

22. Crawford, "World in a Shopping Mall," 21.

23. William Kowinski, *The Malling of America* (New York: William Morrow, 1985), 274.

24. Wall, 99.

25. Wall, 99.

26. In Wall, 110.

27. Christopher B. Leinburger, *The Option*

of Urbanism (Washington, DC: Island Press, 2008), 43.

28. Leinburger, *The Option of Urbanism*, 41. Leinburger notes the term "edge cities" was coined by Joel Garreau in a 1989 book by that name.

29. Kramer, 31.

30. Kramer, 32.

31. ULI, *Shopping Center Development Handbook* (Washington, DC: author, 1985), 4.

32. Kramer, 31.

33. ULI, *Shopping Center Handbook*, 5.

34. David J. Smiley and Mark Robbins, eds., *Sprawl and Public Space: Redressing the Mall* (Washington, DC: National Endowment for the Arts, 2002), 26.

35. ULI, *Shopping Center Handbook*, 14.

36. ULI, *Shopping Center Handbook*, 14.

37. Kowinski, *Malling of America*, 21.

38. Kramer, 33.

39. Leinburger, 46.

40. Kramer, 18.

41. Kramer, 34.

42. Kramer, 18.

43. Daniel Taub and Brian Louis, "General Growth Files Biggest U.S. Property Bankruptcy," April 16, 2009. http://www.bloomberg.com/apps/news?pid=newsarchive&sid=anaZwxRpYcTw (accessed November 11, 2010).

44. Kris Hudson and Vanessa O'Connell, "Recession Turns Malls into Ghost Towns," *Wall Street Journal Online*, April 22, 2009, http://online.wsj.com/article/SB124294047987244803.html (accessed November 11, 2010).

45. Kramer, 37.

46. "Birth, Death and Shopping," *The Economist*, December 19, 2007, http://www.economist.com/node/10278717?story_id=10278717 (accessed December 15, 2010).

47. Ray Oldenburg, *The Great Good Place* (New York: Paragon Books, 1989), 17.

Chapter 2

1. Oldenburg, *Great Good Place*, 4.

2. Norman Bel Geddes, *Magic Motorways* (New York: Random House, 1940), 6.

3. Geddes, *Magic Motorways*, 8.

4. Leinburger, 15.

5. Leinburger, 15.

6. Jon Blackwell, "1951: American Dream Houses, All in a Row," http://www.capitalcentury.com/1951.html (accessed January 11, 2011).

7. Blackwell, "American Dream Houses."

8. Kenneth T. Jackson, "The Baby Boom and the Age of the Subdivision," *Crabgrass Frontier: The Suburbanization of the United States* (New York: Oxford University Press, 1985), 234.

9. Blackwell, "American Dream Houses."

10. Blackwell, "American Dream Houses."

11. Gwendolyn Wright, *Building the Dream: A Social History of Housing in America* (Cambridge, MA: MIT Press, 1983), 258.

12. Chester Liebs, *Main Street to Miracle Mile: American Roadside Architecture* (Toronto: Bulfinch Press, 1985), 28.

13. Oldenburg, 4.

14. Wright, *Building the Dream*, 247.

15. Wright, 247.

16. Jackson, "Baby Boom," 239.

17. Blackwell, "American Dream Houses."

18. Leinburger, 29.

19. Oldenburg, 4.

20. Oldenburg, 4.

21. Jackson, "Baby Boom," 235.

22. Lyndon B. Johnson, *Lyndon B. Johnson, 1963–1964 (In Two Books): Containing the Public Messages, Speeches and Statements of the President* [Book 2] (Ann Arbor: University of Michigan Press, 2005), 669.

23. Oldenburg, 23.

24. Oldenburg, 8.

25. Wright, 258.

26. Wright, 256.

27. Oldenburg, 5.

28. Oldenburg, 8.

29. Chester Liebs, *Main Street to Miracle Mile: American Roadside Architecture* (Toronto: Bulfinch Press, 1985), 29.

30. Oldenburg, 119.

31. Lyn Spigel, *Make Room for the TV: Television and the Family Ideal in Postwar America* (Chicago: University of Chicago Press, 1992), 32.

32. Spigel, *Make Room for the TV*, 33.

33. Spigel, 78.

34. Kowinski, 71.

35. Leinburger, 45.

36. Leinburger, 46.

37. Leinburger, 53.

38. Leinburger, 55.

39. Leinburger, 54.

40. Oldenburg, 4.

41. Leinburger, 52.

42. Leinburger, 52.

43. Kowinski, 67.

44. Sloan Wilson, *The Man in a Grey Flannel Suit* (New York: Simon and Schuster, 1955).

45. Wilson, *Grey Flannel Suit*, 98.

46. In Leinburger, 51–52.

47. *American Beauty*, directed by Sam Mendes (1999; Universal City, CA: Dreamworks Video, 2000), DVD.

Chapter 3

1. Leinburger, 29.

2. D. Bradford Hunt, "Model Cities,"

http://www.encyclopedia.chicagohistory.org/pages/832.html (accessed July 7, 2011).

3. Wall, 184.

4. Victor Gruen, *The Heart of Our Cities* (New York: Simon and Schuster, 1964), 27.

5. Gruen, *Heart of Our Cities*, 212.

6. Gruen, *Heart of Our Cities*, 217.

7. Gruen, *Heart of Our Cities*, 318.

8. Gruen, *Heart of Our Cities*, 320.

9. Gruen, *Heart of Our Cities*, 320.

10. Gruen, *Heart of Our Cities*, 223.

11. Victor Gruen, *Centers for the Urban Environment* (New York: Van Nostrand Company, 1973), 196.

12. Leinburger, 29.

13. Barry Maitland, *Shopping Malls Planning and Design* (London: Construction, 1985), 66.

14. ULI, *Shopping Center Handbook*, 7.

15. Maitland, *Planning and Design*, 67.

16. Maitland, 68.

17. ULI, *Shopping Center Handbook*, 8.

18. Maitland, 69.

19. Alexandra Lange, "Rebooting the Festival Marketplace," *Design Observer*, January 21, 2009, http://observatory.designobserver.com/feature/rebooting-the-festival-marketplace/7927/cookplusfox.com (accessed July 7, 2011).

20. Lange, "Rebooting the Festival Marketplace."

21. Kramer, 15.

22. Leinburger, 68.

23. Edward Glaeser, *Triumph of the City* (London: Macmillan, 2011), 53.

24. Glaeser, *Triumph of the City*, 54.

25. Glaeser, 41.

26. Alex P. Kellogg, "Detroit Shrinks Itself, Historic Homes and All," *The Wall Street Journal*, May 14, 2010, http://online.wsj.com/article/SB10001424052748703950804575242433435338728.html (accessed July 7, 2011).

27. Dejan Sudjic, "Making Cities Work: Detroit," *BBC News*, July 10, 2006, http://news.bbc.co.uk/2/hi/americas/5165808.stm (accessed July 7, 2011).

28. Jodi Wilgoren, "Detroit Urban Renewal Without the Renewal," *The New York Times*, July 7, 2002, http://nytimes.com/2002/07/07/national/07DETR.html (accessed July 7, 2011).

29. Wilgoren, "Detroit Urban Renewal Without the Renewal."

30. Justin Sondel, "No Vacancy," *Artvoice Daily*, November 11, 2010, http://artvoice.com/issues/v9n45/no_vacancy (accessed July 7, 2011).

31. Sondel, "No Vacancy."

32. Glaeser, 67.

33. Leinburger, 67.

34. Leinburger, 60.

Chapter 4

1. David R. Loy, "Religion and the Market," http://www.religiousconsultation.org/loy.htm (accessed June 7, 2010).

2. Max Weber, *The Protestant Ethic and the Spirit of Capitalism* (London: Unwin University Books, 1970).

3. Loy, "Religion and the Market."

4. Loy, "Religion and the Market."

5. Jon Pahl, *Shopping Malls and Other Sacred Spaces: Putting God in Place* (Grand Rapids, MI: Brazos Press, 2003), 69.

6. Weber, *Protestant Ethic*, 65.

7. Karl Polanyi, *The Great Transformation: The Political and Economic Origins of Our Time* (Boston: Beacon Press, 2001), 73.

8. Polanyi, *Great Transformation*, 73.

9. Weber, 117.

10. Weber, 118.

11. Weber, 118.

12. Weber, 121.

13. Polanyi, 73.

14. Polanyi, 79.

15. Weber, 64.

16. Weber, 53.

17. Weber, 53.

18. Weber, 53.

19. Weber, 63.

20. Weber, 72.

21. Pahl, 67.

22. Loy, "Religion and the Market."

23. Ira G. Zepp, *The New Religious Image of Urban America: The Shopping Mall as Ceremonial Center* (Niwot: University of Colorado Press, 1997), 144.

24. Pahl, 75.

25. Zepp, *New Religious Image*, 31.

26. Zepp, 57.

27. Zepp, 59.

28. Zepp, 59.

29. Zepp, 60.

30. Zepp, 53.

31. Zepp, 35.

32. Zepp, 37.

33. Zepp, 37.

34. Pahl, 72.

35. Zepp, 127.

36. Pahl, 72.

37. Pahl, 72.

38. Pahl, 73.

39. Jonathan Gruber and Daniel M. Hungerman, "The Church Versus the Mall: What Happens When Religion Faces Increased Secular Competition?" *The Quarterly Journal of Economics* (May 2008): 831.

40. Pahl, 67.

41. Pahl, 68.

42. Russell H. Conwell, *Acres of Diamonds* (New York: Harpers and Brothers, 1933), 16.

43. Conwell, *Acres of Diamonds*, 20.
44. Pahl, 68.
45. Pahl, 69.
46. Gruber and Hungerman, "Church Versus the Mall," 883.
47. Gruber and Hungerman, 832.
48. Gruber and Hungerman, 857.
49. Mall Area Religious Council, "MARC—The Basics," http://www.meaning store.org/marcdescription.htm (accessed June 7, 2010).
50. Diane Dietz, "Churches, Shopping Centers Forge Uneasy Bonds in Tight Economy," *The Register-Guard*, August 8, 2010, http://spe cial.registerguard.com/csp/cms/sites/web/business/25115202-41/mall-church-churches-gateway-space.csp (accessed January 20, 2011).
51. Dietz, "Uneasy Bonds."
52. Dietz, "Uneasy Bonds."
53. Dietz, "Uneasy Bonds."
54. Polanyi, 75.
55. Loy, "Religion and the Market."
56. Loy, "Religion and the Market."
57. Gruber and Hungerman, 859.
58. Loy, "Religion and the Market."
59. James Howard Kunstler, *Geography of Nowhere: The Rise and Decline of America's Man-made Landscape* (New York: Simon and Schuster, 1993), 27.
60. Dietz, "Uneasy Bonds."
61. Dietz, "Uneasy Bonds."
62. Pahl, 75.
63. Zepp, 192.
64. Pahl, 74.
65. Zepp, 14.

Chapter 5

1. Richard V. Francaviglia, *Main Street Revisited: Time, Space, and Image Building in Small-Town America* (Iowa City: University of Iowa Press, 1996), 1.
2. Francaviglia, 2.
3. Francaviglia, 145.
4. Francaviglia, 151.
5. Francaviglia, 155.
6. Francaviglia, 9.
7. Liebs, 7.
8. Liebs, 9.
9. Francaviglia, 10.
10. Francaviglia, 11.
11. Francaviglia, 20.
12. Francaviglia, 22.
13. Francaviglia, 23.
14. Francaviglia, 35.
15. Francaviglia, 19.
16. Francaviglia, 28.
17. Francaviglia, 35.
18. Francaviglia, 35.
19. Liebs, 9.
20. Liebs, 14.
21. Oldenburg, 112.
22. Kunstler, 185.
23. Liebs, 8.
24. Oldenburg, 107.
25. Kunstler, 121.
26. Francaviglia, 68.
27. Francaviglia, 154.
28. In Francaviglia, 158.
29. Oldenburg, 118.
30. Francaviglia, 104.
31. Kramer, 347.
32. ULI, *Shopping Center Handbook*, 259.
33. Francaviglia, 166.
34. Oldenburg, 119.
35. Francaviglia, 167.
36. Francaviglia, 179.
37. Francaviglia, 192.

Chapter 6

1. Zepp, 70.
2. Ann Sloan Devlin, *What Americans Build and Why: Psychological Perspectives* (New York: Cambridge University Press, 2010), 250.
3. Devlin, 251.
4. *Cambridge Dictionaries Online*, http://dictionary.cambridge.org/dictionary/british/mall-rat?q=mall+rat (accessed November 11, 2010).
5. *Mallrats*, directed by Kevin Smith (1995; Universal City, CA: Universal Studios Home Video, 1999), DVD.
6. Kowinski, 33–34.
7. *Clueless*, directed by Amy Heckerling (1995; Hollywood, CA: Paramount Home Entertainment, 2005), DVD.
8. Paco Underhill, *The Call of the Mall* (New York: Simon and Schuster, 2004), 132.
9. Devlin, 252.
10. Devlin, 252.
11. Susan Kuchinskas, "Market Focus: Best Behavior," *OMMA: The Magazine of Online Media, Marketing and Advertising*, November 1, 2009, http://www.mediapost.com/publications/?fa=Articles.showArticle&art_aid=116122 (accessed November 11, 2010).
12. Devlin, 250.
13. Devlin, 250.
14. Kowinski, 351.
15. James J. Farrell, *One Nation Under Goods: Malls and the Seductions of American Shopping* (Washington, DC: Smithsonian Books, 2003), 102.
16. Andra Case, interviewed by Lisa Scharoun, 15 November 2010, Pyramid Companies, Syracuse, New York.
17. Kowinski, 351.

18. Farrell, *Nation Under Goods*, 101.

19. Devlin, 252.

20. Youn-Kyung Kim, Eun Young Kim, and Jikyeong Kang, "Teens' Mall Shopping Motivations: Functions of Loneliness and Media Usage," *Family and Consumer Sciences Research Journal* 32, No. 2 (December 2003): 141–142.

21. Kim, Kim, and Kang, "Teens' Mall Shopping Motivations: Functions of Loneliness and Media Usage," 145.

22. Farrell, 103.

23. Larry M. Elkin, "Teenagers and 'Sense of Mall.'" *Business Insider*, December 28, 2010. http://www.businessinsider.com/teenagers-and-sense-of-mall-2010-12 (accessed January 20, 2011)

24. Kowinski, 251.

25. Teresa Pitman, "Hanging Out at the Mall: Why Does Your Teen Always Want to Hang Out at the Mall — Without You?" *Today's Parent* (August 2003), http://www.todaysparent.com/teen/behaviordevelopment/article.jsp?content=20030709_103106_4216 (accessed January 20, 2011).

26. Kuchinskas, "Market Focus: Best Behavior."

27. Seung-Hee Lee, Sharron J. Lennon, and Nancy A. Rudd. "Compulsive Consumption Tendencies Among Television Shoppers." *Family and Consumer Sciences Research Journal* 28, No. 4 (2000): 463–488.

28. Julie Baker and Diana Haytko, "The Mall as Entertainment: Exploring Teen Girls' Total Shopping Experiences," *Journal of Shopping Center Research*, 7 (2000): 29–58.

29. Mark Howard Moss, *Shopping as an Entertainment Experience* (Lanham, MD: Lexington Books, 2007), 3.

30. Devlin, 251.

31. Sarah B. Miller, "At Shopping Malls, Teens' Hanging Out Is Wearing Thin," *The Christian Science Monitor*, August 11, 2005, http://www.csmonitor.com/2005/0811/p01s01-ussc.html (accessed January 20, 2011).

32. Devlin, 251.

33. Devlin, 251.

34. Miller, "At Shopping Malls, Teens' Hanging Out Is Wearing Thin."

35. Pitman, "Hanging Out at the Mall: Why Does Your Teen Always Want to Hang Out at the Mall — Without You?"

36. Andrea Chang, "Free-spending Teens Return to Malls."

37. Kuchinskas, "Market Focus: Best Behavior."

38. Megan L. Thomas, "For Teens, Bleak Job Picture Not Looking Brighter," http://www.msnbc.msn.com/id/38666248/ns/business-eye_on_the_economy/# (accessed January 24, 2011).

39. Thomas, "For Teens, Bleak Job Picture Not Looking Brighter."

40. Thomas, "For Teens, Bleak Job Picture Not Looking Brighter."

41. Jason Damas and Ross Schendel, *Labelscar.com* (blog), http://www.labelscar.com/.

42. J.J. Buechner, "Mohawk Mall: Schenectady, NY," *Deadmalls.com* (blog), June 30, 2009, http://www.deadmalls.com/malls/mohawk_mall.html (accessed January 20, 2011).

43. Brett Castleberry, "Colonial Plaza Mall: Orlando, FL," *Deadmalls.com* (blog), December 2, 2006, http://www.deadmalls.com/malls/colonial_plaza_mall.html (accessed January 20, 2011).

44. Erica Hayes, "Rainbow Centre Factory Outlet Mall," *Deadmalls.com* (blog), July 8, 2003, http://www.deadmalls.com/malls/rainbow_centre_factory_outlet_mall.html (accessed January 20, 2011).

Chapter 7

1. David Lindberg, "Mall Walking — a Great Way For Seniors and Elderly to Exercise and Interact," http://www.examiner.com/eldercare-in-pittsburgh/mall-walking-a-great-way-for-seniors-and-elderly-to-exercise-and-interact (accessed February 8, 2011).

2. George H. Lewis, "Community Through Exclusion and Illusion: The Creation of Social Worlds in an American Shopping Mall," *Journal of Popular Culture* 24, No. 2 (Fall 1990): 126.

3. Lewis, "Community Through Exclusion and Illusion," 126.

4. Danielle Frascone, "The Mall and the Value of Social Interactions," http://www.helium.com/items/775991-the-mall-and-the-value-of-social-interactions (accessed February 8, 2011).

5. U.S. Census Bureau, "The Next Four Decades: The Older Population in the United States: 2010 to 2050," http://www.census.gov/population/www/projections/reports.html (accessed January 11, 2011).

6. MetLife Mature Market Institute, "A Demographic Profile of Americans 65+," http://www.metlife.com/assets/cao/mmi/publications/Profiles/mmi-65+-demographic-profile.pdf (accessed January 11, 2011).

7. MetLife Mature Market Institute, "A Demographic Profile."

8. James R. Lumpkin, "Shopping Orientation Segmentation of the Elderly Consumer," *Journal of the Academy of Marketing Science* 13, No. 2 (Spring 1985): 282.

9. Lumpkin, "Shopping Orientation Segmentation of the Elderly Consumer," 284.

10. Stringy, Joseph M., *Handbook of Quality-of-life Research: An Ethical Marketing Perspective* (Norwell, MA: Kluwer, 2001), 241.

11. Dawn Fowler Graham, I. Graham, and M.J. MacLean, "Going to the Mall: A Leisure Activity of Urban Elderly People," *Canadian Journal on Aging* 10, No. 4 (Winter 1991): 345–358.

12. Lewis, "Community Through Exclusion and Illusion," 126.

13. Lewis, "Community Through Exclusion and Illusion," 128.

14. Lewis, "Community Through Exclusion and Illusion," 134.

15. Zepp, 70.

16. Zepp, 72.

17. Devlin, 253.

18. Zepp, 71.

19. Zepp, 72.

20. Zepp, 20.

21. In Dorene Internicola, "These Malls Are Made for Walking," *Reuters*, January 25, 2010, http://www.reuters.com/article/2010/01/25/us-fitness-malls-walking-idUSTRE60O24F20100125 (accessed November 11, 2010).

22. Zepp, 67.

23. Zepp, 67.

24. Lewis, "Community Through Exclusion and Illusion," 134.

25. Oldenburg, 50.

26. Oldenburg, 49.

27. Alexandra Cawthorne, "Elderly Poverty: The Challenge Before Us," Center for American Progress, http://www.americanprogress.org/issues/2008/07/elderly_poverty.html (accessed August 2, 2010), 4.

28. Lewis, "Community Through Exclusion and Illusion," 134.

29. Cawthorne, "Elderly Poverty: The Challenge Before Us," 1.

30. Cawthorne, "Elderly Poverty: The Challenge Before Us," 3.

31. Zepp, 70.

32. Cawthorne, "Elderly Poverty: The Challenge Before Us," 3.

33. Cawthorne, "Elderly Poverty: The Challenge Before Us," 3.

34. Experience Works, "Older Low-Income Workers Face Historic Crisis," http://www.experienceworks.org/site/PageServer?pagename=Overlooked_and_Underserved (accessed August 2, 2010).

35. In Internicola, "These Malls Are Made for Walking."

36. Ralph E. Warner, *Get a Life: You Don't Need a Million to Retire*, 5th ed. (Berkeley, CA: Nolo, 2004), 72.

37. Warner, *Don't Need a Million*, 72.

38. Lewis, "Community Through Exclusion and Illusion," 127.

39. Lewis, "Community Through Exclusion and Illusion," 134.

40. Lewis, "Community Through Exclusion and Illusion," 134.

41. Kate Stone Lombardi, "In Curbing Walking Sprees, a Mall Sets Off Protests," *The New York Times*, March 2, 2008, http://www.nytimes.com/2008/03/02/nyregion/nyregionspecial2/02mallwe.html?pagewanted=all (accessed June 6, 2011).

42. Lombardi, "In Curbing Walking Sprees, a Mall Sets Off Protests."

43. Zepp, 72.

44. Charles Fishman, *The Wal-Mart Effect: How the World's Most Powerful Company Really Works, and How It's Transforming the American Economy* (New York: Penguin Press, 2006).

45. Hunter Interests Incorporated, "Medical Malls: National Trends," *Medical Mall Planning Study Feasibility of Four Different Medical Malls in Prince George's County.* (December 2007): 11, http://www.pgplanning.org/Projects/Completed_Projects/Medical_Mall_Planning_Study.htm (accessed August 8, 2010).

46. Hunter Interests Incorporated, "Medical Malls: National Trends," 11.

47. Hunter Interests Incorporated, "Medical Malls: National Trends," 12.

48. Hunter Interests Incorporated, "Medical Malls: National Trends," 13.

49. Zepp, 7.

50. Lewis, "Community Through Exclusion and Illusion," 121.

Chapter 8

1. Lynn A. Staeheli and Don Mitchell, "USA's Destiny? Regulating Space and Creating Community in American Shopping Malls," *Urban Studies* 43, No. 5/6 (May 2006): 980, doi: 10.1080/00420980600676493.

2. *Malls R Us*, directed by Helene Klodawsky (2009; New York: Icarus Films, 2009), DVD.

3. Naomi Klein, *No Logo* (Toronto: Knopf Canada, 2000), 183.

4. Klein, *No Logo*, 183.

5. Quoted in Peter J. Kane, "Freedom of Expression in Shopping Centers," *Communication Quarterly* 22, No. 3 (Summer 1974): 45, doi: 10.1080/01463377409369151.

6. Benjamin R. Barber, "Civic Space," in *Sprawl and Public Space*, eds., Smiley and Robbins (Washington, DC: National Endowment for the Arts, 2002), 32.

7. Pahl, 79.

8. Christopher J. Sichok, "The Free Market: An Erosion of Free Speech," *Murdoch University Electronic Journal of Law* 7, No. 3 (September 2000), http://www.murdoch.edu.au/elaw/issues/v7n3/sichok73_text.html (accessed January 20, 2011).

9. Kane, "Freedom of Expression in Shopping Centers," 48.

10. *PruneYard Shopping Center v. Robins*, 447 U.S. 74 (1980).

11. Crawford, 23.

12. Underhill, 37.

13. Jon Goss, "The 'Magic of the Mall': An Analysis of Form, Function, and Meaning in the Contemporary Retail Built Environment," *Annals of the Association of American Geographers* 83, No. 1 (March 1993): 26.

14. Goss, "Magic of the Mall," 26.

15. Pamela Mebane, "ULS-P&A Settles Discrimination Lawsuit Against City Place Mall," *The Protection & Advocacy Program for the District of Columbia* 1, Issue 1 (Summer 2004):1–2.

16. Kowinski, 355.

17. John S. Dempsey, *Introduction to Private Security* (Belmont, CA: Thomson Wadsworth, 2008), 174.

18. Dempsey, *Introduction to Private Security*, 174.

19. Goss, "Magic of the Mall," 27.

20. Quoted in Goss, "Magic of the Mall," 27.

21. Kowinski, 309.

22. Ronald van Steden and Mahesh K. Nalla, "Citizen Satisfaction with Private Security Guards in the Netherlands: Perceptions of an Ambiguous Occupation," *European Journal of Criminology* 7, No. 3 (2010): 217, doi: 10.1177/1477370809359264.

23. *Paul Blart: Mall Cop*, directed by Steve Carr (2009; Culver City, CA: Sony Pictures, 2009), DVD.

24. Steden and Nalla, "Citizen Satisfaction with Private Security," 73.

25. Steden and Nalla, "Citizen Satisfaction with Private Security," 230.

26. J.R. Roberts, "Who Will Guard the Guards?" http://www.jrrobertssecurity.com/Who WillTheGuards.pdf (accessed January 3, 2011).

27. Dempsey, *Introduction to Private Security*, 158.

28. Roberts, "Who Will Guard the Guards?"

29. Roberts, "Who Will Guard the Guards?"

30. Jon Hurdle, "U.S. Army Recruiting at the Mall with Video Games," *Reuters*, January 9, 2009, http://www.reuters.com/article/2009/01/09/us-usa-army-recruiting-idUSTRE50819 H20090109 (accessed January 11, 2010).

31. Hurdle, "U.S. Army Recruiting."

32. Hurdle, "U.S. Army Recruiting."

33. Hurdle, "U.S. Army Recruiting."

34. Fox News, "Nebraska Mall Shooter Broke Up with Girlfriend, Lost Job Before Massacre," December 6, 2007, http://www.foxnews. com/story/0,2933,315441,00.html (accessed January 11, 2011).

35. CNN, "Police: Nine Killed in Shooting at Omaha Mall, Including Gunman," December 6, 2007, http://edition.cnn.com/2007/US/12/05/mall.shooting/index.html (accessed January 11, 2011).

36. Fox News, "Gunman Kills 5 in Shooting Spree at Salt Lake City Mall Before Being Killed by Police," February 13, 2007, http://www.foxnews.com/story/0,2933,251603,00.html (accessed January 11, 2011).

37. Sarah Coffey, "Happy Shopping, and Watch Out for Mall Shootings," *Reuters*, October 20, 2008, http://blogs.reuters.com/shoptalk/2008/10/20/happy-shopping-and-watch-out-for-mall-shootings/ (accessed January 11, 2011).

38. Coffey, "Happy Shopping, and Watch Out for Mall Shootings."

39. Coffey, "Happy Shopping, and Watch Out for Mall Shootings."

40. Access Control and Security Systems, "Mall Shooting Sparks Security Debate," December 11, 2007, http://securitysolutions.com/news/mall-security-debate/ (accessed January 11, 2011).

41. Access Control and Security Systems, "Mall Shooting Sparks Security Debate."

42. Access Control and Security Systems, "Mall Shooting Sparks Security Debate."

43. Parija B. Kavilanz, "One More Merchant Worry: Mall Violence," *CNN Money*, February 12, 2008, http://money.cnn.com/2008/02/11/news/companies/retail_crime/index.htm (accessed January 11, 2011).

44. Kavilanz, "One More Merchant Worry: Mall Violence."

45. Underhill, 40.

46. Staeheli and Mitchell, "USA's Destiny?" 980.

Chapter 9

1. Zepp, 148.

2. Wall, 180.

3. Charles Redell, "Dead Malls," http://sustainableindustries.com/articles/2009/03/dead-malls?page=3 (accessed June 11, 2011).

4. Underhill, 37.

5. ULI, *Shopping Center Handbook*, 16.

6. ULI, *Shopping Center Handbook*, 16.

7. ULI, *Shopping Center Handbook*, 16.

8. Kramer, 31.

9. ULI, *Shopping Center Handbook*, 16–17.

10. Kunstler, 59.

11. Kunstler, 73.

12. Kunstler, 78.

13. Kunstler, 84.

14. Gruen, *Heart of Our Cities*, 190.

15. Gruen, *Heart of Our Cities*, 190.

16. Crawford, 21.

17. Kunstler, 39.

18. Zepp, 148.

19. Wall, 183.

20. Mark Robbins, "Redressing the Mall," in *Sprawl and Public Space*, eds., Smiley and Robbins (Washington, DC: National Endowment for the Arts, 2002), 4.

21. Zepp, 63.

22. Farrell, 51.

23. U.S. Fish and Wildlife Service, *Karner Blue Butterfly Recovery Plan* (Fort Snelling, MN: U.S. Fish and Wildlife Services, 2003).

24. Lynne Jackson, "The Karner Blues vs. Crossgates Mall," http://www.savethepinebush.org/News/DecJan97/Xgates.html (accessed June 11, 2011).

25. Jackson, "The Karner Blues vs. Crossgates Mall."

26. Kowinski, 204.

27. Michelle Ma, "Thornton Creek Breathes Again at Northgate," *The Seattle Times*, June 19, 2009, http://seattletimes.nwsource.com/html/localnews/2009357492_thorntoncrk19m0.html (accessed June 11, 2011).

28. Kowinski, 204.

29. Ma, "Thornton Creek Breathes Again at Northgate."

30. Ma, "Thornton Creek Breathes Again at Northgate."

31. Frederick W. Langrehr, "Retail Shopping Mall Semiotics and Hedonic Consumption," *Advances in Consumer Research* 18 (1991): 430.

32. Jeffrey Hopkins, "Orchestrating an Indoor City: Ambient Noise Inside a Mega-Mall," *Environment and Behavior* 26, No. 6 (November 1994): 786, doi: 10.1177/0013916594266004.

33. Hopkins, "Orchestrating an Indoor City," 790.

34. Hopkins, "Orchestrating an Indoor City," 790.

35. Underhill, 31.

36. Underhill, 48.

37. Wall, 227.

38. Wall, 227.

39. Gruen, *Heart of Our Cities*, 42.

40. Gruen, *Heart of Our Cities*, 72.

41. Gruen, *Heart of Our Cities*, 42–43.

42. Gruen, *Heart of Our Cities*, 191.

43. Gruen, *Heart of Our Cities*, 191.

44. Underhill, 22.

45. Kunstler, 120.

46. Underhill, 22.

47. Kunstler, 121.

48. Karen Stabiner, "New Lives for 'Dead' Suburban Malls," *The New York Times*, June 28, 2011, http://newoldage.blogs.nytimes.com/2011/01/21/new-lives-for-dead-suburban-malls/ (accessed June 11, 2011).

49. Kimberley Mok, "Dead Malls: Tragedy or Opportunity," http://www.treehugger.com/files/2009/04/death-of-shopping-malls-dead-malls.php (accessed December 15, 2010).

50. Smiley and Robbins, 14.

51. Smiley and Robbins, 93.

52. Oldenburg, 203.

Chapter 10

1. Devlin, 254.

2. Stabiner, "New Lives for 'Dead' Suburban Malls."

3. Hudson and O'Connell, "Recession Turns Malls into Ghost Towns."

4. Redell, "Dead Malls."

5. Congress for the New Urbanism and PricewaterhouseCoopers, *Greyfields into Goldfields: From Failing Shopping Centers to Great Neighborhoods* (San Francisco: Congress for the New Urbanism, 2001), 3.

6. Martha S. Peyton, *Investing in Retail Real Estate: Identifying the Winners* (New York: Teachers Insurance and Annuity Association-College Retirement Equities Fund [TIAA-CREF], 2010), 4.

7. Matt Brownell, "The Future of American Malls," http://www.mainstreet.com/article/smart-spending/future-american-malls?page=1 (accessed July 11, 2011).

8. Bindu Nair, "Keeping Track of the Mall Count," *ICSC Research Quarterly* 10, No. 2 (Summer 2003): 5.

9. "Malls: Time to Think Outside the (Big) Box," *Knowledge@Emory*, http://knowledge.emory.edu/article.cfm?articleid=1356 (accessed July 11, 2011).

10. Congress for the New Urbanism and PricewaterhouseCoopers, *Greyfields into Goldfields*, 1.

11. Congress for the New Urbanism, 2.

12. Congress for the New Urbanism, 3.

13. Peyton, *Investing in Retail Real Estate*, 2.

14. "Malls: Time to Think Outside the (Big) Box."

15. Devlin, 256.

16. Greg Lindsay, "How Much Longer Can Shopping Malls Survive?" *Fast Company*, February 23, 2010, http://www.fastcompany.com/1557242/dead-malls (accessed July 11, 2011).

17. James R. DeLisle, *Shopping Center Classifications: Challenges and Opportunities* (New York: International Council of Shopping Centers, 2005), 14.

18. DeLisle, *Shopping Center Classifications*, 14.

19. Lindsay, "How Much Longer?"

20. Lindsay, "How Much Longer?"

21. Taub and Louis, "General Growth Files Biggest U.S. Property Bankruptcy."

22. Kris Hudson, "Mall Owner Ready to Emerge," *The Wall Street Journal*, October 22, 2010, http://online.wsj.com/article/SB10001424 0527023040238045755662736121 80224.html (accessed July 11, 2011).

23. Crawford, 8.

24. Michael D. Beyard, et al., *Ten Principles for Rethinking the Mall* (Washington, DC: Urban Land Institute, 2006), iv.

25. Beyard, et al., *Rethinking the Mall*, vi.

26. *The Economist*, "Birth, Death and Shopping."

27. Beyard, et al., v.

28. Beyard, et al., v.

29. Devlin, 269.

30. Beyard, et al., v.

31. Beyard, et al., v.

32. Devlin, 261.

33. Beyard, et al., v.

34. Beyard, et al., v.

35. Devlin, 265.

36. Beyard, et al., vi.

37. Devlin, 269.

38. Boscov's, "About Boscov's," http://www.boscovs.com/static/about_boscov/history.html (accessed July 11, 2011).

39. Dawn McCarty and Lauren Coleman-Lochner, "Boscov's Department Stores Seek Bankruptcy Protection," *Bloomberg*, August 4, 2008, http://www.bloomberg.com/apps/news?pid=newsarchive&sid=a2fCiNWU8sI8 (accessed July 11, 2011).

40. Dawn McCarty and Lauren Coleman-Lochner, "Boscov's Department Stores Seek Bankruptcy Protection."

41. Andrew Cannarsa and Aaron Cahall, "Boscov's Bankruptcy May Cause Malls to Move Away from Department Stores," *The Examiner*, August 6, 2008, http://washingtonexaminer.com/bankruptcy/boscovs-bankruptcy-may-cause-malls-move-away-department-stores#ixzz1PnAhvlQS (accessed July 11, 2011).

42. Devlin, 273.

43. Erick Schonfeld, "Forrester Forecast: Online Retail Sales Will Grow to $250 Billion by 2014," http://techcrunch.com/2010/03/08/forrester-forecast-online-retail-sales-will-grow-to-250-billion-by-2014/ (accessed July 7, 2011).

44. James Thomson, "Borders Collapses into Bankruptcy in the U.S.," http://www.smartcompany.com.au/retail/20110217-borders-collapses-into-bankruptcy-in-the-us.html (accessed July 7, 2011).

45. Devlin, 273.

46. Devlin, 274.

47. Devlin, 273.

48. Underhill, 215.

49. Kramer, 37.

50. Devlin, 265.

51. ULI, *Shopping Center Handbook*, 5.

52. Fishman, *The Wal-Mart Effect*, 5.

53. Fishman, 9.

54. Andra Case, interviewed by Lisa Scharoun, 15 November 2010, Pyramid Companies, Syracuse, New York.

55. Kramer, 145.

56. Richard Reep, "The Future of the Shopping Mall," http://www.newgeography.com/content/00501-the-future-shopping-mall (accessed November 11, 2010).

57. "Birth, Death and Shopping," The Economist.

58. Kramer, 137.

59. "Birth, Death and Shopping," The Economist.

60. Kramer, 138.

61. Reep, "The Future of the Shopping Mall."

62. In Devlin, 268.

63. Zepp, 159.

64. Hudson and O'Connell, "Recession Turns Malls into Ghost Towns."

Chapter 11

1. Hudson and O'Connell, "Recession Turns Malls into Ghost Towns."

2. Givens in Zepp, 159.

3. Fishman, 9.

4. Matthew A. Zook and Mark Graham, "Wal-Mart Nation: Mapping the Reach of a Retail Colossus," in *Wal-Mart World: The World's Biggest Corporation in the Global Economy*, ed., Stanley D. Brunn (New York: Routledge, 2006), 20.

5. Parachuri, et al., in Tom Angotti, Brian Paul, Tom Gray and Dom Williams, "Walmart's Economic Footprint: A Literature Review Prepared by Hunter College Center for Community Planning and Development and New York City Public Advocate Bill de Blasio," Center for Community Planning and Development, Hunter College, January 10, 2010: 8. http://advocate.nyc.gov/files/Walmart.pdf (accessed March 19, 2011).

6. Zook and Graham, "Wal-Mart Nation," in Brunn, 24.

7. Steve Burt and Leigh Sparks, "Wal-Mart's World," in *Wal-Mart World: The World's Biggest Corporation in the Global Economy*, ed., Stanley D. Brunn (New York: Routledge, 2006), 29.

8. Jane Dunnett and Stephen J. Arnold,

"Falling Prices, Happy Faces: Organizational Culture at Wal-Mart," in *Wal-Mart World: the World's Biggest Corporation in the Global Economy*, ed. Stanley D. Brunn (New York: Routledge, 2006), 82.

9. Jane Dunnett and Stephen J. Arnold, 82.

10. Sam Walton with John Huey, 158.

11. Ellen I. Rosen, "Wal-Mart: The New Retail Colossus," in *Wal-Mart World: The World's Biggest Corporation in the Global Economy*, ed., Stanley D. Brunn (New York: Routledge, 2006), 92.

12. Jesse LeCavalier, "All Those Numbers: Logistics, Territory and Walmart," *Design Observer*, May 24, 2010, http://places.designobserver.com/feature/walmart-logistics/13598/ (accessed August 3, 2011).

13. Angotti, et al., "Walmart's Economic Footprint," 3.

14. Nelson Lichtenstein and Erin Johansson, "Creating Hourly Careers: A New Vision for Walmart and the Country," American Rights at Work, http://americanrightsatwork.org/publications/general/creating-hourly-careers-2011 0119-974-116-116.html (accessed January 24, 2011).

15. Angotti, et al., "Walmart's Economic Footprint," 5.

16. "Fact Sheet — Wages," *Walmart Watch*, http://walmartwatch.org/get-the-facts/fact-sheet-wages (accessed August 3, 2011).

17. Rosen, "Wal-Mart: The New Retail Colossus," in Brunn, 94.

18. Rosen in Brunn, 95.

19. Sam Walton with John Huey, 157.

20. Jane Dunnett and Stephen J. Arnold, 83.

21. Sam Walton with John Huey, 177.

22. Barney Warf and Thomas Chapman, "Cathedrals of Consumption: A Political Phenomenology of Wal-Mart," in *Wal-Mart World: The World's Biggest Corporation in the Global Economy*, ed., Stanley D. Brunn (New York: Routledge, 2006), 171.

23. Warf and Thomas, "Cathedrals of Consumption," in Brunn, 170.

24. Sam Walton with John Huey, 173.

25. Dunnett and Arnold, "Falling Prices, Happy Faces," in Brunn, 87.

26. Warf and Chapman in Brunn, 178.

27. Warf and Chapman in Brunn, 173.

28. Sam Walton with John Huey, 241.

29. Holly R. Barcus, "Wal-Mart-scapes in Rural and Small-Town America," in *Wal-Mart World: The World's Biggest Corporation in the Global Economy*, ed. Stanley D. Brunn (New York: Routledge, 2006), 68.

30. Emily Anderson, Geoff DeOld, Corey Hoelker, "Waltropolis: City in a Box," *Architectural Design* 76, Issue 1 (January-February 2006): 96–99. Doi: 10.1002/ad.218. This article was first published online June 5, 2006, http://theboxtank.typepad.com/walmartbox/public_space/ (accessed March 19, 2011).

31. Barcus, "Wal-Mart-scapes," in Brunn, 69.

32. Anderson, et al., "Waltropolis: City in a Box."

33. Anderson, et al., "Waltropolis: City in a Box."

34. LeCavalier, "All Those Numbers: Logistics, Territory and Walmart."

35. Barcus in Brunn, 74.

36. "Walmart=pro vs. the mall=con," *Debate.org*, http://www.debate.org/debates/Walmart-pro-vs.-themall-con/1/ (accessed August 1, 2011).

37. Benjamin Smith, "Visualising Wal-Mart as Home: *Where the Heart Is* and *King of the Hill*," in *Wal-Mart World: The World's Biggest Corporation in the Global Economy*, ed., Stanley D. Brunn (New York: Routledge, 2006), 191.

38. Warf and Chapman in Brunn, 169.

39. The BoxTank, "Wal-Mart Promotes Parking Lot Living," first published online October 3, 2004. Posted October 4, 2004, http://dialogic.blogspot.com/2004/10/wal-mart-promotes-parking-lot-living.html (accessed March 19, 2011).

40. The BoxTank, "Wal-Mart Promotes Parking Lot Living."

41. "About The People of Walmart," *People of Walmart*, http://www.peopleofwalmart.com/about-the-people-of-walmart (accessed August 3, 2011).

42. Arnold, et al., "The Institutional Semiotics of Wal-Mart Flyers and Signage in United States, United Kingdom, Germany and China," in *Wal-Mart World: The World's Biggest Corporation in the Global Economy*, ed., Stanley D. Brunn (New York: Routledge, 2006), 157.

43. Fishman, 247.

44. Smith, "Visualising Wal-Mart as Home," in Brunn, 191.

45. Fishman, 108.

46. "Walmart=pro vs. the mall=con." *Debate.org*,

47. LeCavalier, "All Those Numbers: Logistics, Territory and Walmart."

48. Fishman, 247.

49. "Our History: Through the Years," *Target.com*, http://sites.target.com/site/en/company/page.jsp?contentId=WCMP04-031697 (accessed August 13, 2011).

50. "Our History: Through the Years," *Target.com*.

51. "Our History: Through the Years," *Target.com*.

52. Vivian M. Baulch, "How J.L. Hudson

changed the way we shop," *The Detroit News,* March 17, 2000, http://apps.detnews.com/apps/history/index.php?id=29 (accessed August 1, 2011).

53. "Our History: Through the Years," *Target.com.*

54. Associated Press, "Macy's Turns up the Charm to Court Chicagoans," last updated November 8, 2007, http://www.msnbc.msn.com/id/21693664 (accessed August 3, 2011).

55. "Our History: Through the Years," *Target.com.*

56. Constance L. Hays, "Can Target Thrive in Wal-Mart's Cross Hairs?" *The New York Times,* June 9, 2002, http://www.nytimes.com/2002/06/09/business/can-target-thrive-in-wal-mart-s-cross-hairs.html?src=pm (accessed August 5, 2011).

57. Hays, "Can Target Thrive in Wal-Mart's Cross Hairs?"

58. Hays, "Can Target Thrive in Wal-Mart's Cross Hairs?"

59. Smith in Brunn, 191.

60. Steve Kaufman, "Target, Multiple Locations," June 28, 2010, http://vmsd.com/content/target-multiple-locations?page=0%2C0 (accessed August 5, 2011).

61. Lea S. VanderVelde, "Wal-Mart as a Phenomenon in the Legal World: Matters of Scale, Scale Matters," in *Wal-Mart World: the World's Biggest Corporation in the Global Economy,* ed. Stanley D. Brunn (New York: Routledge, 2006), 122.

62. Warf and Chapman in Brunn, 172.

63. Associated Press, "Strong Holiday Season Lifted the Bottom Line at Target, Kohl's and Gap," *The New York Times,* February 24, 2011, http://www.nytimes.com/2011/02/25/business/economy/25shop.html?ref=targetcorporation (accessed August 5, 2011).

64. Reuters, "Profits at Target and BJ's Rise as Shoppers Buy Essentials," *The New York Times,* May 18, 2011, http://www.nytimes.com/2011/05/19/business/19retail.html?_r=1&ref=targetcorporation (accessed August 5, 2011).

Chapter 12

1. Smiley and Robbins, 47.

2. U.S. Census Bureau, "Monthly and Annual Retail Trade," http://www.census.gov/retail/ (accessed July 22, 2011).

3. U.S. Census Bureau, "The 2011 Statistical Abstract," http://www.census.gov/compendia/statab/ (accessed July 22, 2011).

4. Ken Allen, "Nanuet Mall: Nanuet, NY." *Deadmalls.com* (blog), March 10, 2008, http://deadmalls.com/malls/nanuet_mall.html (accessed July 11, 2011).

5. U.S. Census Bureau, "State and County QuickFacts: Rockland County, New York," http://quickfacts.census.gov/qfd/sates/36/36087.html (accessed July 22, 2011).

6. Stephanie Landsman, "Dead Mall Hunting," *CNBC,* May 12, 2011, http://www.cnbc.com/id/42959125/ (accessed July 22, 2011).

7. Kevin Kenyon, "Palisades Delivering Promise, Finally," *Shopping Centers Today,* April 1998, http://www.icsc.org/srch/sct/sct9804/13.php (access July 22, 2011).

8. Kenyon, "Palisades Delivering Promise, Finally."

9. Kenyon, "Palisades Delivering Promise, Finally."

10. Tim Stelloh, "The Crowds Are Gone, the Walls Are Next," *The New York Times,* May 1, 2011, http://www.nytimes.com/2011/05/02/nyregion/nanuet-malls-demolition-plans-stun-workers.html (access July 25, 2011).

11. "I Don't Care, the Nanuet Mall Will Always Be Part of My Childhood," *Facebook.com* (blog), http://www.facebook.com/group.php?gid=11567352942&v=wall (accessed July 25, 2011).

12. Gary Endlich, "I Don't Care, the Nanuet Mall Will Always Be Part of My Childhood," *Facebook.com* (blog), May 23, 2009, http://www.facebook.com/group.php?gid=1156735294 2&v=wall (accessed July 11, 2011).

13. Mariann Cedo Simpson, "I Don't Care, the Nanuet Mall Will Always Be Part of My Childhood," *Facebook.com* (blog), May 22, 2009, http://www.facebook.com/group.php?gid=11567352942&v=wall (accessed July 11, 2011).

14. Karen F. Guth Holland, "I Don't Care, the Nanuet Mall Will Always Be Part of My Childhood," *Facebook.com* (blog), January 30, 2009, http://www.facebook.com/group.php?gid=11567352942&v=wall (accessed July 11, 2011).

15. Ava, "Nanuet Mall Soon to Close; Nanuet, New York," *Labelscar.com* (blog), March 31, 2008, http://www.labelscar.com/new-york/nanuet-mall-closing#comment-61076 (accessed July 11, 2011).

16. Peggy Sullivan, "Nanuet Mall Soon to Close; Nanuet, New York," *Labelscar.com* (blog), April 15, 2008, http://www.labelscar.com/new-york/nanuet-mall-closing#comment-62421 (accessed July 11, 2011).

17. Andra Case, interviewed by Lisa Scharoun, 15 November 2010, Pyramid Companies, Syracuse, New York.

18. Max, "Nanuet Mall Soon to Close; Nanuet, New York," *Labelscar.com* (blog), March 4, 2008, http://www.labelscar.com/new-york/nanuet-mall-closing#comment-58341 (accessed July 11, 2011).

19. Eric, "Nanuet Mall Soon to Close; Nanuet, New York," *Labelscar.com* (blog), March

24, 2008, http://www.labelscar.com/new-york/
nanuet-mall-closing#comment-60527 (accessed
July 11, 2011).

20. Jasn, "Nanuet Mall Soon to Close;
Nanuet, New York," *Labelscar.com* (blog), March
30, 2008, http://www.labelscar.com/new-york/
nanuet-mall-closing#comment-61020 (accessed
July 11, 2011).

21. Lindsay Nichols, "I Don't Care, the
Nanuet Mall Will Always Be Part of My Childhood," *Facebook.com* (blog), October 23, 2008,
http://www.facebook.com/group.php?gid=1156
7352942&v=wall (accessed July 11, 2011).

22. Afua Adjei-Brenjah, "I Don't Care, the
Nanuet Mall Will Always Be Part of My Childhood," *Facebook.com* (blog), November 18, 2008,
http://www.facebook.com/group.php?gid=
11567352942&v=wall (accessed July 11, 2011).

23. Jeff, "Nanuet Mall Soon to Close;
Nanuet, New York," *Labelscar.com* (blog), April
6, 2008, http://www.labelscar.com/new-york/
nanuet-mall-closing#comment-61563 (accessed
July 11, 2011).

24. Sean, "Nanuet Mall Soon to Close;
Nanuet, New York," *Labelscar.com* (blog), April
10, 2008, http://www.labelscar.com/new-york/
nanuet-mall-closing#comment-61919 (accessed
July 11, 2011).

25. Dan Sabbatino, "The Birth of a Mall,"
Spotlightnews, January 28, 2010, http://spot-
lightnews.com/news/view_news.php?news_id=1
264696894 (accessed July 25, 2011).

26. Michael DeMasi, "Latham Circle
Owners Ask for Time as Lender Files $25M
Foreclosure Petition," *The Business Review*, last
modified June 5, 2008, http://www.bizjournals.
com/albany/stories/2008/06/09/story5.html
(accessed July 25, 2011).

27. Michael DeMasi, "Redevelopment Plan
Shows Whole Foods at Latham Circle Mall,"
The Business Review, July 12, 2011, http://www.
bizjournals.com/albany/news/2011/07/12/rede
velopment-plan-shows-whole-foods.html (accessed July 25, 2011).

28. U.S. Bureau of Labor Statistics, "New
York–New Jersey Information Office," http://
www.bls.gov/ro2/ro2_ny.htm (accessed July 11,
2011).

29. Sabbatino, "The Birth of a Mall."

30. Derek Ewing, "Latham Circle Mall;
Latham, NY," *Deadmalls.com* (blog), March 31,
2005, http://deadmalls.com/malls/latham_cir
cle_mall.html (accessed July 11, 2011).

31. Stavros interviewed by Lisa Scharoun,
11 November 2010, Latham Circle Mall, Albany
County, New York.

32. Patrick, "Latham Circle Mall; Latham,
NY," *Labelscar.com* (blog), March 31, 2007, http:
//www.labelscar.com/new-york/latham-circle-
mall#comment-5993 (accessed July 11, 2011).

33. Scott, "Latham Circle Mall; Latham,
NY," *Labelscar.com* (blog), April 7, 2007, http:
//www.labelscar.com/new-york/latham-circle-
mall#comment-7412 (accessed July 11, 2011).

34. Dan Sabbatino, "What Went Wrong?"
Spotlightnews, February 11, 2010, http://www.
spotlightnews.com/news/views_news.php?news
_id=1265924496 (accessed July 25, 2011).

35. Caldor, "Shoppingtown Mall; De-
Witt, New York," *Labelscar.com* (blog), October
21, 2006, http://www.labelscar.com/new-york/
shoppingtown-mall (accessed July 22, 2011).

36. The Macerich Company, "Macerich
Announces $2.333 Billion Agreement to Acquire
Wilmorite," December 23, 2004, http://invest
ing.macerich.com/phoenix.zhtml?c=80539&p=
irol-newArticle&t=Regular&id=657356& (accessed July 22, 2011).

37. Rick Moriarty, "DeWitt Approves
$800,000 Per Year Tax Break for Struggling
Shopping Town Mall," *The Post-Standard*, January 14, 2011, http://www.syracuse.com/news/
index.ssf/2011/01/shoppingtown_malls_tax_bill_
to.html (accessed July 22, 2011).

38. U.S. Census Bureau, "State and
County QuickFacts: Onondaga County, New
York," http://quickfacts.census.gov/qfd/states/
36/36067.html (accessed July 22, 2011).

39. U.S. Bureau of Labor Statistics, "Economy at a Glance: Syracuse, NY," http://www.
bls.gov/eag/eag.ny_syracuse_msa.htm (accessed
July 22, 2011).

40. Erik, "Shoppingtown Mall: Shoppingtown, New York," *Labelscar.com* (blog), October
27, 2008, http://www.labelscar.com/new-york/
shoppingtown-mall#comment-75776 (accessed
July 11, 2011).

41. Jim, "Shoppingtown Mall: Shoppingtown, New York," *Labelscar.com* (blog), February
12, 2008, http://www.labelscar.com/new-york/
shoppingtown-mall#comment-151259 (accessed
July 11, 2011).

42. Caldor, "Shoppingtown Mall: Shoppingtown, New York," *Labelscar.com* (blog),
April 3, 2008, http://www.labelscar.com/new-
york/shoppingtown-mall#comment-61418 (accessed July 11, 2011).

43. Ruth, "Shoppingtown Mall: Shoppingtown, New York," *Labelscar.com* (blog),
June 18, 2008, http://www.labelscar.com/new-
york/shoppingtown-mall#comment-102797
(accessed July 11, 2011).

44. Timothy, "Shoppingtown Mall: Shoppingtown, New York," *Labelscar.com* (blog),
February 7, 2008, http://www.labelscar.com/
new-york/shoppingtown-mall#comment-85150
(accessed July 11, 2011).

45. Frank Thomas Croisdale, "Summit
Closing a Sad Day for Niagara," *Niagara Falls
Reporter*, May 19, 2009, http://www.niagarafalls

reporter.com/croisdale5.19.09.html (accessed July 22, 2011).

46. Mark Sheer, "Mall Goes into Bankruptcy: Summit Owners Cite Economy," *Niagara Gazette*, May 6, 2009, http://niagara-gazette.com/breakingnews/x681342885/MALL-GOES-INTO-BANKRUPTCY-Summit-owners-cite-economy (accessed July 22, 2011).

47. U.S. Census Bureau, "State and County QuickFacts: Niagara County, New York," http://quickfacts.census.gov/qfd/states/36/36063.html (accessed July 22, 2011).

48. U.S. Bureau of Labor Statistics, "Economy at a Glance: Buffalo–Niagara Falls, NY," http://www.bls.gov/eag/eag.ny_buffalo_msa.htm (accessed July 22, 2011).

49. Croisdale, "Summit Closing a Sad Day for Niagara."

50. Croisdale, "Summit Closing a Sad Day for Niagara."

51. John Grdovich, "Summit Park Mall/Summit Park Center: Wheatfield (Niagara Falls), NY," *Deadmalls.com* (blog), April 3, 2005, http://www.deadmalls.com/malls/summit_park_mall.html (accessed July 11, 2011).

52. Croisdale, "Summit Closing a Sad Day for Niagara."

53. Deborah Perry, "Summit Park Mall/Summit Park Center: Wheatfield (Niagara Falls), NY," *Deadmalls.com* (blog), April 3, 2005, http://www.deadmalls.com/malls/summit_park_mall.html (accessed July 11, 2011).

54. "Lockport Mall," *Wikipedia*, http://en.wikipedia.org/wiki/Lockport_Mall (accessed July 22, 2011).

55. Thomas J. Prohaska, "Demolition of Lockport Mall Begins," *Buffalo News*, April 13, 2011, http://www.buffalonews.com/city/communities/lockport/article391973.ece (accessed July 22, 2011).

56. U.S. Census Bureau, "State and County QuickFacts: Niagara County, New York."

57. U.S. Bureau of Labor Statistics, "Economy at a Glance: Buffalo–Niagara Falls, NY."

58. Prohaska, "Demolition of Lockport Mall Begins."

59. Prohaska, "Demolition of Lockport Mall Begins."

60. Joe Olenick, "Lockport Mall Could Be Gone by Month's End," *Lockport Union-Sun and Journal*, April 14, 2011, http://lockportjournal.com/local/x1142035511/Lockport-mall-could-be-gone-by-months-end (accessed July 22, 2011).

61. D34dm4n, "Lockport Mall to Be Demolished," *Buffalorange.com* (blog), March 29, 2011, http://www.buffalorange.com/showthread.php?187797-Lockport-Mall-to-be-Demolished_ (accessed July 11, 2011).

62. Erica Hayes, "Lockport Mall: Lockport, NY," Deadmalls.com (blog), May 5, 2008, http://www.deadmalls.com/malls/lockport_mall.html (accessed July 11, 2011).

63. Jewel Kazacami, "The End: Lockport Mall," *Deviantart.com* (blog), May 6, 2011, http://jewelkazacami.deviantart.com/art/The-End-Lockport-Mall-207874632 (accessed July 22, 2011).

64. Jewel Kazacami, "The End: Lockport Mall," *Deviantart.com* (blog), May 7, 2011, http://jewelkazacami.deviantart.com/art/The-End-Lockport-Mall-207874632 (accessed July 22, 2011).

65. Sabredan17, "Lockport Mall to Be Demolished," *Buffalorange.com* (blog), March 29, 2011, http://www.buffalorange.com/showthread.php?187797-Lockport-Mall-to-be-Demolished_ (accessed July 11, 2011).

66. Micgaes, "Lockport Mall to Be Demolished," *Buffalorange.com* (blog), April 10, 2011, http://www.buffalorange.com/showthread.php?187797-Lockport-Mall-to-be-Demolished_ (accessed July 11, 2011).

67. "Medley Center," *Wikipedia*, http://en.wikipedia.org/wiki/Medley_Centre (accessed July 25, 2011).

68. Phillip Dampier, "Irondequoit Mall/Medley Centre: Rochester, NY," Deadmalls.com (blog), April 9, 2007, http://www.deadmalls.com/malls/irondequoit_mall.html (accessed July 25, 2011).

69. Medley Center Information, "Proposed Medley Center Redevelopment Plan: Issues That Need to Be Addressed," https://sites.google.com/site/medleycenterinfomation/Home (accessed July 25, 2011).

70. U.S. Bureau of Labor Statistics, "Economy at a Glance: Rochester, NY," http://www.bls.gov/eag/eag.ny_rochester_msa.htm (accessed July 25, 2011).

71. U.S. Census Bureau, "State and County QuickFacts: Rochester (City), New York," http://quickfacts.census.gov/qfd/states/36/3663000.html (accessed July 25, 2011).

72. Prange Way, "Irondequoit Mall/Medley Centre/Lake Ridge Centre; Irondequoit (Rochester), New York," *Labelscar.com* (blog), December 29, 2010, http://www.labelscar.com/new-york/medley-centre-irondequoit-mall-lakeridge-centre (accessed July 25, 2011).

73. Way, "Irondequoit Mall/Medley Centre/Lake Ridge Centre; Irondequoit (Rochester), New York."

74. "Eastview Mall," *Wikipedia*, http://en.wikipedia.org/wiki/Eastview_Mall (accessed July 25, 2011).

75. Way, "Irondequoit Mall/Medley Centre/Lake Ridge Centre; Irondequoit (Rochester), New York."

76. Phillip Dampier, "Irondequoit Mall/

Medley Centre: Rochester, NY," Deadmalls.com (blog), June 28, 2007, http://www.deadmalls.com/malls/irondequoit_mall.html (accessed July 25, 2011).

77. Way, "Irondequoit Mall/Medley Centre/Lake Ridge Centre; Irondequoit (Rochester), New York."

78. Mallguy, "Irondequoit Mall/Medley Centre/Lake Ridge Centre; Irondequoit (Rochester), New York," *Labelscar.com* (blog), December 29, 2010, http://www.labelscar.com/new-york/medley-centre-irondequoit-mall-lake ridge-centre (accessed July 25, 2011).

79. Rich, "Irondequoit Mall/Medley Centre/Lake Ridge Centre; Irondequoit (Rochester), New York," *Labelscar.com* (blog), December 29, 2010, http://www.labelscar.com/new-york/med ley-centre-irondequoit-mall-lakeridge-centre (accessed July 25, 2011).

80. Michelle, "Irondequoit Mall/Medley Centre/Lake Ridge Centre; Irondequoit (Rochester), New York," *Labelscar.com* (blog), December 30, 2010, http://www.labelscar.com/new-york/medley-centre-irondequoit-mall-lake ridge-centre (accessed July 25, 2011).

81. IronWest, "Irondequoit Mall/Medley Centre/Lake Ridge Centre; Irondequoit (Rochester), New York," *Labelscar.com* (blog), March 21, 2011, http://www.labelscar.com/new-york/medley-centre-irondequoit-mall-lakeridge-centre (accessed July 25, 2011).

82. Meami Craig, "Medley Center: Are You Kidding Me?" *HerRochester.com* (blog), November 22, 20008, http://blogs.democratand chronicle.com/her2/2008/11/22/medley-center-are-you-kidding-me/ (accessed July 25, 2011).

83. Sean, "Irondequoit Mall/Medley Centre/Lake Ridge Centre; Irondequoit (Rochester), New York," *Labelscar.com* (blog), December 29, 2010, http://www.labelscar.com/new-york/med ley-centre-irondequoit-mall-lakeridge-centre (accessed July 25, 2011).

Chapter 13

1. David Sokol, "Morphing Mega Malls," *Retail Traffic*, October 1, 2002, http://retailtraffic mag.com/development/trends/retail_morphing_mega_malls/ (accessed August 11, 2011).

2. Kenyon, "Palisades Delivering Promise, Finally."

3. Debra West, "Palisades Center, the Rumor Mall; Rosie O'Donnell Wants to Know: Is It Really Going to Sink?" *The New York Times*, January 8, 1999, http://www.nytimes.com/1999/01/08/nyregion/palisades-center-rumor-mall-rosie-o-donnell-wants-know-it-really-going-sink.html?src=pm (accessed July 22, 2011).

4. Andra Case, interviewed by Lisa Scharoun, 15 November 2010, Pyramid Companies, Syracuse, New York.

5. U.S. Bureau of Labor Statistics, "Unemployment in the New York Area by County — April 2011," http://www.bls.gov/ro2/countyun emp.htm (accessed August 11, 2011).

6. U.S. Census Bureau, "State and County QuickFacts: Rockland County, New York," http://quickfacts.census.gov/qfd/states/36/36087.html (accessed August 11, 2011).

7. Yaffi Spodek, "The Malls Are All Right," *The Real Deal*, January 1, 2011, http://therealdeal.com/newyork/articles/the-malls-are-all-right (accessed August 11, 2011).

8. Milford Prewitt, "Mall Trends and Hurdles Send Chains Shopping for Site Solutions," April 24, 2000, http://findarticles.com/p/articles/mi_m3190/is_17_34/ai_61948437/pg_2/?tag=content;col1 (accessed August 15, 2011).

9. West, "Palisades Center, the Rumor Mall."

10. West, "Palisades Center, the Rumor Mall."

11. *Megamall*, directed by Sarah Mondale, Vera Aronwo and Roger Grange (2009; Oley, PA: Bullfrog Films, 2009), DVD. http://stonelanternfilms.org/megamall.html.

12. Christina P., "Palisades Center," *Yelp.com* (blog), May 5, 2011, http://www.yelp.com/biz/palisades-center-west-nyack (accessed August 15, 2011).

13. Jennifer D., "Palisades Center," *Yelp.com* (blog), April 25, 2010, http://www.yelp.com/biz/palisades-center-west-nyack (accessed August 15, 2011).

14. Eva K., "Palisades Center," *Yelp.com* (blog), July 8, 2011, http://www.yelp.com/biz/palisades-center-west-nyack (accessed August 15, 2011).

15. "Walden Galleria," *Wikipedia*, http://en.wikipedia.org/wiki/Walden_Galleria (accessed August 11, 2011).

16. Andra Case, interviewed by Lisa Scharoun, 15 November 2010, Pyramid Companies, Syracuse, New York.

17. James Fink, "Walden Galleria Getting Bigger," *Buffalo Business First*, June 19, 2006, http://www.bizjournals.com/buffalo/stories/2006/06/19/story1.html (August 15, 2011).

18. Andra Case, interviewed by Lisa Scharoun, 15 November 2010, Pyramid Companies, Syracuse, New York.

19. U.S. Census Bureau, "State and County QuickFacts: Erie County, New York," http://quickfacts.census.gov/qfd/states/36/36029.html (accessed August 11, 2011).

20. Andra Case, interviewed by Lisa Scharoun, 15 November 2010, Pyramid Companies, Syracuse, New York.

21. Ashley S., "Walden Galleria," *Yelp.com*

(blog), May 22, 2011, http://www.yelp.com/biz/walden-galleria-mall-buffalo.

22. Naureen H., "Walden Galleria," *Yelp.com* (blog), February 14, 2010, http://www.yelp.com/biz/walden-galleria-mall-buffalo.

23. Erica M., "Walden Galleria," *Yelp.com* (blog), January 10, 2010, http://www.yelp.com/biz/walden-galleria-mall-buffalo.

24. Cookie x., "Walden Galleria," *Yelp.com* (blog), January 25, 2009, http://www.yelp.com/biz/walden-galleria-mall-buffalo.

25. "Carousel Center," *Carousel Center*, http://www.carouselcenter.com (accessed August 13, 2011).

26. Staeheli and Mitchell, 979.

27. "Carousel Center," *Wikipedia*, http://en.wikipedia.org/wiki/Carousel_Center (accessed August 13, 2011).

28. Straheli and Mitchell, 979.

29. Rick Moriarty, "Faded 'Green' Promises Could Cost Destiny USA Millions," *The Post-Standard*, February 20, 2011, http://www.syracuse.com/news/index.ssf/2011/02/faded_green_promises_could_cos.html (accessed August 15, 2011).

30. Tim Knauss, "Syracuse Gives Carousel Center Mall a 6-Month Tax Reprieve for $1 Million," *The Post-Standard*, June 6, 2011, http://www.syracuse.com/news/index.ssf/2011/06/syracuse_gives_carousel_center.html (accessed August 15, 2011).

31. Rick Moriarty, "Outlet Stores Are Coming to Carousel Center's Addition After Developer Robert Congel Scraps His Earlier Plans," *The Post-Standard*, June 15, 2011, http://www.syracuse.com/news/index.ssf/2011/06/congels_outlet.html (accessed August 15, 2011).

32. U.S. Bureau of Labor Statistics, "Economy at a Glance: Syracuse, NY."

33. Straheli and Mitchell, 979.

34. Daryl A., "Carousel Center," *Yelp.com* (blog), March 10, 2011, http://www.yelp.com/biz/carousel-center-syracuse (accessed August 15, 2011).

35. Mark Kyle E., "Carousel Center," *Yelp.com* (blog), June 14, 2010, http://www.yelp.com/biz/carousel-center-syracuse (accessed August 15, 2011).

36. Mark M., "Carousel Center," *Yelp.com* (blog), February 7, 2011, http://www.yelp.com/biz/carousel-center-syracuse (accessed August 15, 2011).

37. Samantha H., "Carousel Center," *Yelp.com* (blog), January 3, 2008, http://www.yelp.com/biz/carousel-center-syracuse (accessed August 15, 2011).

38. Rachel C., "Carousel Center," *Yelp.com* (blog), January 8, 2011, http://www.yelp.com/biz/carousel-center-syracuse (accessed August 15, 2011).

39. Jasmine A., "Carousel Center," *Yelp.com* (blog), May 25, 2011, http://www.yelp.com/biz/carousel-center-syracuse (accessed August 15, 2011).

40. Caldor, "Clifton Park Center (Clifton Country Mall; Clifton, New York," *Labelscar.com* (blog), February 22, 2007, http://www.labelscar.com/new-york/clifton-park-center (accessed July 15, 2011).

41. Alicia Jacobs, "Local Malls Headed in a Different Direction," *Your News Now*, June 9, 2007, http://capitalregion.ynn.com/content/103903/local-malls-headed-in-a-different-direction/ (accessed August 15, 2011).

42. U.S. Census Bureau, "State and County QuickFacts: Saratoga County, New York," http://quickfacts.census.gov/qfd/states/36/36091.html (accessed August 11, 2011).

43. U.S. Bureau of Labor Statistics, "Local Area Unemployment Statistics Map," http://data.bls.gov/map/MapToolServlet?state=36&datatype=unemployment&year=2011&period=M05&survey=la&map=county&seasonal=u (accessed August 11, 2011).

44. Chris Churchill, "J.C. Penney Renovating at Clifton Park Center," *Timesunion.com*, June 29, 2011, http://www.timesunion.com/business/article/J-C-Penney-renovating-at-Clifton-Park-Center-1446391.php (accessed August 11, 2011).

45. Droman, "Clifton Park Center (Clifton Country Mall); Clifton, New York," *Labelscar.com* (blog), February 22, 2007, http://www.labelscar.com/new-york/clifton-park-center (accessed July 15, 2011).

46. Xismzero, "Clifton Park Center (Clifton Country Mall); Clifton, New York," *Labelscar.com* (blog), February 23, 2007, http://www.labelscar.com/new-york/clifton-park-center (accessed July 15, 2011).

47. Steve, "Clifton Park Center (Clifton Country Mall); Clifton, New York," *Labelscar.com* (blog), February 23, 2007, http://www.labelscar.com/new-york/clifton-park-center (accessed July 15, 2011).

48. Kristina T., "Mocha Lisa's Cafe," *Insiderpages.com* (blog), November 1, 2009, http://www.insiderpages.com/b/15239792330/mocha-lisas-caffe-clifton-park (accessed August 15, 2011).

49. sp123311, "Wonderful Cappucinos and Paninis," *Citysearch.com* (blog), July 13, 2010, http://albany.citysearch.com/review/44839129?reviewId=86638691 (accessed August 15, 2011).

50. Caldor, "The Shops at Ithaca Mall (Pyramid Mall)/Triphammer Mall; Ithaca, New York," *Labelscar.com* (blog), April 12, 2007, http://www.labelscar.com/new-york/pyramid-mall-and-triphammer-mall (accessed June 29, 2011).

51. Dan Veaner, "Business Profile: The

Shops at Ithaca Mall," *The Lansing Star*, July 12, 2007, http://www.lansingstar.com/component/content/article/141/3100-business-profile-the-shops-at-ithaca-mall (accessed August 18, 2011).

52. Dan Veaner, "BJ's to Come to the Shops at Ithaca Mall," *The Lansing Star*, July 29, 2010, http://www.lansingstar.com/news-archive/6377-bjs-to-come-to-the-shops-at-ithaca-mall (accessed August 18, 2011).

53. Byron Kittle, "BJs Wholesale Club Construction Begins Near Ithaca Mall," *The Cornell Daily Sun*, April 20, 2011, http://cornellsun.com/section/news/content/2011/04/20/bj%E2%80%99s-wholesale-club-construction-begins-near-ithaca-mall (accessed August 18, 2011).

54. U.S. Census Bureau, "State and County QuickFacts: Tompkins County, New York," http://quickfacts.census.gov/qfd/states/36/36109.html (accessed August 11, 2011).

55. U.S. Bureau of Labor Statistics, "Local Area Unemployment Statistics Map," http://data.bls.gov/map/MapToolServlet?state=36&datatype=unemployment&year=2011&period=M05&survey=la&map=county&seasonal=u (accessed August 11, 2011).

56. Johanh Norason, "The Shops at Ithaca Mall (Pyramid Mall)/Triphammer Mall; Ithaca, New York," *Labelscar.com* (blog), September 8, 2007, http://www.labelscar.com/new-york/pyramid-mall-and-triphammer-mall (accessed June 29, 2011).

57. Xismzero, "The Shops at Ithaca Mall (Pyramid Mall)/Triphammer Mall; Ithaca, New York," *Labelscar.com* (blog), April 12, 2007, http://www.labelscar.com/new-york/pyramid-mall-and-triphammer-mall (accessed June 29, 2011).

58. Paul Allen, "Fingerlake Mall Gains New Owners," *CNY Business Journal*, April 7, 2000, http://findarticles.com/p/articles/mi_qa3718/is_200004/ai_n8889117/ (accessed August 15, 2011).

59. Parker Stanton, "Fingerlakes Mall: Auburn, NY," *Deadmalls.com* (blog), April 24, 2011, http://www.deadmalls.com/malls/fingerlakes_mall.html (accessed August 12, 2011).

60. Fran LeFort, "On the Waterfront," *Shopping Centers Today* (December 2005), http://www.icsc.org/srch/sct/sct1205/Bass_pro_buffalo.php (accessed August 15, 2011).

61. U.S. Census Bureau, "State and County QuickFacts: Cayuga County, New York," http://quickfacts.census.gov/qfd/states/36/36011.html (accessed August 18, 2011).

62. U.S. Bureau of Labor Statistics, "Local Area Unemployment Statistics Map."

63. Timbo50, "Fingerlakes Mall," *FingerLakes1.com* (blog), July 26, 2010, http://forums.fingerlakes1.com/ubbthreads.php?ubb=showflat&Number=1202652&page=3 (accessed August 18, 2011).

64. runner 97, "Fingerlakes Mall," *FingerLakes1.com* (blog), July 25, 2010, http://forums.fingerlakes1.com/ubbthreads.php?ubb=showflat&Number=1202652&page=3 (accessed August 18, 2011).

65. Josephus, "Fingerlakes Mall," *FingerLakes1.com* (blog), July 26, 2010, http://forums.fingerlakes1.com/ubbthreads.php?ubb=showflat&Number=1202652&page=3 (accessed August 18, 2011).

66. Sokol, "Morphing Mega Malls."

67. Kramer, 237.

Chapter 14

1. Leinburger, 176.

2. Yestercuse, "Syracuse Today," http://www.yestercuse.com/today.htm (accessed July 27, 2011).

3. Ken Allan, "St. Louis Centre: St. Louis, MO," *Deadmalls.com* (blog), March 25, 2005, http://deadmalls.com/malls/st_louis_centre.html (accessed July 27, 2011).

4. Yestercuse, "Syracuse Today."

5. Yestercuse, "South Salina Street — the Heart of Downtown," http://www.yestercuse.com/salina.htm (accessed July 27, 2011).

6. Yestercuse, "South Salina Street — the Heart of Downtown."

7. U.S. Bureau of Labor Statistics, "Economy at a Glance: Syracuse, NY."

8. Don Cazentre, "Dey's Fresh Market in Downtown Syracuse is Still a Work in Progress," *The Post-Standard*, June 8, 2011, http://blog.syracuse.com/cny/2011/06/deys_fresh_market_in_downtown_syracuse_is_still_a_work_in_progress.html (accessed July 27, 2011).

9. "Apartments Set to Open in Redeveloped Downtown Building," News Channel 9, August 28, 2010, http://www.9wsyr.com/news/local/story/Apartments-set-to-open-in-redeveloped-downtown/VylD5l62Xku_FZ6Nf63a1A.cspx (accessed July 27, 2011).

10. Armory Square Association, "History," http://www.armorysquareofsyracuse.com/about/history.php (accessed July 27, 2011).

11. Yestercuse, "Syracuse Today."

12. Jack Thomas, "Main Place Mall: Buffalo, NY," *Deadmalls.com* (blog), October 5, 2003, http://www.deadmalls.com/malls/main_place_mall.html (accessed July 27, 2011).

13. Main Place Liberty Group, "Main Place Liberty Group," http://www.mainliberty.com (accessed July 27, 2011).

14. "History of Buffalo, New York," *Wikipedia*, http://en.wikipedia.org/wiki/History_of_Buffalo,_New_York (accessed July 27, 2011).

15. Niagara Frontier Transportation Authority, "History of Metro," http://metro.nfta.

com/About/History.aspx (accessed July 27, 2011).

16. "Buffalo Metro Rail," *Wikipedia*, http://en.wikipedia.org/wiki/Buffalo_Metro_Rail (accessed July 27, 2011).

17. U.S. Census Bureau, "State and County QuickFacts: Buffalo (City), New York," http://quickfacts.census.gov/gfd/states/36/3611000.html (accessed July 27, 2011).

18. U.S. Bureau of Labor Statistics, "Economy at a Glance: Buffalo–Niagara Falls, NY."

19. Christian Calleri, "Elmwood Avenue District," July 13, 2005, http://www.pps.org/great_public_spaces/one?public_place_id=852&type_id=3 (accessed July 27, 2011).

20. Mark Sommer and Jonathan D. Epstein, "Canal Side Ready to Speed Ahead," *Buffalo News*, July 20, 2011, http://www.buffalonews.com/city/communities/downtown/article493896.ece (accessed July 27, 2011).

21. Buffalo Waterfront, "Welcome to Buffalo's Waterfront," http://www.buffalowaterfront.com/ (accessed July 27, 2011).

22. WBEN, "WBEN Extra: Bye-Bye Big Box, but Now What?" *WBEN News Radio*, December 9, 2010, http://www.wben.com/pages/8741935.php? (accessed July 27, 2011).

23. Sommer and Epstein, "Canal Side Ready to Speed Ahead."

24. Rochester Downtown Development Corporation and Downtown Special Services Inc., "Midtown Plaza Timeline," http://www.rochesterdowntown.com/downloads/Midtown_2011).

25. Rochester Downtown, "Midtown Plaza Timeline."

26. Rochester Downtown, "Midtown Plaza Timeline."

27. Will Astor, "Trial Puts Focus on Midtown," *Rochester Business Journal*, February 12, 2010, http://www.rbj.net/article.asp?aID=183013 (accessed July 30, 2011).

28. U.S. Bureau of Labor Statistics, "Economy at a Glance: Rochester, NY."

29. U.S. Census Bureau, "State and County QuickFacts: Rochester (City), New York."

30. Urban Land Institute (ULI), *An Advisory Services Panel Report: Rochester, New York* (Washington, DC: author, 2005), 15, http://rochesterdowntown.com/news/PDF/ULIreport.pdf (accessed July 27, 2011).

31. ULI, *Rochester New York*, 11.

32. ULI, *Rochester New York*, 15.

33. ULI, *Rochester New York*, 11.

34. Will, "The Rainbow Centre Mall — Niagara Falls, NY," *4640.com* (blog), August 8, 2010, http://www.4640.com/2010/08/08/the-rainbow-centre-mall-niagara-falls-ny/ (accessed July 30, 2011).

35. Rick Forgione, "Niagara Falls: Last Call for Wintergarden," *Niagara Gazette*, August 9, 2008, http://niagara-gazette.com/local/x681318069/NIAGARA-FALLS-Last-call-for-Wintergarden (accessed July 30, 2011).

36. U.S. Environmental Protection Agency, "Love Canal: Press Releases and Articles," http://www.epa.gov/aboutepa/history/topics/lovecanal/ (accessed July 30, 2011).

37. Rochester Downtown Development Corporation and Downtown Special Services Inc., "Gaming in Rochester and New York State," http://rochesterdowntown.com/news/rdc_casino/ROCHESTER/ROCH11.pdf (accessed July 30, 2011).

38. USA Niagara Development Corporation, "Old Falls Street–East Mall Project," http://www.usaniagara.com/projects_display.asp?id=14 (accessed July 30, 2011).

39. Nick Mattera, "Rainbow Centre Tour Whets Appetite," *The Tonawanda News*, January 27, 2011, http://tonawanda-news.com/local/x1472873746/Rainbow-Centre-tour-whets-appetite (accessed July 30, 2011).

40. U.S. Census Bureau, "State and County QuickFacts: Niagara Falls (City), New York," http://quickfacts.census.gov/qfd/states/36/3651055.html (accessed July 30, 2011).

41. U.S. Bureau of Labor Statistics, "Economy at a Glance: Buffalo-Niagara Falls, NY."

42. David Staba, "New Passport Rules Bring Worry Over Tourism at Niagara Falls," *The New York Times*, June 11, 2007, http://www.nytimes.com/2007/06/11/nyregion/11border.html (accessed July 30, 2011).

43. Buffalo Rising, "Project to Bring Retail Back to Downtown Niagara Falls, NY," March 4, 2011, http://www.buffalorising.com/2011/03/project-to-bring-retailing-back-to-downtown-niagara-falls-ny.html (accessed July 30, 2011).

44. Robert Berner, "Wal-Mart's Urban Renewal," *Businessweek*, April 4, 2006, http://www.businessweek.com/investor/content/apr2006/pi20060404_285531.htm (accessed July 30, 2011).

45. Jayne O'Donnell, "Wal-Mart Plans for Smaller, Urban Stores with Fresh Food," *USA Today*, September 20, 2010, http://www.usatoday.com/money/industries/retail/2010-09-20-walmart-urban_N.htm (accessed July 30, 2011).

46. Sloane Burwell, "Viva El Mercado: Supercado De Walmart," *NewTimesPhoenix.com* (blog), June 17, 2009, http://blogs.phoenixnewtimes.com/bella/2009/06/viva_el_mercado_supermercado_d.php (accessed July 30, 2011).

47. Fishman, 269.

48. Julie Davis, et al., *The Impact of an Urban Wal-Mart Store on Area Business: An Evaluation of One Chicago Neighborhood's Experience* (Chicago: Loyola University, 2009), ii.

49. Jonathan Birchall, "Walmart Strikes Deal with Unions in Chicago," *Financial Times*, June 22, 2010, http://www.ft.com/intl/cms/s/0/da01f27a-7e20-11df-94a8-00144feabdc0.html#axzz1TGpTwgTu (accessed July 30, 2011).

50. "Chicago Wal-Mart Approved by City Council," *Huffington Post Chicago*, June 30, 2010, http://www.huffingtonpost.com/2010/06/30/chicago-wal-mart-approved_n_631386.html (accessed July 30, 2011).

51. Nicole Maestri, "Marketside Getting Walmart's Name Added to Its Own," *Reuters*, June 15, 2009, http://www.reuters.com/article/2009/06/15/walmart-food-idUSN15208609200 90615 (accessed July 30, 2011).

52. Lisa Baertlein, "Wal-Mart Marketside Test Feels Economic Hit," *Reuters.com* (blog), June 5, 2009, http://blogs.reuters.com/shoptalk/2009/06/05/wal-mart-marketside-test-feels-economic-hit/ (accessed July 30, 2011).

53. David Schwartz and Nicole Maestri, "Wal-Mart Woos Hispanics with New Supermercado," *Reuters*, July 8, 2009, http://www.reuters.com/article/2009/07/08/us-walmart-su permercado-idUSTRE5676N820090708 (accessed July 30, 2011).

54. Peter Finocchiaro, "Wal-Mart Continues March Towards Urban Domination," *Salon*, February 10, 2011, http://www.salon.com/news/feature/2011/02/10/walmart_new_york_washing ton (accessed July 30, 2011).

Chapter 15

1. Gruen and Smith, *Shopping Towns USA*, 267.

2. Gruen and Smith, 269.

3. Gruen and Smith, 269–270.

4. Gruen and Smith, 271

5. ULI, *Shopping Center Handbook*, 304.

6. ULI, *Shopping Center Handbook*, 307.

7. ULI, *Shopping Center Handbook*, 307.

8. ULI, *Shopping Center Handbook*, 318.

9. ULI, *Shopping Center Handbook*, 313.

10. ULI, *Shopping Center Handbook*, 313.

11. Kevin Mattson, "Antidotes to Sprawl," in *Sprawl and Public Space*, eds., Smiley and Robbins (Washington, DC: National Endowment for the Arts, 2002), 37.

12. Kramer, 438.

13. Mattson, "Antidotes to Sprawl," 43.

14. "Willingboro Town Center going 'green,'" *Entrepreneur.com*, August 22, 2001, http://www.entrepreneur.com/tradejournals/article/78059083.html (accessed August 18, 2011).

15. Mattson, "Antidotes to Sprawl," 43.

16. Kramer, 440.

17. Beyard, et al., 20.

18. Kramer, 433.

19. Kramer, 433.

20. Kramer, 435.

21. Gruen, *Centers for the Urban Environment*, 39.

22. Kramer, 435.

23. Fishman, 267.

24. Leinburger, 161.

25. Leinburger, 169–170.

26. Kramer, 436.

27. Kramer, 426.

28. Kramer, 427.

29. Kramer, 427.

30. Kramer, 430.

31. Kramer, 431.

32. Kramer, 431.

33. Leinburger, 175.

34. Bel Geddes, 283.

35. Mattson, "Antidotes to Sprawl," 45.

36. Bel Geddes, 269.

37. Mattson, "Antidotes to Sprawl," 45.

38. Oldenburg, 296.

39. Oldenburg, 296.

40. Farrell, 265.

Bibliography

Access Control and Security Systems. "Mall Shooting Sparks Security Debate." December 11, 2007. http://securitysolutions.com/news/mall-security-debate/ (accessed January 11, 2011).

Allen, Paul. "Fingerlake Mall Gains New Owners." *CNY Business Journal*, April 7, 2000. http://findarticles.com/p/articles/mi_qa3718/is_200004/ai_n8889117/ (accessed August 15, 2011).

American Beauty. Directed by Sam Mendes. 1999. Universal City, CA: Dreamworks Video. DVD.

Anderson, Emily, Geoff DeOld, and Corey Hoelker. "Waltropolis: City in a Box." *Architectural Design* 76, Issue 1 (January–February 2006): 96–99. Doi: 10.1002/ad.218. First published online June 5, 2006. http://theboxtank.typepad.com/walmartbox/public_space/ (accessed March 19, 2011).

Angotti, Tom, Brian Paul, Tom Gray and Dom Williams. "Walmart's Economic Footprint: A Literature Review Prepared by Hunter College Center for Community Planning and Development and New York City Public Advocate Bill de Blasio." Center for Community Planning and Development, Hunter College. January 10, 2010. http://advocate.nyc.gov/files/Walmart.pdf (accessed March 19, 2011).

Armory Square Association. "History." http://www.armorysquareofsyracuse.com/about/history.php (accessed July 27, 2011).

Arnold, Stephen J., and Nailin Bu, Ulrike Gerhard, Elke Pioch, and Zhengxin Sun. "The Institutional Semiotics of Wal-Mart Flyers and Signage in United States, United Kingdom, Germany and China." *Wal-Mart World: The World's Biggest Corporation in the Global Economy*, edited by Stanley D. Brunn, 143–162. New York: Routledge, 2006.

Associated Press. "Macy's Turns Up the Charm to Court Chicagoans." Last updated November 8, 2007. http://www.msnbc.msn.com/id/21693664 (accessed August 3, 2011).

_____. "Strong Holiday Season Lifted the Bottom Line at Target, Kohl's and Gap." *The New York Times*, February 24, 2011. http://www.nytimes.com/2011/02/25/business/economy/25shop.html?ref=targetcorporation (accessed August 5, 2011).

Astor, Will. "Trial Puts Focus on Midtown." *Rochester Business Journal*, February 12, 2010. http://www.rbj.net/article.asp?aID=183013 (accessed July 30, 2011).

Baker, Julie, and Diana Haytko. "The Mall as Entertainment: Exploring Teen Girls' Total Shopping Experiences." *Journal of Shopping Center Research*, 7, Issue 1 (2000): 29–58.

Barber, Benjamin R. "Civic Space." *Sprawl and Public Space*, edited by David J. Smiley and Mark Robbins, 31–36. Washington, DC: National Endowment for the Arts, 2002.

Barcus, Holly R. "Wal-Mart-scapes in Rural and Small-Town America." *Wal-Mart World: The World's Biggest Corporation in the Global Economy*, edited by Stanley D. Brunn, 63–75. New York: Routledge, 2006.

Baulch, Vivian M. "How J.L. Hudson Changed the Way We Shop." *The Detroit News*, March 17, 2000. http://apps.detnews.com/apps/history/index.php?id=29 (accessed August 1, 2011).

Beauvais, Jean-Marie. *Setting Up Superstores and Climate Change*. Tours, France: Beauvais Consultants, 2008.

Bel Geddes, Norman. *Magic Motorways*. New York: Random House, 1940.

Berner, Robert. "Wal-Mart's Urban Renewal." *Businessweek*, April 4, 2006. http://www.businessweek.com/investor/content/apr2006/pi20060404_285531.htm (accessed July 30, 2011).

Beyard, Michael D., Mary Beth Corrigan, Anita Kramer, Michael Pawlukiewicz and Alexa Bach. *Ten Principles for Rethinking the Mall*. Washington, DC: Urban Land Institute, 2006.

Bhatnager, Parija. "Not a Mall, It's a Lifestyle

Center." *CNN Money*, January 12, 2005. http: //money.cnn.com/2005/01/11/news/fortune 500/retail_lifestylecenter/ (accessed June 22, 2010).

Birchall, Jonathan. "Walmart Strikes Deal with Unions in Chicago." *Financial Times*, June 22, 2010. http://www.ft.com/intl/cms/s/0/da 01f27a-7e20-11df-94a8-00144feabdc0.html# axzz1TGpTwgTu (accessed July 30, 2011).

Blackbird, Peter and Brian Florence. *Deadmalls. com* (blog). http://www.deadmalls.com/ (accessed November 11, 2010).

Blackwell, Jon. "1951: American Dream Houses, All in a Row." http://www.capitalcentury. com/1951.html (accessed January 11, 2011).

Boscov's. "About Boscov's." http://www.bos covs.com/static/about_boscov/history.html (accessed July 11, 2011).

The Brady Bunch. Season 1, Episode 12, first broadcast 19 December 1969 by ABC. Directed by Oscar Rudolph and written by Sherwood Schwartz and John Fenton Murray.

Brownell, Matt. "The Future of American Malls." http://www.mainstreet.com/article/ smart-spending/future-american-malls?page =1 (accessed July 11, 2011).

Brunn, Stanley D., ed. *Wal-Mart World: The World's Biggest Corporation in the Global Economy*. New York: Routledge, 2006.

Buffalo Rising. "Project to Bring Retail Back to Downtown Niagara Falls, NY." March 4, 2011. http://www.buffalorising.com/2011/03/ project-to-bring-retailing-back-to-down-town-niagara-falls-ny.html (accessed July 30, 2011).

Buffalo Waterfront. "Welcome to Buffalo's Waterfront." http://www.buffalowaterfront.com/ (accessed July 27, 2011).

Burt, Steve, and Leigh Sparks. "Wal-Mart's World." In *Wal-Mart World: the World's Biggest Corporation in the Global Economy*, edited by Stanley D. Brunn, 27–43. New York: Routledge, 2006.

Calleri, Christian. "Elmwood Avenue District." July 13, 2005. http://www.pps.org/great_pub lic_spaces/one?public_place_id=852&type_ id=3 (accessed July 27, 2011).

Cannarsa, Andrew, and Aaron Cahall. "Boscov's Bankruptcy May Cause Malls to Move Away from Department Stores." *The Examiner*, August 6, 2008. http://washingtonexaminer.com/ bankruptcy/boscovs-bankruptcy-may-cause-malls-move-away-department-stores#ixzz1Pn AhvlQS (accessed July 11, 2011).

Carousel Center. "Carousel Center." http://www. carouselcenter.com (accessed August 13, 2011).

Case, Andra, interviewed by Lisa Scharoun, 15 November 2010, Pyramid Companies, Syracuse, New York.

Cawthorne, Alexandra. "Elderly Poverty: The Challenge Before Us." Center for American Progress. http://www.americanprogress.org/ issues/2008/07/elderly_poverty.html (accessed August 2, 2010).

Cazentre, Don. "Dey's Fresh Market in Downtown Syracuse in Still a Work in Progress." *The Post-Standard*, June 8, 2011. http://blog. syracuse.com/cny/2011/06/deys_fresh_mar ket_in_downtown_syracuse_is_still_a_work_ in_progress.html (accessed July 27, 2011).

Chang, Andrea. "Free-spending Teens Return to Malls." *Los Angeles Times*, March 28, 2010. http://articles.latimes.com/2010/mar/28/busi ness/la-fi-cover-teen-spending28-2010mar28 (accessed January 24, 2011).

Churchill, Chris. "J.C. Penney Renovating at Clifton Park Center." *Timesunion.com*, June 29, 2011. http://www.timesunion.com/busi ness/article/J-C-Penney-renovating-at-Clif ton-Park-Center-1446391.php (accessed August 11, 2011).

Clever Dude Personal Finance and Money. "Dead Stores = Dead Malls = Unruly Teens in Your Hometown!" http://www.cleverdude. com/content/dead-stores-dead-malls-unruly-teens-in-your-hometown/ (accessed January 24, 2011).

Clueless. Directed by Amy Heckerling. 1995. Hollywood, CA: Paramount Home Entertainment, 2005. DVD.

CNN. "Police: Nine Killed in Shooting at Omaha Mall, Including Gunman." December 6, 2007. http://edition.cnn.com/2007/ US/12/05/mall.shooting/index.html (accessed January 11, 2011).

Coffey, Sarah. "Happy Shopping, and Watch Out for Mall Shootings." *Reuters*, October 20, 2008. http://blogs.reuters.com/shop-talk/ 2008/10/20/happy-shopping-and-watch-out-for-mall-shootings/ (accessed January 11, 2011).

Cohen, Lizabeth. "From Town Center to Shopping Center: The Reconfiguration of Community Marketplaces in Postwar America." *American Historical Review* (October 1996): 1050–1081.

Congress for the New Urbanism and PricewaterhouseCoopers. *Greyfields into Goldfields: From Failing Shopping Centers to Great Neighborhoods*. San Francisco, CA: Congress for the New Urbanism, 2001.

Conwell, Russell H. *Acres of Diamonds*. New York: Harpers and Brothers, 1933.

Crawford, Margaret. "The World in a Shopping Mall." In *Variations of a Theme Park*, edited by Michael Sorkin, 3–30. New York: Hill and Wang, 1992.

Croisdale, Frank Thomas. "Summit Closing a Sad Day for Niagara." *Niagara Falls Reporter*, May 19, 2009. http://www.niagarafallsreporter.com/croisdale5.19.09.html (accessed July 22, 2011).

Cyphert, Dale. "Economic Epideitic: The Virtuous Business of Main Street, USA." In *Proceedings of the 75th Annual Convention of the Association for Business Communication, October 27–30, 2010.* Chicago: Association for Business Communication.

Damas, Jason, and Ross Schendel. *Labelscar.com* (blog). http://www.labelscar.com/ (accessed November 11, 2010).

Davies, Julie, David Merriman, Lucia Samayoa, Brian Flanagan, Ron Baiman, and Joe Persky. *The Impact of an Urban Wal-Mart Store on Area Business: An Evaluation of One Chicago Neighborhood's Experience.* Chicago: Loyola University, 2009.

Debate.org. "Walmart=pro vs. the mall=con." http://www.debate.org/debates/Walmart-pro-vs.-themall-con/1/ (accessed August 1, 2011).

DeLisle, James R. *Shopping Center Classifications: Challenges and Opportunities.* New York: International Council of Shopping Centers, 2005.

DeMasi, Michael. "Latham Circle Owners Ask for Time as Lender Files $25M Foreclosure Petition." *The Business Review,* last modified June 5, 2008. http://www.bizjournals.com/albany/stories/2008/06/09/story5.html (accessed July 25, 2011).

_____. "Redevelopment Plan Shows Whole Foods at Latham Circle Mall." *The Business Review,* July 12, 2011. http://www.bizjournals.com/albany/news/2011/07/12/redevelopment-plan-shows-whole-foods.html (accessed July 25, 2011).

Dempsey, John S. *Introduction to Private Security.* Belmont, CA: Thomson Wadsworth, 2008.

Dery, Mark. "Dawn of the Dead Mall." *Change Observer,* December 11, 2009. http://changeobserver.designobserver.com/feature/dawn-of-the-dead-mall/11747/ (accessed 11 November 2010).

Devlin, Ann Sloan. *What Americans Build and Why: Psychological Perspectives.* New York: Cambridge University Press, 2010.

Dietz, Diane. "Churches, Shopping Centers Forge Uneasy Bonds in Tight Economy." *The Register-Guard,* August 8, 2010. http://special.registerguard.com/csp/cms/sites/web/business/25115202-41/mall-church-churches-gateway-space.csp (accessed January 20, 2011).

Dokoupil, Tony. "Is the Mall Dead?" *Newsweek,* November 12, 2008. http://newsweek.com/2008/11/11/is-the-mall-dead.html (accessed December 20, 2010).

Dunnett, Jane, and Stephen J. Arnold. "Falling Prices, Happy Faces: Organizational Culture

at Wal-Mart." In *Wal-Mart World: the World's Biggest Corporation in the Global Economy,* edited by Stanley D. Brunn, 79–90. New York: Routledge, 2006.

The Economist. "Birth, Death and Shopping." December 19, 2007. http://www.economist.com/node/10278717?story_id=10278717 (accessed December 15, 2010)

Elkin, Larry M. "Teenagers and 'Sense of Mall.'" *Business Insider,* December 28, 2010. http://www.businessinsider.com/teenagers-and-sense-of-mall-2010-12 (accessed January 20, 2011).

Experience Works. "Older Low-Income Workers Face Historic Crisis." http://www.experienceworks.org/site/PageServer?pagename=Overlooked_and_Underserved (accessed August 2, 2010).

Farrell, James J. *One Nation Under Goods: Malls and the Seductions of American Shopping.* Washington, DC: Smithsonian Books, 2003.

Fink, James. "Walden Galleria Getting Bigger." *Buffalo Business First,* June 19, 2006. http://www.bizjournals.com/buffalo/stories/2006/06/19/story1.html (August 15, 2011).

Finocchiaro, Peter. "Wal-Mart Continues March Towards Urban Domination." *Salon,* February 10, 2011. http://www.salon.com/news/feature/2011/02/10/walmart_new_york_washington (accessed July 30, 2011).

Fishman, Charles. *The Wal-Mart Effect: How the World's Most Powerful Company Really Works, and How It's Transforming the American Economy.* New York: Penguin Press, 2006.

Forgione, Rick. "Niagara Falls: Last Call for Wintergarden." *Niagara Gazette,* August 9, 2008. http://niagara-gazette.com/local/x681318069/NIAGARA-FALLS-Last-call-for-Wintergarden (accessed July 30, 2011).

Fox News. "Gunman Kills 5 in Shooting Spree at Salt Lake City Mall Before Being Killed by Police." February 13, 2007. http://www.foxnews.com/story/0,2933,251603,00.html (accessed January 11, 2011).

_____. "Nebraska Mall Shooter Broke Up with Girlfriend, Lost Job Before Massacre." December 6, 2007. http://www.foxnews.com/story/0,2933,315441,00.html (accessed January 11, 2011).

Fox, Robin. "Shopping Malls: The New Village Green." http://www.sirc.org/articles/foxmalls.html (accessed January 20, 2011).

Francaviglia, Richard V. *Main Street Revisited: Time, Space, and Image Building in Small-Town America.* Iowa City: University of Iowa Press, 1996.

Frascone, Danielle. "The Mall and the Value of Social Interactions." http://www.helium.com/items/775991-the-mall-and-the-value-of-social-interactions (accessed February 8, 2011).

Full House. [TV series, 1987–1995, broadcast on ABC] Created by Jeff Franklin.

Glaeser, Edward. *Triumph of the City.* London: Macmillan, 2011.

Goss, Jon. "The 'Magic of the Mall': An Analysis of Form, Function, and Meaning in the Contemporary Retail Built Environment." *Annals of the Association of American Geographers* 83, No. 1 (March 1993): 18–47.

Gottdiener, Mark. *Postmodern Semiotics: Material Culture and the Forms of Postmodern Life.* Oxford: Blackwell, 1995.

Graham, D.F., I. Graham, and M.J. MacLean. "Going to the Mall: A Leisure Activity of Urban Elderly People." *Canadian Journal on Aging* 10, No. 4 (Winter 1991): 345–358.

Greenseth, Morgan. "The Future of Shopping Malls: An Image Essay." http://www.worldchanging.com/local/seattle/archives/008250.html (accessed October 19, 2010).

Gruber, Jonathan, and Daniel M. Hungerman, "The Church Versus the Mall: What Happens When Religion Faces Increased Secular Competition?" *The Quarterly Journal of Economics* (May 2008): 831–862.

Gruen, Victor. *Centers for the Urban Environment.* New York: Van Nostrand, 1973.

_____. *The Heart of Our Cities.* New York: Simon and Schuster, 1964.

_____, and Larry Smith. *Shopping Towns USA.* New York: Reinhold, 1960.

Hays, Constance L. "Can Target Thrive in Wal-Mart's Cross Hairs?" *The New York Times,* June 9, 2002. http://www.nytimes.com/2002/06/09/business/can-target-thrive-in-wal-mart-s-cross-hairs.html?src=pm (accessed August 5, 2011).

Hepp, Mike. "Penn Can Mall." http://www.penncanmall.com/ (accessed November 20, 2010).

Hopkins, Jeffrey. "Orchestrating an Indoor City: Ambient Noise Inside a Mega-Mall." *Environment and Behavior* 26, No. 6 (November 1994): 785–812. doi: 10.1177/0013916594266004.

Hudson, Kris. "Mall Owner Ready to Emerge." *The Wall Street Journal,* October 22, 2010. http://online.wsj.com/article/SB10001424052702304023804575566273612180224.html (accessed July 11, 2011).

_____, and Vanessa O'Connell. "Recession Turns Malls into Ghost Towns." *The Wall Street Journal,* April 22, 2009. http://online.wsj.com/article/SB124294047987244803.html (accessed November 11, 2010).

Huffington Post Chicago. "Chicago Wal-Mart Approved by City Council." June 30, 2010. http://www.huffingtonpost.com/2010/06/30/chicago-wal-mart-approved_n_631386.html (accessed July 30, 2011).

Hunt, D. Bradford. "Model Cities." http://www.encyclopedia.chicagohistory.org/pages/832.html (accessed July 7, 2011).

Hunter Interests Incorporated. "Medical Malls: National Trends." In *Medical Mall Planning Study Feasibility of Four Different Medical Malls in Prince George's County.* (December 2007): 11–17. http://www.pgplanning.org/Projects/Completed_Projects/Medical_Mall_Planning_Study.htm (accessed August 8, 2010).

Hurdle, Jon. "U.S. Army Recruiting at the Mall with Video Games." *Reuters,* January 9, 2009. http://www.reuters.com/article/2009/01/09/us-usa-army-recruiting-idUSTRE50819H20090109 (accessed January 11, 2010).

Internicola, Dorene. "These Malls Are Made for Walking." *Reuters,* January 25, 2010. http://www.reuters.com/article/2010/01/25/us-fitness-malls-walking-idUSTRE60O24F20100125 (accessed November 11, 2010).

Jackson, Kenneth T. "The Baby Boom and the Age of the Subdivision." Chapter 13 in *Crabgrass Frontier: The Suburbanization of the United States.* New York: Oxford University Press, 1985.

Jackson, Lynne. "The Karner Blues vs. Crossgates Mall." http://www.savethepinebush.org/News/DecJan97/Xgates.html (accessed June 11, 2011).

Jacobs, Alicia. "Local Malls Headed in a Different Direction." *Your News Now,* June 9, 2007. http://capitalregion.ynn.com/content/103903/local-malls-headed-in-a-different-direction/ (accessed August 15, 2011).

Johnson, Lyndon B. *Lyndon B. Johnson, 1963–1964 (In Two Books): Containing the Public Messages, Speeches and Statements of the President* [Book 2] (Ann Arbor: University of Michigan Press, 2005).

Kane, Peter J. "Freedom of Expression in Shopping Centers." *Communication Quarterly* 22, No. 3 (Summer 1974): 45–48. doi: 10.1080/01463377409369151.

Kaufman, Steve. "Target, Multiple Locations." June 28, 2010. http://vmsd.com/content/target-multiple-locations?page=0%2C0 (accessed August 5, 2011).

Kavilanz, Parija B. "One More Merchant Worry: Mall Violence." *CNN Money,* February 12, 2008. http://money.cnn.com/2008/02/11/news/companies/retail_crime/index.htm (accessed January 11, 2011).

Kellogg, Alex P. "Detroit Shrinks Itself, Historic Homes and All." *The Wall Street Journal,* May 14, 2010. http://online.wsj.com/article/SB10001424052748703950804575242433453338728.html (accessed July 7, 2011).

Kenyon, Kevin. "Palisades Delivering Promise, Finally." *Shopping Centers Today,* April 1998.

http://www.icsc.org/srch/sct/sct9804/13.php (access July 22, 2011).

Kim, Youn-Kyung, Eun Young Kim, and Jikyeong Kang. "Teens' Mall Shopping Motivations: Functions of Loneliness and Media Usage." *Family and Consumer Sciences Research Journal* 32, No. 2 (December 2003): 140–167.

Kittle, Byron. "BJ's Wholesale Club Construction Begins Near Ithaca Mall." *The Cornell Daily Sun*, April 20, 2011. http://cornellsun.com/section/news/content/2011/04/20/bj%E2%80%99s-wholesale-club-construction-begins-near-ithaca-mall (accessed August 18, 2011).

Klein, Naomi. *No Logo*. Toronto: Knopf Canada, 2000.

Knauss, Tim. "Syracuse Gives Carousel Center Mall a 6-Month Tax Reprieve for $1 Million." *The Post-Standard*, June 6, 2011. http://www.syracuse.com/news/index.ssf/2011/06/syracuse_gives_carousel_center.html (accessed August 15, 2011).

Knowledge@Emory. "Malls: Time to Think Outside the (Big) Box." http://knowledge.emory.edu/article.cfm?articleid=1356 (accessed July 11, 2011).

Kowinski, William. *The Malling of America*. New York: William Morrow, 1985.

Kramer, Anita. *Retail Development*. 4th ed. Washington, DC: Urban Land Institute, 2008.

Kuchinskas, Susan. "Market Focus: Best Behaviour." *OMMA*, November 1, 2009. http://www.mediapost.com/publications/?fa=Articles.showArticle&art_aid=116122 (accessed November 11, 2010).

Kunstler, James Howard. *Geography of Nowhere: The Rise and Decline of America's Man-made Landscape*. New York: Simon and Schuster, 1993.

Landsman, Stephanie. "Dead Mall Hunting." *CNBC*, May 12, 2011. http://www.cnbc.com/id/42959125// (accessed July 22, 2011).

Lange, Alexandra. "Rebooting the Festival Marketplace." *Design Observer*, January 21, 2009. http://observatory.designobserver.com/feature/rebooting-the-festival-marketplace/7927/cookplusfox.com (accessed July 7, 2011).

Langrehr, Frederick W. "Retail Shopping Mall Semiotics and Hedonic Consumption." *Advances in Consumer Research* 18 (1991): 428–433.

LeCavalier, Jesse. "All Those Numbers: Logistics, Territory and Walmart." *Design Observer*, May 24, 2010. http://places.designobserver.com/feature/walmart-logistics/13598/ (accessed August 3, 2011).

Lee, Seung-Hee, Sharron J. Lennon, and Nancy A. Rudd. "Compulsive Consumption Tendencies Among Television Shoppers." *Family and Consumer Sciences Research Journal* 28, No. 4 (2000): 463–488.

LeFort, Fran. "On the Waterfront." *Shopping Centers Today* (December 2005). http://www.icsc.org/srch/sct/sct1205/Bass_pro_buffalo.php (accessed August 15, 2011).

Leichenko, Robin M. "Growth and Change in U.S. Cities and Suburbs." *Growth and Change*, 32 (Summer 2010): 326–354.

Leinburger, Christopher B. *The Option of Urbanism*. Washington, DC: Island Press, 2008.

Lewis, George H. "Community Through Exclusion and Illusion: The Creation of Social Worlds in an American Shopping Mall." *Journal of Popular Culture* 24, No. 2 (Fall 1990): 121–136.

Lichtenstein, Nelson, and Erin Johansson. "Creating Hourly Careers: A New Vision for Walmart and the Country." *American Rights at Work*. http://americanrightsatwork.org/publications/general/creating-hourly-careers-2011 0119-974-116-116.html (accessed January 24, 2011).

Liebs, Chester. *Main Street to Miracle Mile: American Roadside Architecture*. Toronto: Bulfinch Press, 1985.

Lindberg, David. "Mall Walking — A Great Way for Seniors and Elderly to Exercise and Interact." http://www.examiner.com/elder-care-in-pittsburgh/mall-walking-a-great-way-for-seniors-and-elderly-to-exercise-and-interact (accessed February 8, 2011).

Lindsay, Greg. "How Much Longer Can Shopping Malls Survive?" *Fast Company*, February 23, 2010. http://www.fastcompany.com/1557242/dead-malls (accessed July 11, 2011).

Loftsgarden, Tanja. "Shopping Malls in Scandinavia Planning Regulations as a Policy Instrument for Reducing Greenhouse Gas Emissions." In *Session 14—Transport Economics and Behavior, Young Researchers Seminar June 3–5, 2009*. Torino, Italy: European Conference of Transport Research Institutes.

Lombardi, Kate Stone. "In Curbing Walking Sprees, a Mall Sets Off Protests." *The New York Times*, March 2, 2008. http://www.nytimes.com/2008/03/02/nyregion/nyregionspecial2/02mallwe.html?pagewanted=all (accessed June 6, 2011).

Loomis, Alan A. "Locating Victor Gruen." http://www.deliriousla.net/essays/2000-gruen.htm (accessed August 17, 2010).

Loy, David R. "Religion and the Market." http://www.religiousconsultation.org/loy.htm (accessed June 7, 2010).

Lumpkin, James R. "Shopping Orientation Segmentation of the Elderly Consumer." *Journal of the Academy of Marketing Science* 13, No. 2 (Spring 1985): 271–289.

Ma, Michelle. "Thornton Creek Breathes Again at Northgate." *The Seattle Times*, June 19, 2009. http://seattletimes.nwsource.com/html/local news/2009357492_thorntoncrk19m0.html (accessed June 11, 2011).

Macerich Company. "Macerich Announces $2.333 Billion Agreement to Acquire Wilmorite." December 23, 2004. http://investing. macerich.com/phoenix.zhtml?c=80539&p=ir ol-newArticle&t=Regular&id=657356& (accessed July 22, 2011).

Maestri, Nicole. "Marketside Getting Walmart's Name Added to Its Own." *Reuters*, June 15, 2009. http://www.reuters.com/article/2009/06/15/walmart-food-idUSN1520860920090 615 (accessed July 30, 2011).

Main Place Liberty Group. "Main Place Liberty Group." http://www.mainliberty.com (accessed July 27, 2011).

Maitland, Barry. *Shopping Malls Planning and Design*. London: Construction, 1985.

Mall Area Religious Council. "MARC — The Basics." http://www.meaningstore.org/marc description.htm (accessed June 7, 2010).

Mallrats. DVD. Directed by Kevin Smith. 1995. Universal City, CA: Universal Studios Home Video, 1999.

Malls R Us. Directed by Helene Klodawsky. 2009. New York: Icarus Films, 2009. DVD.

Max, Sarah. "Malls: Death of an American Icon." *CNN*, June 4, 2003. http://www.cnnmoney.com (accessed December 15, 2010).

Manzo, John. "Social Control and the Management of 'Personal' Space in Shopping Malls." *Space and Culture* 8, No. 1 (February 2005): 83–97. doi: 10.1177/1206331204265991.

Mattera, Nick. "Rainbow Centre Tour Whets Appetite." *The Tonawanda News*, January 27, 2011. http://tonawanda-news.com/local/x147 2873746/Rainbow-Centre-tour-whets-app etite (accessed July 30, 2011).

Mattson, Kevin. "Antidotes to Sprawl." In *Sprawl and Public Space*, edited by David J. Smiley and Mark Robbins, 37–45. Washington, DC: National Endowment for the Arts, 2002.

McCarty, Dawn, and Lauren Coleman-Lochner. "Boscov's Department Stores Seek Bankruptcy Protection." *Bloomberg*, August 4, 2008. http://www.bloomberg.com/apps/news ?pid=newsarchive&sid=a2fCiNWU8sI8 (accessed July 11, 2011).

Mebane, Pamela. "ULS-P&A Settles Discrimination Lawsuit Against City Place Mall." *The Protection and Advocacy Program for the District of Columbia* 1, Issue 1 (Summer 2004): 1–2.

Medley Center Information. "Proposed Medley Center Redevelopment Plan: Issues That Need to Be Addressed." https://sites.google. com/site/medleycenterinfomation/Home (accessed July 25, 2011).

Megamall. Directed by Sarah Mondale, Vera Aronwo, and Roger Grange. 2009. Oley, PA: Bullfrog Films, 2009. DVD. http://stonelan ternfilms.org/megamall.html.

MetLife Mature Market Institute. "A Demographic Profile of Americans 65+." http:// www.metlife.com/assets/cao/mmi/publicat ions/Profiles/mmi-65+-demographic-profile. pdf (accessed January 11, 2011).

Miller, Sara B. "At Shopping Malls, Teens' Hanging Out Is Wearing Thin." *The Christian Science Monitor*, August 11, 2005. http:// www.csmonitor.com/2005/0811/p01s01-ussc. html (accessed January 20, 2011).

Mok, Kimberley. "Dead Malls: Tragedy or Opportunity." http://www.treehugger.com/files/2009/04/death-of-shopping-malls-dead-malls.php (accessed December 15, 2010).

Moriarty, Rick. "DeWitt Approves $800,000 Per Year Tax Break for Struggling Shopping Town Mall." *The Post-Standard*, January 14, 2011. http://www.syracuse.com/news/index. ssf/2011/01/shoppingtown_malls_tax_bill_to. html (accessed July 22, 2011).

_____. "Faded 'Green' Promises Could Cost Destiny USA Millions." *The Post-Standard*, February 20, 2011. http://www.syracuse.com/news/index.ssf/2011/02/faded_green_prom ises_could_cos.html (accessed August 15, 2011).

_____. "Outlet Stores Are Coming to Carousel Center's Addition After Developer Robert Congel Scraps His Earlier Plans." *The Post-Standard*, June 15, 2011. http://www.syracuse. com/news/index.ssf/2011/06/congels_outlet. html (accessed August 15, 2011).

Morris, Les, Simon Group, interviewed by Lisa Scharoun, 15 February 2011, via e-mail.

Moss, Mark Howard. *Shopping as an Entertainment Experience*. Lanham, MD: Lexington Books, 2007.

Nair, Bindu. "Keeping Track of the Mall Count." *ICSC Research Quarterly* 10, No. 2 (Summer 2003): 1–5.

News Channel 9. "Apartments Set to Open in Redeveloped Downtown Building." August 28, 2010. http://www.9wsyr.com/news/local/story/Apartments-set-to-open-in-redevelop ed-downtown/VylD5l62Xku_FZ6Nf63a1A. cspx (accessed July 27, 2011).

Niagara Frontier Transportation Authority. "History of Metro." http://metro.nfta.com/About/History.aspx (accessed July 27, 2011).

O'Connell, Jonathan. "Lifestyle Centers Are Growing in Popularity, but Some Say Malls Will Win Out." *The Washington Post*, May 31, 2010. http://www.washingtonpost.com/capi talbusiness (accessed November 10, 2010).

O'Donnell, Jayne. "Wal-Mart Plans for Smaller, Urban Stores with Fresh Food." *USA Today*, September 20, 2010. http://www.usatoday.com/money/industries/retail/2010-09-20-walmart-urban_N.htm (accessed July 30, 2011).

Oldenburg, Ray. *The Great Good Place: Cafes, Coffee Shops, Community Centers, General Stores, Bars, Hangouts and How They Get You Through the Day.* New York: Paragon Books, 1989.

Olenick, Joe. "Lockport Mall Could Be Gone by Month's End." *Lockport Union-Sun and Journal*, April 14, 2011. http://lockportjournal.com/local/x1142035511/Lockport-mall-could-be-gone-by-months-end (accessed July 22, 2011).

Pahl, Jon. *Shopping Malls and Other Sacred Spaces: Putting God in Place.* Grand Rapids, MI: Brazos Press, 2003.

Paul Blart: Mall Cop. Directed by Steve Carr. 2009. Culver City, CA: Sony Pictures, 2009. DVD.

People of Walmart. "About the People of Walmart." http://www.peopleofwalmart.com/about-the-people-of-walmart (accessed August 3, 2011).

Peyton, Martha S. *Investing in Retail Real Estate: Identifying the Winners.* New York: Teachers Insurance and Annuity Association-College Retirement Equities Fund (TIAA-CREF), 2010.

Pitman, Teresa. "Hanging Out at the Mall: Why Does Your Teen Always Want to Hang Out at the Mall—Without You?" *Today's Parent* (August 2003). http://www.todaysparent.com/teen/behaviordevelopment/article.jsp?content=20030709_103106_4216 (accessed January 20, 2011).

Polanyi, Karl. *The Great Transformation: the Political and Economic Origins of Our Time.* Boston, MA: Beacon Press, 2001.

Prewitt, Milford. "Mall Trends and Hurdles Send Chains Shopping for Site Solutions." April 24, 2000. http://findarticles.com/p/articles/mi_m3190/is_17_34/ai_61948437/pg_2/?tag=content;col1 (accessed August 15, 2011).

Prohaska, Thomas J. "Demolition of Lockport Mall Begins." *Buffalo News*, April 13, 2011. http://www.buffalonews.com/city/communities/lockport/article391973.ece (accessed July 22, 2011).

Readdick, Christine A., and Ronald L. Mullis. "Adolescents and Adults at the Mall: Dyadic Interactions." http://findarticles.com/p/articles/mi_m2248/is_n126_v32/ai_19619412/ (accessed January 24, 2011). Previously published in *Adolescence* 32, No. 126 (Summer 1997): 313–322.

Real Estate Weekly. "Willingbro Town Center Going 'Green.'" *Entrepreneur*, August 22, 2001.

http://www.entrepreneur.com/tradejournals/article/78059083.html (accessed August 18, 2011).

Redell, Charles. "Dead Malls." http://sustainbleindustries.com/articles/2009/03/dead-malls?page=3 (accessed November 20, 2010).

Reep, Richard. "The Future of the Shopping Mall." http://www.newgeography.com/content/00501-the-future-shopping-mall (accessed November 11, 2010).

Reuters. "Profits at Target and BJ's Rise as Shoppers Buy Essentials." *The New York Times*, May 18, 2011. http://www.nytimes.com/2011/05/19/business/19retail.html?_r=1&ref=targetcorporation (accessed August 5, 2011).

Robbins, Mark. "Redressing the Mall." In *Sprawl and Public Space*, edited by David J. Smiley and Mark Robbins, 3–8. Washington, DC: National Endowment for the Arts, 2002.

Roberts, J.R. "Who Will Guard the Guards?" http://www.jrrobertssecurity.com/WhoWillTheGuards.pdf (accessed January 3, 2011).

Rochester Downtown Development Corporation and Downtown Special Services, Inc. "Gaming in Rochester and New York State." http://rochesterdowntown.com/news/rddc_casino/ROCHESTER/ROCH11.pdf (accessed July 30, 2011).

_____. "Midtown Plaza Timeline." http://www.rochesterdowntown.com/downloads/Midtown_Plaza_Timeline.pdf (accessed July 30, 2011).

Rosen, Ellen I. "Wal-Mart: The New Retail Colossus." In *Wal-Mart World: The World's Biggest Corporation in the Global Economy*, edited by Stanley D. Brunn, 91–97. New York: Routledge, 2006.

Rubenstein, Harvey M. *Pedestrian Malls, Streetscapes and Urban Spaces.* New York: John Wiley and Sons, 1992.

Ruff, Joshua. "Levittown: The Archetype for Suburban Development." *American History*, December, 2007. http://www.historynet.com/levittown-the-archetype-for-suburban-development.htm (accessed January 11, 2011).

Sabbatino, Dan. "The Birth of a Mall." *Spotlightnews*, January 28, 2010. http://spotlightnews.com/news/view_news.php?news_id=1264696894 (accessed July 25, 2011).

_____. "What Went Wrong?" *Spotlightnews*, February 11, 2010. http://www.spotlightnews.com/news/views_news.php?news_id=1265924496 (accessed July 25, 2011).

Salcedo, Rodrigo. "When the Global Meets the Local at the Mall." *American Behavioral Scientist* 46, No. 8 (April 2003): 1084–1103. doi: 10.1177/0002764202250500.

Sampson, Christine. "Kamer Predicts Slow Recovery for Long Island Economy." *Levittown Patch*, October 26, 2010. http://levittown-ny.

patch.com/articles/kamer-predicts-slow-re covery-for-long-island-economy-5 (accessed January 11, 2011).

Schonfeld, Erick. "Forrester Forecast: Online Retail Sales Will Grow to $250 Billion by 2014." http://techcrunch.com/2010/03/08/forrester-forecast-online-retail-sales-will-grow-to-250-billion-by-2014/ (accessed July 7, 2011).

Schwartz, David, and Nicole Maestri. "Wal-Mart Woos Hispanics with New Supermercado." *Reuters*, July 8, 2009. http://www.reuters.com/article/2009/07/08/us-walmart-supermercado-idUSTRE5676N820090708 (accessed July 30, 2011).

Sheer, Mark. "Mall Goes into Bankruptcy: Summit Owners Cite Economy." *Niagara Gazette*, May 6, 2009. http://niagara-gazette.com/breakingnews/x681342885/MALL-GOES-INTO-BANKRUPTCY-Summit-owners-cite-economy (accessed July 22, 2011).

Shepherd, Steven L. "The Popular Condition: Mall Culture." *The Humanist* (November-December 1998): 40–41.

Shim, Soyeon, Mary Ann Eastlick, and Sherry Lotz. "Assessing the Impact of Internet Shopping on Store Shopping Among Mall Shoppers and Internet Users." *Journal of Shopping Center Research* 7, No. 2: 7–43.

Sichok, Christopher J. "The Free Market: An Erosion of Free Speech." *Murdoch University Electronic Journal of Law* 7, No. 3 (September 2000). http://www.murdoch.edu.au/elaw/issues/v7n3/sichok73_text.html (accessed January 20, 2011).

Smiley, David J., and Mark Robbins, eds. *Sprawl and Public Space: Redressing the Mall*. Washington, DC: National Endowment for the Arts, 2002.

Smith, Benjamin. "Visualising Wal-Mart as Home: *Where the Heart Is* and *King of the Hill*." In *Wal-Mart World: The World's Biggest Corporation in the Global Economy*, edited by Stanley D. Brunn, 179–192. New York: Routledge, 2006.

Sokol, David. "Morphing Mega Malls." *Retail Traffic*, October 1, 2002. http://retailtrafficmag.com/development/trends/retail_morphing_mega_malls/ (accessed August 11, 2011).

Sommer, Mark, and Jonathan D. Epstein. "Canal Side Ready to Speed Ahead." *Buffalo News*, July 20, 2011. http://www.buffalonews.com/city/communities/downtown/article493896.ece (accessed July 27, 2011).

Sondel, Justin. "No Vacancy." *Artvoice Daily*, November 11, 2010. http://artvoice.com/issues/v9n45/no_vacancy (accessed July 7, 2011).

Spigel, Lyn. *Make Room for the TV: Television and the Family Ideal in Postwar America*. Chicago: University of Chicago Press, 1992.

Spodek, Yaffi. "The Malls Are All Right." *The Real Deal*, January 1, 2011. http://therealdeal.com/newyork/articles/the-malls-are-all-right (accessed August 11, 2011).

Staba, David. "New Passport Rules Bring Worry Over Tourism at Niagara Falls." *The New York Times*, June 11, 2007. http://www.nytimes.com/2007/06/11/nyregion/11border.html (accessed July 30, 2011).

Stabiner, Karen. "New Lives for 'Dead' Suburban Malls." *The New York Times*, June 28, 2011. http://newoldage.blogs.nytimes.com/2011/01/21/new-lives-for-dead-suburban-malls/ (accessed January 25, 2011).

Staeheli, Lynn A., and Don Mitchell. "USA's Destiny? Regulating Space and Creating Community in American Shopping Malls." *Urban Studies* 43, No. 5/6 (May 2006): 977–992. doi: 10.1080/00420980600676493.

Steden, Ronald van, and Mahesh K. Nalla. "Citizen Satisfaction with Private Security Guards in the Netherlands: Perceptions of an Ambiguous Occupation." *European Journal of Criminology* 7, No. 3 (2010): 214–234. doi: 10.1177/1477370809359264.

Stelloh, Tim. "The Crowds Are Gone, the Walls Are Next." *The New York Times*, May 1, 2011. http://www.nytimes.com/2011/05/02/nyregion/nanuet-malls-demolition-plans-stun-workers.html (access July 25, 2011).

Stringy, Joseph M., *Handbook of Quality-of-life Research: An Ethical Marketing Perspective*. Norwell, MA: Kluwer, 2001.

Sudjic, Dejan. "Making Cities Work: Detroit." *BBC News*, July 10, 2006. http://news.bbc.co.uk/2/hi/americas/5165808.stm (accessed July 7, 2011).

Target.com. "Our History: Through the Years." http://sites.target.com/site/en/company/page.jsp?contentId=WCMP04-031697 (accessed August 13, 2011).

Taub, Daniel, and Brian Louis. "General Growth File Biggest U.S. Property Bankruptcy." *Bloomberg*, April 16, 2009. http://www.bloomberg.com/apps/news?pid=newsarchive&sid=anaZwxRpYcTw (accessed November 11, 2010).

Thomas, Megan L. "For Teens, Bleak Job Picture Not Looking Brighter." http://www.msnbc.msn.com/id/38666248/ns/business-eye_on_the_economy/# (accessed January 24, 2011).

Thompson, Mark. "Why Are Army Recruiters Killing Themselves?" *Time*, April 2, 2009. http://www.time.com/time/magazine/article/0,9171,1889152,00.html (accessed January 11, 2011).

Thomson, James. "Borders Collapses into Bankruptcy in the U.S." http://www.smartcompany.com.au/retail/20110217-borders-collapses-into-bankruptcy-in-the-us.html (accessed July 7, 2011).

Underhill, Paco. *The Call of the Mall*. New York: Simon and Schuster, 2004.

Urban Land Institute. *An Advisory Services Panel Report: Rochester, New York*. Washington, DC: Urban Land Institute, 2005. http://rochester downtown.com/news/PDF/ULIreport.pdf (accessed July 27, 2011).

_____. *Shopping Center Development Handbook*. 2nd ed. Washington, DC: Urban Land Institute, 1985.

USA Niagara Development Corporation. "Old Falls Street — East Mall Project." http://www. usaniagara.com/projects_display.asp?id=14 (accessed July 30, 2011).

U.S. Bureau of Labor Statistics. "Economy at a Glance: Buffalo–Niagara Falls, NY." http:// www.bls.gov/eag/eag.ny_buffalo_msa.htm (accessed July 22, 2011).

_____. "Economy at a Glance: Rochester, NY." http://www.bls.gov/eag/eag.ny_rochester_msa. htm (accessed July 25, 2011).

_____. "Economy at a Glance: Syracuse, NY." http://www.bls.gov/eag/eag.ny_syracuse_msa. htm (accessed July 22, 2011).

_____. "Local Area Unemployment Statistics Map." http://data.bls.gov/map/MapToolServ let?state=36&datatype=unemployment&year =2011&period=M05&survey=la&map=county &seasonal=u (accessed August 11, 2011).

_____. "New York–New Jersey Information Office." http://www.bls.gov/ro2/ro2_ny.htm (accessed July 11, 2011).

_____. "Unemployment in the New York Area by County — April 2011." http://www.bls. gov/ro2/countyunemp.htm (accessed August 11, 2011).

U.S. Census Bureau. "Monthly and Annual Retail Trade." http://www.census.gov/retail/ (accessed July 22, 2011).

_____. "The Next Four Decades: The Older Population in the United States, 2010 to 2050." http://www.census.gov/population/www/ projections/reports.html (accessed January 11, 2011).

_____. "State and County QuickFacts: Buffalo (City), New York." http://quickfacts.census. gov/qfd/states/36/3611000.html (accessed July 27, 2011).

_____. "State and County QuickFacts: Cayuga County, New York." http://quickfacts.census. gov/qfd/states/36/36011.html (accessed August 18, 2011).

_____. "State and County QuickFacts: Erie County, New York." http://quickfacts.census. gov/qfd/states/36/36029.html (accessed August 11, 2011).

_____. "State and County QuickFacts: Niagara County, New York." http://quickfacts.census. gov/qfd/states/36/36063.html (accessed July 22, 2011).

_____. "State and County QuickFacts: Niagara Falls (City), New York." http://quickfacts. census.gov/qfd/states/36/3651055.html (accessed July 30, 2011).

_____. "State and County QuickFacts: Onondaga County, New York." http://quickfacts. census.gov/qfd/states/36/36067.html (accessed July 22, 2011).

_____. "State and County QuickFacts: Rochester (City), New York." http://quickfacts. census.gov/qfd/states/36/3663000.html (accessed July 25, 2011).

_____. "State and County QuickFacts: Rockland County, New York." http://quickfacts. census.gov/qfd/sates/36/36087.html (accessed July 22, 2011).

_____. "State and County QuickFacts: Saratoga County, New York." http://quickfacts.census. gov/qfd/states/36/36091.html (accessed August 11, 2011).

_____. "State and County QuickFacts: Tompkins County, New York." http://quickfacts. census.gov/qfd/states/36/36109.html (accessed August 11, 2011).

_____. "The 2011 Statistical Abstract." http:// www.census.gov/compendia/statab/ (accessed July 22, 2011).

U.S. Environmental Protection Agency. *A Guide to Waste Reduction at Shopping Centers*. Washington, DC: U.S. Environmental Protection Agency, 2004.

_____. "Love Canal: Press Releases and Articles." http://www.epa.gov/aboutepa/history/ topics/lovecanal/ (accessed July 30, 2011).

U.S. Fish and Wildlife Service. *Karner Blue Butterfly Recovery Plan*. Fort Snelling, MN: U.S. Fish and Wildlife Services, 2003.

VanderVelde, Lea S. "Wal-Mart as a Phenomenon in the Legal World: Matters of Scale, Scale Matters." In *Wal-Mart World: the World's Biggest Corporation in the Global Economy*, edited by Stanley D. Brunn, 115–140. New York: Routledge, 2006.

Veaner, Dan. "BJ's to Come to the Shops at Ithaca Mall." *The Lansing Star*, July 29, 2010. http://www.lansingstar.com/news-archive/ 6377-bjs-to-come-to-the-shops-at-ithaca- mall (accessed August 18, 2011).

_____. "Business Profile: The Shops at Ithaca Mall." *The Lansing Star*, July 12, 2007. http: //www.lansingstar.com/component/content/ article/141/3100-business-profile-the-shops- at-ithaca-mall (accessed August 18, 2011).

Voyce, Malcolm. "Shopping Malls in Australia: The End of Public Space and the Rise of 'Consumerist Citizenship'?" *Journal of Sociology* 42, No. 3 (2006): 269–286. doi: 10.1177/ 1440783306066727.

Wall, Alex. *Victor Gruen: From Urban Shop to New City*. Barcelona: Actar, 2005.

Walmart Watch. "Fact Sheet — Wages." http://walmartwatch.org/get-the-facts/fact-sheet-wages (accessed August 3, 2011).

Walton, Sam, with John Huey. *Sam Walton: Made in America — My Story.* New York: Doubleday, 1992.

Warf, Barney, and Thomas Chapman. "Cathedrals of Consumption: A Political Phenomenology of Wal-Mart." In *Wal-Mart World: the World's Biggest Corporation in the Global Economy,* edited by Stanley D. Brunn, 163–178. New York: Routledge, 2006.

Warner, Ralph E. *Get a Life: You Don't Need a Million to Retire.* 5th ed. Berkeley, CA: Nolo, 2004.

Way, Prange. *Labelscar.com* (blog). http://www.labelscar.com/new-york/medley-centre-iron dequoit-mall-lakeridge-centre (accessed July 25, 2011).

WBEN. "WBEN Extra: Bye-Bye Big Box, but Now What?" *WBEN News Radio,* December 9, 2010. http://www.wben.com/pages/8741935.php? (accessed July 27, 2011).

Weber, Max. *The Protestant Ethic and the Spirit of Capitalism.* London: Unwin University Books, 1970.

West, Debra. "Palisades Center, the Rumor Mall; Rosie O'Donnell Wants to Know: Is It Really Going to Sink?" *The New York Times,* January 8, 1999. http://www.nytimes.com/1999/01/08/nyregion/palisades-center-rumor-mall-rosie-o-donnell-wants-know-it-really-going-sink.html?src=pm (accessed July 22, 2011).

Wikipedia. "Buffalo Metro Rail." http://en.wikipedia.org/wiki/Buffalo_Metro_Rail (accessed July 27, 2011).

_____. "Carousel Center." http://en.wikipedia.org/wiki/Carousel_Center (accessed August 13, 2011).

_____. "Eastview Mall." http://en.wikipedia.org/wiki/Eastview_Mall (accessed July 25, 2011).

_____. "History of Buffalo, New York." http://en.wikipedia.org/wiki/History_of_Buffalo,_New_York (accessed July 27, 2011).

_____. "Lockport Mall." http://en.wikipedia.org/wiki/Lockport_Mall (accessed July 22, 2011).

_____. "Medley Center." http://en.wikipedia.org/wiki/Medley_Centre (accessed July 25, 2011).

_____. "Walden Galleria." http://en.wikipedia.org/wiki/Walden_Galleria (accessed August 11, 2011).

Wilgoren, Jodi. "Detroit Urban Renewal Without the Renewal." *The New York Times,* July 7, 2002. http://nytimes.com/2002/07/07/national/07DETR.html (accessed July 7, 2011).

Wilson, Sloan. *The Man in a Grey Flannel Suit.* New York: Simon and Schuster, 1955.

The Wonder Years. Season 3, Episode 3, first broadcast 24 October 1989 by ABC. Directed by Bethany Rooney and written by Carol Black, Neal Marlens and Mark B. Perry.

Wright, Gwendolyn. *Building the Dream: A Social History of Housing in America.* Cambridge, MA: MIT Press, 1983.

Yestercuse. "South Salina Street — The Heart of Downtown." http://www.yestercuse.com/salina.htm (accessed July 27, 2011).

_____. "Syracuse Today." http://www.yestercuse.com/today.htm (accessed July 27, 2011).

Zepp, Ira G. *The New Religious Image of Urban America: The Shopping Mall as Ceremonial Center.* Colorado: University of Colorado Press, 1997.

Zook, Matthew A., and Mark Graham. "Wal-Mart Nation: Mapping the Reach of a Retail Colossus." In *Wal-Mart World: the World's Biggest Corporation in the Global Economy,* edited by Stanley D. Brunn, 15–25. New York: Routledge, 2006.

Index